W9-CGR-145

The Pastoral Circle Revisited

The Pastoral Circle Revisited

*A Critical Quest
for Truth and Transformation*

Frans Wijsen
Peter Henriot
Rodrigo Mejía
EDITORS

ORBIS BOOKS

Maryknoll, New York 10545

Founded in 1970, Orbis Books endeavors to publish works that enlighten the mind, nourish the spirit, and challenge the conscience. The publishing arm of the Maryknoll Fathers and Brothers, Orbis seeks to explore the global dimensions of the Christian faith and mission, to invite dialogue with diverse cultures and religious traditions, and to serve the cause of reconciliation and peace. The books published reflect the views of their authors and do not represent the official position of the Maryknoll Society. To learn more about Maryknoll and Orbis Books, please visit our website at www.maryknoll.org.

Copyright © 2005 by Frans Wijsen, Peter Henriot, and Rodrigo Mejía.

Published by Orbis Books, Maryknoll, New York 10545-0308.
Manufactured in the United States of America.
Manuscript editing and typesetting by Joan Weber Laflamme.

All rights reserved. No part of this publication may be reproduced or transmitted in any form or by any means, electronic or mechanical, including photocopying, recording or any information storage or retrieval system, without prior permission in writing from the publisher.

Queries regarding rights and permissions should be addressed to: Orbis Books, P.O. Box 308, Maryknoll, New York 10545-0308.

Library of Congress Cataloging-in-Publication

The pastoral circle revisited : a critical quest for truth and transformation / Frans Wijsen, Peter Henriot, Rodrigo Mejía, editors.
    p. cm.
    Includes bibliographical references and index.
    ISBN-13: 978-1-57075-620-7 (pbk.)
    1. Christian sociology—Catholic Church—Methodology. I. Wijsen, Frans Jozef Servaas, 1956- II. Henriot, Peter J. III. Mejía, Rodrigo.
    BX1753.P342 2005
    253'.7—dc22
                       2005009141

We dedicate this book to the memory of Archbishop Oscar A. Romero, the martyred archbishop of San Salvador, El Salvador. His assassination occurred twenty-five years ago, the same year as the publication of Social Analysis: Linking Faith and Justice. *His life and the memory of his heroic dedication continue to inspire all of us to a more authentic and effective linking of our faith and justice.*

Contents

Part I
The Use in Pastoral Situations

Part II
The Use in Academic Settings

Foreword

Faith, Justice, and Injustice

Jon Sobrino

In 1980 Joe Holland and Peter Henriot published *Social Analysis: Linking Faith and Justice*, a book that has had a great impact in many regions of the world. Now, twenty-five years later, *The Pastoral Circle Revisited: A Critical Quest for Truth and Transformation* offers a critical rethinking of that work and a reflection on the challenges it represents for the future.

The new book is dedicated to Archbishop Oscar Romero, who was martyred in the same year the book appeared, and I have been asked to put in a few words. This is not intended to introduce the new book but rather to offer some reflections that I consider necessary in order to understand and analyze the present reality. I refer specifically to the need to allow ourselves to be affected by reality in order to analyze it properly; as a way of working for justice, we must reclaim the categories of injustice and justice in order to grasp the truth of the world we live in and to understand faith with Jesus of Nazareth as the starting point.

Allowing Ourselves to Be Affected by Reality

Holland and Henriot propose the pastoral circle as a way of analyzing reality. In my opinion this means, fundamentally, that our intelligence is affected by reality through the appropriate processes. I have seen this first-hand in the work of Ignacio Ellacuría, not only as a method of social analysis but as a more adequate way of exercising one's intelligence.

There are three dimensions to human intellectual activity, each in an essential relationship to humanity. The first is "getting a grip on reality," which requires us *to be truly and actively involved* in reality, affected by things as they are; it is not sufficient to be intellectually face to face with their meaning and concepts. The second is "taking on the burden of reality," that is, taking charge of reality in order to transform it; this is the

ix

praxic dimension of intelligence. The third is "taking responsibility for reality," that is, accepting the demands of reality and bearing its hardships; this is the *ethical dimension* of intelligence. To this I would add what I believe Ellacuría was saying implicitly: "letting reality carry us," that is, letting ourselves be enlightened by reality. This is the *dimension of grace* in the exercise of intelligence.

To put it more simply, focusing on its anthropological effects: in order to know and analyze reality we need to insert ourselves in it (in Christian terms, incarnation); we need to develop a transforming praxis (in Christian terms to build or, more modestly, to initiate the reign of God, guided by prophecy and utopia in following Jesus); we need to accept the risks that entails (in Christian terms, persecution and the cross); we need to be open to the leading, the energy, values, and salvation that reality offers (in Christian terms the grace, the gift, the fire of God most naturally found on the underside of history).

Archbishop Romero embraced this theoretical understanding of intellectual activity, though he saw it more in pastoral terms. Clearly, he allowed himself to be deeply affected by reality; he reacted to it with love for his people, with prophetic lucidity, and with utopian hope; he took responsibility, unto death, for reality; and he let reality carry him. "It's not hard to be a good shepherd with these people," he said. This enabled him to understand and analyze reality. Let us remember how he spoke of his people's reality: "You are the suffering servant of Yahweh. You are the pierced divinity, the crucified people." It seems easy to say that, but it isn't. Indeed very few people, if any, have seen and analyzed reality as he did.

The conclusion is important. Whatever details we need to focus on in the pastoral circle, the most important thing is to let ourselves be affected by what is most real in reality. This affectedness is prior to methodology as such; it can be seen in our openness to conversion, our honesty toward reality, our faithfulness unto death toward reality, and our openness to what reality gives us, that is, grace. When this happens, as Karl Rahner described it, "reality wants to have a word" (to speak). Reality speaks, and the analyst listens.

Reclaiming the Categories of Justice and Injustice

This second reflection is not about method but about content. At Medellín in 1968, and more explicitly at the XXXII General Congregation of the Society of Jesus in 1975, the categories of *injustice* and *justice* were seen as normal and essential for a reading of reality; but the West and its democracies—and the churches too, to a large extent—have been trying to bury those concepts. This has been happening in practice, but the need to do so has also been argued in principle. For some, to understand our world in terms of justice and injustice would mean "returning" to outdated paradigms, which are customarily rejected in the name of postmodernity.

In my opinion, although new paradigms have emerged throughout history, we must always ask if some realities are not "transparadigmatic." For me, What have you done with your brother? is a transparadigmatic question. It echoes through history, and no paradigm can silence it. Our essential humanity is at stake when we listen or don't listen, when we respond or don't respond to that question. When we ignore it, devalue it, or try to bury it in "ifs," "ands," or "buts," we are witnessing the end, the disintegration, the failure of the human. Some readers may question what I have just said, but it is what I firmly believe.

Certainly we need to understand as best we can the paradigm in which we live, but where justice and injustice are concerned, we must also refuse to absolutize the present—and be prepared, if need be, to "return" to the past. This may sound politically incorrect today and offend the Western sensibilities of those who consider their perspective appropriate (or at least irreversible) as a way of understanding reality.

In this context I propose, provocatively, to "return" to what was done a generation ago, admittedly more in the Third World than in the First, which in turn was a "return" to other traditions like the narratives of the Yahwist and the Elohist, the synoptic gospels, and the letter of James—historicizing them for our time, of course. This is the great tradition that, sometimes more and sometimes less, has held up injustice and justice as central human realities. We must emphasize that this great tradition has always maintained a dialectical perspective, which is fading today: justice *against* injustice, oppression and repression, murderous poverty, and culture-killing colonialism.

That great tradition is disappearing. Therefore I would like to analyze here some attitudes that—although strictly speaking they come before the analysis of reality, justice, and injustice—I consider fundamental and necessary today, because without them it is even more difficult to reclaim the categories of justice and injustice in our analysis.[1]

The Importance of Language

Let us begin with the need to win the *language battle*, since whoever controls the language, and especially the definitions, has already won most of the other battles. The "powers that be" take control of words, shamelessly inventing some and burying others. For example, after what happened in the Rwanda catastrophe, US Secretary of State Madeleine Albright prohibited the use of the word *genocide* to describe the massacres; it would have obligated the United Nations to intervene. At the end of April 1994, UN Secretary General Boutros Boutros-Ghali was still speaking of civil war, not genocide. The reason? "Nobody was interested in coming to Rwanda and risking casualties," as General Dallaire—the UN envoy to Rwanda in 1994—said recently.

In another recent example, the United States and the West have enshrined the memory of 9/11—and consigned to total silence that of 10/7 (October 7 of the same year, when the bombing of Afghanistan began). They have also silenced the memory of another 9/11 (1973, when Chilean president Allende was violently overthrown), and a 12/11 (December 1981, when the US-trained Atlacatl battalion massacred some thousand people in El Mozote, El Salvador). The calendar is used, paradoxically and hypocritically, to prevent reality in its temporal dimension from having its word.

A final example. We live in a time of *empire*, that of the United States, but the language of empire is carefully silenced. The free and democratic West has silenced that reality. As José Comblin reminds us, "St. Augustine called the Roman empire an immense case of banditry, *'magnum latrocinium.'* And the same can be said of today's empires. They are sins and sources of sin."

No genocide, no 10/7, no empire. And something similar is happening with justice and injustice. The negative side of reality is expressed today in terms like *underdevelopment, developing countries, less-privileged classes.* War and terrorism are also mentioned, of course, but only selectively and when they become impossible to avoid. And we almost never speak of *injustice.* The positive side is expressed in terms like *democracy, dialogue, international cooperation and solidarity, prosperity, progress, human rights, the state of law*—good things, obviously, although they are affirmed with various degrees of truth and hypocrisy. But we almost never speak of *justice.*

The reason for such deafening silence seems to be this: the language of injustice *unmasks* the truth and the tragedy of this world as no other language can, and the language of justice *insists*—as no other language can—on the radicality, urgency, and ultimacy of what we human beings must do. What is more, the language of justice and injustice expresses dialectical realities and, above all, the conflictive nature of reality. Since that is inconvenient, dialectical language is replaced by a more positive but finally innocuous way of speaking: *dialogue, tolerance, complementarity.* This language is good because of what it tries to achieve and cruel because of what it tries to hide.

The reality of our world is what it is: deplorable. It is a dialectical reality, with injustice as its principal cause. In José Comblin's sharp description, "in reality, humanity is divided between the oppressors and the oppressed."

So we need to win the battle of language, to reclaim the language of justice and injustice, but that is not easy. Three fundamental attitudes are necessary.

Honesty toward reality. People are reluctant to recognize it, but there is a glaring lack of respect for reality, a failure to let reality be what it is without ignoring it, covering it up, or whitewashing it. An abundance of knowledge masks an ignorance of concrete facts, but truth is seldom able to overcome lies and coverups. Does Iraq exist? Is it a reality in and for itself, or is it only real when it interacts, for good or ill, with the West? Is it by chance that the West decides what is substantial in Iraq and what is not? To say nothing of Africa, its resources of colton, a rare mineral used in the manufacture of cell phones, and the four million people killed in the Congo in recent years. Do they exist?

The will to be real. In Christology it is said that from the beginning the greatest danger to Christianity (along with gnosticism) was docetism, which held that Christ was not a man of flesh and especially that he did not have *sarx*, the weakness of the flesh. His physical body was not real but only apparent. This kind of docetism still exists in our world.

It is docetism to live in Western islands of abundance and luxury in a mostly poor and oppressed planet, as if the abundance were real and the poverty unreal, when in fact it is quite the opposite. This is justified by affirming that abundance is the manifest destiny of the West, a belief invoked in practice to exploit and oppress the rest of the world. And it is still being done today. To put it in sophisticated terms, this manifest destiny consists primarily of living not just any existence, but of *living well.*

It has been so for a long time. Divine election and predestination have often been invoked to justify this manifest destiny, but they are expressed in secular language. "We are human," say the Europeans and North Americans; "we," not the indigenous Latin Americans, Africans, and Asians. "We are the measure of all things," says the West; the Greeks only said that about human beings. The West measures reality but does not let itself be measured by the more global reality of the planet. That is its destiny. And it does not accept that being real is what happens among the poor and victimized majorities.

The audacity to name what is beyond debate. Debates often take place in the West, and that is good. The word *controversial* is often used in the United States, and people often think that the best approach to reality is to focus on its controversial points. So what happens? There is no longer anything *self-evident*, beyond controversy, beyond discussion. Everything, no matter how horrible it is, can be relativized by describing it as controversial, as a topic of debate. But the grotesqueness of the African reality, and the silence surrounding it, should not be a topic of debate. It should now be beyond controversy that the war in Iraq has produced a series of lies, injustices, atrocious violations of human rights, and civilian deaths, and that people and institutions are responsible for all of them.

With due respect for the Anglo-Saxon tradition's great contribution to debate, we must insist that some realities impose themselves, without debate, on the human conscience. If they are not seen as real and self-evident, they will always be debatable and will eventually cease to be obvious, important—even to exist. Western injustice and cruelty? It's debatable, people will say. And nothing of substance will change.

The conclusion? Without honesty toward reality, without the audacity to be real, and without the will to name the truth, injustice will smugly forge ahead with nothing standing in its way. There will then be no need to speak of justice but only of aid, negotiations, globalization . . .

The Central Contribution of Christian Faith to Justice

Let us now ask how faith can help us "return" to the centrality of justice and injustice. Clearly the faith-justice correlation is theologically, christologically, and ecclesiologically globalizing, and it is above all a two-way correlation: faith enlightens and empowers justice; justice enlightens and empowers faith.

We shall not analyze the globality of the correlation now. We shall ask more modestly about some of the things that faith can offer to justice today. In the biblical tradition, and more specifically by focusing on Jesus of Nazareth, I think faith offers three things:

- a denunciation of what is wrong in the world, with reference not only to injustice but to the ills that surround and express it;
- the call to a praxis that takes the side of the weak; and
- witness to the death and resurrection of Jesus.

Throughout history these have been explained in terms of Jesus' struggle for justice, so that without it the central truth of our faith would remain a distant enigma to us humans. Let us look at each of these.

First, the denunciation of evil. Jesus does not offer a definition of justice and injustice but says in different ways that "this is not right." Let us recall two basic gospel passages.

The scandal of comparative harm. The rich man and the poor Lazarus (Lk 16:19–31). Although in theory the coexistence of rich and poor is not the result of injustice, it expresses a monumental and fundamental failure in the human family. This is the primordial law of comparative harm, which, logically speaking, comes even before the need to let ourselves be affected by injustice, and without which the praxis of justice loses dynamism and vigor.

The story of the rich man and the poor Lazarus is the parable of today's world, and the abyss between them grows wider every year. As the United Nations Development Programme regularly reports, the income of the wealthy was thirty times that of the poor in 1969, sixty times in 1990, seventy-four times in 1997. A baby in the United States consumes 420 times more resources than a baby in Ethiopia. On a soccer field in Madrid three years ago, the salaries of the twenty-two players in the game were equivalent to more than twice the national budget of Chad. No more examples are needed.

Although it doesn't seem important, let us note that Jesus gives a name to the poor man, Lazarus, but not to the rich man. And bringing the point alarmingly close to home, he spoke of how hard it is for the rich to overcome the seriousness of their offense. They won't be convinced, Jesus said at the end of the parable, "even if someone should rise from the dead."

Indignation; denouncing oppression and hypocrisy. "Woe also to you lawyers! For you load people with burdens heavy to bear, and you yourselves do not lift a finger to help them" (Lk 11:46). Jesus has no tolerance for those who demean or ignore the poor, let alone those who offend them directly by giving them unbearable burdens. In Luke 22:24–25, which places his words in the setting of the Last Supper to emphasize them, Jesus summarizes centuries of history: "The kings of the Gentiles lord it over them."

That is the fundamental sin, but more than that, "those in authority over them are called benefactors." The UN Security Council, the World Bank, the International Monetary Fund, the World Trade Organization often appear in this guise. And in Jesus' denunciation the "injustice" of the lawyers is linked with the "hypocrisy" of the Pharisees—which is equally relevant when we ask about the relationship between the injustice of the Western world and the hypocrisy of the "democracies" that claim to be spreading democracy in Iraq. Jesus' solemn admonition is important: "But not so with you."

Second, a liberating praxis that takes sides. *The justice of the Messiah who takes sides.* Jesus proclaimed the reign of God and participated in its messianic hopes, including the coming of a just king who would establish justice. The role of those we now call judges was exclusively to help those whose weakness made them defenseless; the others don't need it. When the Bible speaks of Yahweh as a judge, it refers to God's will to save the oppressed from injustice.

This is worth remembering, especially in the West, because democracy—even theoretically—places citizens, not the poor, at the center of society. It is true that democracies have succeeded somewhat in improving the lot of the poor, albeit often by mechanisms that cause injustice to the poor in the Third World. But taking sides is not central to democracy. That theoretical limitation may well explain why real democracies—there is no other kind—have not, from the viewpoint of most of the planet, brought life to the poor. Often what they bring is death.

In the Jesuanic tradition, taking sides also reflects the fact that salvation comes from the small, from the victims. Utopia is a civilization that eradicates the now-prevailing civilization of wealth, that allows all to have life, that makes room for the spirit and humanizes everyone, as Ignacio Ellacuría used to say.

Historical praxis and gratuity. The experience of love freely given. Here we need to emphasize the praxic dimension and consequences of Jesus' mission for modern believers, because for several reasons these have been diluted at both the ecclesial and theological levels.

The omission is happening, first, because a praxis of justice can be costly. It is true that we have had a galaxy of martyrs, and we can take pride in them, but to imitate them is obviously scary. We try to ignore them by explaining them away. Although no one says so, it is out of fashion to relate martyrdom with the praxis of Jesus.

There is also an undeniable insistence on spirituality and love freely given alone, which can lead to a kind of "Christianity light." This may stop short of being a "cheap" Christianity (like the cheap grace of which Bonhoeffer wrote), but it does lead us away from the "costly" Christianity of Jesus (like Bonhoeffer's costly grace). The praxis of justice requires spirituality and gratuity, in the sense of the experience of love freely given, or it becomes dehumanizing as all human things can. But we cannot appeal to spirituality and gratuity as a way of avoiding the praxis of responding to basic human needs. "Give them to eat" and "bring the crucified people down from the cross" have an ultimacy that nothing should be allowed to diminish.

The ultimacy of mercy. In the parable of the Good Samaritan (Lk 10:29–37) highway robbers attack people, beat them, and leave them half dead. Others, a priest and a Levite, pass by, deliberately going around them. Only the Samaritan helps.

For Jesus, mercy is first and ultimate, coming from the depth of a human being, from the very guts—*splachnizomai*—because the suffering of the victims has reached that deeply. Mercy needs no justification, not even to be commanded by God's law; it is an obligation from which nothing can excuse us. Mercy is also an obligation of "due obedience" to an authority that truly can order and demand action: the authority of those who suffer.

Third is to be crucified by human injustice and resurrected by the justice of God. Jesus' fate—like that of Martin Luther King Jr., Archbishop Romero, Bishop Munzihirwa of Bukavu, Congo (assassinated in 1996)—is the clearest expression of the need to reclaim the reality of injustice and justice in social analysis and Christian praxis. Jesus was condemned to die on a cross not by chance but because of his struggle against injustice. To forget this is not only a grave mutilation of history, but it ignores the fact that the millions of crosses in today's world do not drop down from heaven but are the result of injustice, and it also falsifies any analysis of reality.

But people do ignore it. Even theology perhaps, after years of keeping it in mind, has not been paying much attention to it. Years ago things were different. Fr. [José] Miranda once wrote: "No authority can declare everything permissible; injustice and exploitation are not that hard to discern, and Christ died to show that not everything is permissible. But not just any Christ. It is the historical Jesus that accommodation and opportunism can never claim for themselves."[2]

Years ago, too, people didn't ignore the conflictive dimension of reality. Ignacio Ellacuría wrote then: "Jesus and his enemies represent two different kinds of totality, pushing human life in opposite directions; they are practical totalities, which infuse everyday life with contradiction."[3]

Neither the life nor the death of Jesus is understandable without his struggle against injustice and the reaction of the unjust. Or, in more positive terms, his life and death cannot be understood without his love for and defense of the oppressed and without his struggle to turn that oppression around in real life. The same is true of his resurrection. God resurrected Jesus in order to do him justice, and in that way to enable all victims to have hope.

These are my reflections. I hope that the book by Joe Holland and Peter Henriot, and the new book that brings it into our time, will shed light on our reality and help to resolve the new problems of our age. I would be happy if its guidelines for a Christian response to suffering in the world included an insistence on these three things, which I consider absolutely necessary: (1) to let ourselves be affected by the reality we are analyzing, (2) to reclaim justice and injustice as essential categories, and (3) to place faith on the side of justice and against injustice. Not only can the practice of justice be nourished by faith, but it can also help faith be faith in the mystery of God, as made present in Jesus of Nazareth.

—TRANSLATED BY MARGARET WILDE

Notes

[1] For more detail, see "Reflexiones sobre Jesús y la justicia para Occidente," *Revista Latinoamericana de teología* 62 (2004): 179–98.

[2] José Miranda, *El ser y el Mesías* (Salamanca: Sigueme, 1973), 9.

[3] Ignacio Ellacuría, "Por qué muere Jesús y por qué lo matan," *Diakonía* 8 (1978): 66.

Preface

In 1980, Joe Holland and Peter Henriot, who were then on the staff of the Center of Concern in Washington, D.C., published a working paper entitled *Social Analysis* as an integral part of the ministry for social justice. To their surprise the working paper, published as a book first by the Center of Concern, became very popular and remains popular up to the present. The working paper grew out of notes they had put together for a seminar given to major superiors of women religious in the United States. In 1983 Orbis Books, the publishing arm of Maryknoll, together with the Center of Concern, published a second and enlarged edition. Since then the book has had twenty reprints, the most recent in 2004, and has been translated into seven languages. It has been in all continents and in many ministries other than justice and peace work.

In 1996 Peter Henriot wrote an article on the pastoral circle for a booklet entitled *Zeichen der Zeit: Pastoraler Zirkel, Gesellschaftsanalyse, Bibel-Teilen* (signs of the time: pastoral circle, social analysis, Bible sharing), edited by Hermann Jansen and published by Missio Aachen in Germany. In this article Henriot cited several people who were using the pastoral circle and invited other people to share their experiences with him. Frans Wijsen, a professor of mission studies at Radboud University Nijmegen, the Netherlands, responded to this invitation and narrated his experience of using the pastoral circle in ministerial formation in Tanzania and Indonesia. Since then, Henriot and Wijsen have been communicating about their joint interest in using and promoting the pastoral circle for theological reflection and social transformation.

In 1999 Henriot and Wijsen met at a conference entitled "Globalization and Its Victims" in the Indian Social Institute in Delhi, India, facilitated by, among others, Michael Amaladoss, one of the contributors to this book. As this conference focused on global and local forms of exclusion and marginalization, the need for appropriate social analysis and authentic theological reflection became evident. It was during this conference that Henriot and Wijsen took the initiative to commemorate the twenty-fifth anniversary of the first edition of *Social Analysis* and to produce an update on uses of social analysis and the pastoral circle.

It was a risky enterprise as we had no idea where to start or how to proceed. But through God's providence and with the financial help of CORDAID, the Catholic Organisation for Relief and Development Aid in

The Hague, we were able to bring fifteen interested scholars together to work on this volume. The first invitation was sent soon after the Delhi meeting in 1999, and authors were invited based on their experience in working with *Social Analysis* in various contexts. They were asked to describe their experiences, to evaluate them, and to suggest innovations for future use of the pastoral circle. The first response was very positive. Henriot and Wijsen gathered reflections from all continents, from various levels of the church (parish, diocesan, regional, and national), and focused on different concerns (justice and peace, religious pluralism, church development, and Bible sharing). Some were very practical and others more theoretical. It seemed proof that the enterprise was relevant and that the process would be fruitful.

In April 2003, Henriot and Wijsen met in Hekima College, the Jesuit School of Theology in Nairobi, Kenya, to review the suggestions that had been made by various authors, to discover the lacunae, and to make further plans for the project. We had a good exchange about the focus of such a collection of essays, the process to follow in preparation of the book, and the authors proposed to write the essays. Gender balance was lacking in the original team, and we tried to involve some female authors. On the basis of feedback various authors had given, we learned that the use of *Social Analysis* had become much broader than its original focus, expressed in the subtitle, *Linking Faith and Justice.*

The audience we had in mind was neither strictly academic nor popular, but a professional group interested in theological reflection and social transformation. The authors were asked to relate their contributions to the following five areas: the original design of the pastoral circle and how it came about in the context of the book *Social Analysis*; how the pastoral circle enriches the theological project by grounding theology in lived experience; how the pastoral circle contributes to an integral transformation process focusing on justice, development, and peace; how the pastoral circle opens a dialogue with culture in encountering a globalizing world; and agenda for future use of the pastoral circle.

Next, most authors met for a review session in the Conference Centre Soeterbeeck of the Radboud University Nijmegen, the Netherlands, in July 2004, organized by the Nijmegen Institute for Missiology. They came from all parts of the world and from various contexts, some working at the grassroots level, others working in national offices or in academic institutions, some priests, others lay people. But there was one thing that brought them together, and this was their interest in committed theology and social transformation. They had good and open discussions, and they shared their stories and reflections. They discovered hidden roots of the pastoral circle and saw new and unexpected dimensions in its use as well as its future needs.

The authors find it interesting to note that the term *pastoral circle* has been used in different settings, as have the terms *pastoral cycle* and *pastoral spiral.* If you searched the World Wide Web on November 19, 2004, using the popular search engine Google, you would have found 166 hits under *pastoral circle,* 238 hits under *pastoral cycle,* and 7 hits under *pastoral spiral.* You would have found that the term *pastoral circle* is widely used in the United States, Canada, and Africa; *pastoral cycle* is the more popular term in United Kingdom, Australia, and in Asia; and *pastoral spiral* seems an exclusively Asian term. The terms have different connotations. Whereas the original term *circle* was inspired by the "circle of praxis" as developed by Paulo Freire and the "hermeneutic circle" as elaborated by Juan Luis Segundo, some people were of the opinion that the term *circle* was not appropriate. They preferred the term *cycle* to stress the *openness* of the process (the diagram in the first edition of *Social Analysis* shows a closed circle). Still others preferred the term *spiral* to emphasize the *ongoing* character of the process. It is not a project in the sense of having a clear starting point and a defined end.

The term *pastoral circle* is widely used in formation programs for social ministry (justice and peace, social teaching of the church), spiritual renewal, pastoral ministry, mission and ecology; the term *pastoral cycle* seems more popular in pastoral care, pastoral theology, retreat programs, and religious education. The term *pastoral spiral* is most often used in the Federation of Asian Bishops' Conferences, such as the Bishops' Institute for Social Action and the Asian Institute for Social Action, in particular in the Philippines and Indonesia. But the term is also used in course descriptions in academic handbooks of theological schools and colleges.

The editors of this volume met in the Galilee Centre, the Jesuit Centre for Human and Spiritual Renewal in Debre Zeit, Ethiopia, in November 2004, to finalize the manuscript. We found that all contributions were rich in their content, reflecting a variety of experiences, and that none of them would fit exclusively into one of the five areas mentioned earlier. Therefore, we believed that we would be doing them an injustice by forcing them into clear-cut categories. Yet we also thought that we would facilitate reading by placing the fifteen contributions into a structure, albeit a loose and flexible one. We tried a "see, judge, and act" scheme, distinguishing descriptive, evaluative, and innovative contributions, but this did an injustice to most of them. We thought about focusing on personal transformation, societal transformation, ecclesial transformation, and theological transformation, but these distinctions also proved not to be very helpful. Finally we decided to focus on the use of the pastoral circle: its use in pastoral situations (Part I), its use in academic settings (Part II) and its future use (Part III).

In talking about future use we realized how different our present-day context is from the context in which the first edition of *Social Analysis* was written. In 1980 the Berlin Wall was still there, and the Cold War was going on. Certain issues are raised much more strongly now than they were in the 1980s—the issues of gender, ecology and pluralism, to mention but a few. Information-and-communication technology facilitated, among other things, globalization of economy and politics but also caused a "retribalization" (McLuhan), manifest in both in ethnic and religious extremism. The Cold War has been replaced by a War against Terrorism. Postmodernism influenced a personal search for truth and spirituality but also a reaction of neo-conservatism, seeking certainty, both in political institutions and in centralized ecclesial structures. Bio-technologies raise new medical and moral issues, as does the HIV/AIDS epidemic, and the gap between the rich and the poor has become wider, both in the Northern and the Southern hemispheres.

It is hoped that this update and revision of the pastoral circle will stimulate open and critical thinking within and outside the church. Possibly some of the issues mentioned above will have been solved at the fiftieth anniversary of *Social Analysis*. Undoubtedly, in line with the ongoing dialectic between experience and reflection, new and unexpected problems will have emerged by then. We look forward to seeing a new generation of theologians and activists, in the West and in the rest of the world, revisiting *Social Analysis* then.

Introduction _____

Roots of the Pastoral Circle
in Personal Experiences
and Catholic Social Tradition

JOE HOLLAND

It is hard for me to believe that twenty-five years have passed since Peter Henriot and I wrote *Social Analysis*. It is harder to believe that the book still appears even partially relevant. I also find it humbling that so many devoted people in so many diverse places have found and continue to find this little book helpful. Finally, I even find it providential that the book had such an impact, for Peter Henriot and I really did not set out to write a book, and it grew rather unexpectedly out of modest notes that we had casually put together for a seminar given to major superiors of women religious in the United States. The Holy Spirit must have chosen us for a project whose impact would far exceed the limits of our modest talents.

In their invitation to prepare an essay for this seminar, Frans Wijsen and Peter Henriot asked me to offer some "opening reflections" on "how and why the pastoral circle was originally designed." I will respond by offering reflections on (1) the personal roots of my interest in the pastoral circle, and (2) the historical roots of the pastoral circle in the tradition of Catholic social thought and action.

Those who may not be so interested in my personal story may go straight to the second area. My purpose in telling a personal tale is simply to show how historical experiences much larger than my own were at work behind the scenes in the selection and communication of the pastoral circle.

Also, in these reflections, without in any way discounting the rich and diverse complexity of local experiences, I address the "global" perspective of the pastoral circle, since that has been my focus and experience. Peter Henriot has been more skilled with the "local" side, and he continues to do rich work there, as do many others. Certainly the local side is the more important one, but I hope that analyses of the global context are of service to the local.

I also address here the social-analysis dimension of the pastoral circle, since it has been my strongest interest. Others in the seminar will no doubt speak more to the other dimensions of the circle, and do so more eloquently than I might, though perhaps on another occasion there will be opportunity to develop my thoughts regarding theological reflection and pastoral planning.

Personal Experiences

My personal social history has been one source for my interest in the pastoral circle, even if indirectly. I myself have never undergone any harsh social suffering; indeed, my entire life has been bourgeois or middle class, if only at a modest level. But both family history and personal circumstances pressed upon me a profound consciousness of social concern, which in turn pressed me toward social analysis and toward the method of the pastoral circle.

Memories from a Long Oppressed Nation

Growing up originally in New York City within a self-consciously Irish-immigrant ethnic family, I imbibed from my father's parents' home endless stories that early on awakened a sense of social justice. I learned about the British Empire's long oppression of the Irish people, which Karl Marx had claimed was the proving ground for modern Western imperialism. I learned that my grandmother at the age of fourteen had come to New York City from rural Ireland (in Spanish we would call her a *campesina*) to work as a servant for a rich family. I learned too that my grandfather's father in Ireland had been the leader of the anti-British farmers' movement in his native county of Kilkenny, and that British troops had burned the family house to the ground and built an army barracks on its street. From my own father I heard stories of his childhood trip to Ireland—about the dreaded Black and Tans, English prisoners conscripted into the British Army and sent to terrorize the rebellious Irish population, and the equally dreaded Protestant "marching bands" in the North, who also terrorized the poor Northern Irish Catholic population.

I learned that my mother's father and his sister had been orphaned as children in the Boston area, their father dying from post-combat exhaustion as a Union foot soldier in the notoriously bloody US Civil War. My mother's father's family had immigrated to America in the mid-nineteenth century from Ireland's West Kerry (then one of the poorest areas of Ireland) during the deadly famine times. Actually it was not a famine but a legal starvation enforced by British "free-market" policy. There was abundant food in Ireland, but it was grown by British landlords strictly as lucrative cash crops for free-market export to wealthier buyers abroad.

My parents and our extended family members were by and large believers in a progressive social democracy and voted accordingly, as did most of our family friends. Such was the socially conscious world of European industrial-immigrant Catholicism during the middle years of the twentieth century. My father was and remains at ninety-two a man deeply devoted to social justice. Though he held a prestigious position as a real-estate attorney in New York City, and even served as a vice-president of the American Bar Association, his great love was his unpaid "night job," namely, volunteer work in progressive political-reform movements, and especially volunteer work to create affordable housing for low-income families.

Radical Catholic Thought in the Americas

In my early university training and early professional career during the 1960s, I stumbled on and became linked loosely to the Catholic Worker Movement, founded in the United States by Peter Maurin and Dorothy Day. Next I had the privilege of working pastorally at the grassroots level with *campesinos* in rural Puerto Rico. Later I worked with immigrant Puerto Ricans who had come to the mainland United States to seek employment at the bottom rungs of the urban industrial system. In addition, I became involved with the War on Poverty that grew out of the presidency of John F. Kennedy, and I also became an active leader against the Vietnam War, or more widely, the War in Southeast Asia. These were all moving and powerful experiences for a young person, and from them I received much more than I ever gave.

Later circumstances determined that grassroots pastoral work would no longer be a feasible option, though I would have preferred to have stayed in that work. So I decided to go on for advanced university studies to help me think through the meaning of all that I had learned and to try to figure out what to do next with my professional life. I was fortunate to be accepted into a doctoral program in church and society at the University of Chicago, a program led by Gibson Winter, a profound and prophetic social theologian and Anglican priest who would become my teacher, mentor, and dear friend.

During my earlier Spanish-speaking pastoral work with Puerto Rican communities, I had made early contact with the new radical movements in the Latin American church. Indeed, Paulo Freire had come to work with us in our local community to help found an alternative high school for dropouts from the poor Latino and African American communities. It was during those years that the famous Medellín Conference took place, as well as the World Synod of Bishops, Justice in the World. So I brought all that with me to Chicago and began to study the social-scientific and philosophical roots of the new liberation theology.

Freire, Hegel, and Marx, as well as cultural Marxism, were my favorite studies, all set with a wider interdisciplinary dialogue among theology, philosophy, and the human sciences as developed within the limits of the modern Western intellectual tradition. My main focus, however, was the emergence of liberation theology in Latin America, including its distinct expressions in Brazil, Peru, Chile, Uruguay, and elsewhere.

While at Chicago I received a Fulbright Scholarship to the Universidad Católica in Santiago, Chile, to study the interaction of Marxism and Christianity during the socialist government of Dr. Salvador Allende. So my wife, Paquita, and I, with our infant son, Daniel, moved to Chile. The time in Chile proved an extraordinary experience, though one seared by the deep tragedy of the US-supported *golpe del estado*. The impending birth of our second child (a daughter named Natanya) required that we leave Chile a month earlier than planned, and as it turned out, just before the coup. This may have saved our lives, for following the coup many friends and acquaintances were quickly arrested, with some suffering torture and even execution.

Formative Years at the Center of Concern

After the years at Chicago I had the marvelous experience of working fifteen years at the Center of Concern with Peter Henriot and a score of other extraordinary individuals, especially Bill Ryan, the center's founding Jesuit director, who became a close friend and second mentor.

One of my first jobs at the center was to assist the exiled Chilean diocesan priest Sergio Torres (later co-founder of the Ecumenical Association of Third World Theologians) with his new Theology in the Americas project. This project brought together in dialogue Latin American liberation theologians and many older and newer theological traditions in North America, including black theology, Hispanic theology, Native American theology, feminist theology, and what Harvey Cox of Harvard humorously called WHAM theology, that is, White Anglo Saxon male theology. Though ethnically not an Anglo Saxon but a Celt, I nonetheless found a welcome home in that last group.

From the Theology in the Americas experience I learned the concrete complexity of social analysis and, in particular, how conflicting factors of class, race-ethnicity, gender, and geography are bewilderingly intertwined and never exist as autonomous social categories. I also learned that tensions and conflicts within this concrete complexity are not easily or quickly resolved. Using these insights I prepared for the Theology in the Americas Conference a background book titled *The American Journey*. In it I offered what I hope was a prophetic social-analytical perspective on the past, present, and future of the United States. The book attempted to weave together the historically evolutionary holism of society's cultural-spiritual, political-juridical, and technological-economic structures, with all the complexity of their class, racial-ethnic, and gender dimensions. I laid out the analysis within a global context and projected three futurist trends: (1) the growth of the political Right; (2) an attack on the social-welfare state; and (3) a crisis of communism. This was my first attempt at social analysis as part of a theological project.

It was because of the Center of Concern's work with Theology in the Americas that Peter Henriot and I received the invitation to give that seminar to major superiors of women religious, out of which *Social Analysis* grew. So here the story should stop, since it is where the book appears, even though the Holy Spirit later guided me to ever richer experiences that also bear on the pastoral circle. But they are stories for another time and place. Let us turn now to reflections on the wider roots of the pastoral circle in the tradition of Catholic social thought and action.

The Catholic Social Tradition

In tracing the historical roots of the pastoral circle we can discern three historical levels of sources for the method. The first and most obvious level is, of course, Latin American liberation theology. The second level is the older "see, judge, act" tradition of modern lay Catholic Action movements, originally European in character, and growing out of the deep tradition of Catholic social teaching. The third level is the praxis model *(phronesis)* of Aristotelian thought, which entered the Catholic tradition through medieval Scholasticism. I speak at more length of the first level and only briefly of the second and third.

Roots in Latin American Liberation Theology

The pastoral circle comes to us most immediately, of course, from Latin American liberation theology, a rich and still developing theological movement. In addressing this root I first offer some reflections on the historical context of liberation theology and then reflect briefly on each of its three steps.

I do not include here the "insertion" phase of the pastoral circle as found in *Social Analysis*, because it was not found explicitly in the original model of liberation theology or in the earlier "see, judge, act" model. When drafting the manuscript, Peter Henriot and I had a friendly and even humorous disagreement about whether or not to include it, with Peter Henriot in favor and myself opposed. My viewpoint was that the term *insertion* reflected the old Platonic consciousness of dualistic spirituality that saw the religious reality as outside the temporal world. Instead, I argued that everyone was already and always a part of the very fabric of the social reality and, therefore, could not be "inserted" into it. Nonetheless, being self-consciously explicit about our social location is a helpful exercise, so I certainly do not object to its presence in the book.

Clearly Latin American liberation theology arose as a movement linked to the post–World War II revolutionary spirit of overthrowing formal European industrial-capitalist colonialism in Africa and Asia, a form of colonialism that had been implanted following the birth of the second stage of industrial capitalism (the machine revolution) in the second half of the nineteenth century. Latin America had been originally colonized in the form of European mercantile-capitalist colonialism two hundred years earlier, but in the industrial-capitalist era it had come under the control of US neo-colonialism.

Also, one might argue that the new theological movement was a response to the profound social dislocations caused in Latin America by the earliest phase of the global stage of modern industrial capitalism, in turn precipitated by the postmodern electronic revolution. During the years of President John F. Kennedy's Alliance for Progress, international networks of transportation and communication were becoming more sophisticated and US businesses were developing a more active presence within Latin America. Two key results were the growing urban middle classes and the exploding numbers of rural peasants migrating to the expanding urban-industrial centers. Both of these developments undermined the old power of the Latin American landed aristocracies, which had been traditionally allied with the Catholic higher clergy.

Latin American liberation theology, with roots also in the "see, judge, act" methodology of Catholic Action, added richer specificity and deeper prophetic critique to this method (which I address more below). So let us now address each of the three steps of this method.

Radically Prophetic Social Analysis. To the moment of "see" (when one studies the surrounding society) the new theology brought to theological method—for the first time in an integrally and formally theological way— the contribution of the social sciences. It was perhaps no coincidence that Gustavo Gutiérrez had studied at the Catholic University of Louvain in Belgium, the home of the great radical Catholic priest-sociologist François Houtart. At the same time, many church workers in Latin America were turning to the social sciences to understand the vast social and demographic changes shaking the Latin American world. Of course, not all turned radical, for we might recall the case of Roger Veckemanns, SJ, who became a bitter enemy of liberation theology. In contrast to Veckemanns, Latin American liberation theology turned to dialogue with Marxian social analyses (though it did not accept Marxian philosophical assumptions or Marxian strategies).

It also turned, at least in the Brazilian case, back beyond Marx to his precursor in the use of the dialectic, namely, the extraordinary German philosopher G. W. F. Hegel. In many ways the Brazilian "conscientization" movement was a shift from Marx back to Hegel and, I propose, one highly helpful for dealing with the increasing hegemony of the neo-liberal cultural ideology. (While in Chile, I was blessed to be able to study with Paulo Freire's exiled master-teacher and friend from the Catholic University in São Paulo, Ernani María Fiori, himself a neo-Hegelian philosopher.)

Certainly today some criticize early liberation theology for its confinement within the analytical categories of class and colonialism, that is, for not stressing strongly the equally important dimensions of race-ethnicity and gender, as well as ecology. But its radical analysis of the dimensions of class and colonialism was an important development in Catholic social thought, and one that is being richly supplemented by more recent contributions of liberation theology stressing race-ethnicity, gender, and ecology. Others perhaps criticize the original tendency by some to limit the social-scientific perspective to authors heavily influenced by the Marxian tradition. But the integration of a Marxian critique of capitalism was also an important development (and one that John Paul II himself used in his encyclical on human work, *Laborem exercens*). It is hard to imagine how the genius-filled insights of Marx could be left out of any comprehensive social analysis, provided that the insights of other social-analytical traditions are also included, and provided that the mechanistic-materialist foundations of Marxist ideology are not accepted.[1]

Mosaic Turn in Theological Reflection. To the moment of "judge" (reflecting on what has been "seen" and doing so in the light of reason and faith, including the resources of the Bible, the church's tradition, and the *sensus fidelium*), liberation theology proposed a radical shift to the dominant classical heritage of the Catholic theological perspective.

In the Hebrew scriptures we may discern two major poles, a prophetic one centered in the figure of Moses, and a kingly one centered in the figure of the David. Though the two represent polar opposites, there is a historically organic dialectic between them. Moses was a liberator of oppressed Jewish slaves, and David was an anointed warrior-king whose establishment of a hierarchical "Zionist" kingdom of Israel represented the fulfillment of God's liberation of the slaves from Egypt under Moses' leadership. The Jewish priesthood with its Temple ultimately came to symbolize religious leadership for the Davidic perspective, while the Jewish rabbinate, created in the Babylonian Exile, came to provide leadership for the Mosaic perspective in later periods of Judaism.

In his life Jesus had presented himself more in terms of the Mosaic pole. Indeed, he defined himself as a rabbi (again, the religious leader of the post-exilic Mosaic pole) and not as a priest (the religious leader of the Davidic pole). Further, his Jewish name, Joshua or Yeshuah (with Jesus being Greek version) is the biblical name of the one who continued the mission of Moses.

With the Christianization of the Roman Empire under Constantine, and with seminal roots in pro-Roman Pauline theology, the imperial Christian understanding shifted away from the socially prophetic Mosaic pole to the socially legitimating Davidic one, as reflected in the Pauline emphasis on

Jesus' title of Christos, that is, the anointed king like David. In the Davidic pole the social structure is seen as legitimate and not open to fundamental or systemic prophetic critique (while in the Mosaic pole the whole social structure is prophetically called into question). And so it was with classical and modern Catholic Christianity's Davidic legitimating of the original Roman Empire, of the later Holy Roman Empire, and of the still later mercantile-capitalist European empires of the sixteenth-century conquest of the Americas, as well as of the industrial-capitalist European empires of the nineteenth-century conquest of Africa and Asia.

Through its turn to the symbol of the Exodus, grounding symbolically its prophetic critique of the structural captivity of the poor and oppressed, liberation theology proposed a radical shift for the grounding historical symbolism of Catholic Christianity. It was, however, not the first modern Christian tradition to make this turn, for at the birth of modernity African American slaves in the English colonies of what is today the United States had pioneered the way. Where the English Puritan John Winthrop had looked out at the "new land" and proclaimed it in Davidic terms a "New Jerusalem," the oppressed slaves captive in the same land lamented in their soul songs that they were held in a Mosaic "New Egypt."

Call for Transformative Strategy. To the moment of "act" (the point at which the faith-filled reflection on the social reality strategizes how to transform the world), liberation theology added two important contributions, one at the macro level and another at the micro level, with both aimed at systemic transformation.

At the macro level liberation theology sought to change the entire social system of the industrial-capitalist periphery of Latin America. Implicitly, it appears from the literature, the desired transformation would be some revisionist form of socialism, presumably democratic and open to religion, and decentralist and communitarian in orientation—in contrast to the reigning state-centered models of nationalization required in the secular socialist and communist traditions.

Today, with hindsight, we might say that liberation theology's optimistic hopes for dramatic transformations proved naive, especially in the wake of the tens of thousands, perhaps hundreds of thousands, of Latin American victims of repression during the last three decades of the twentieth century. But naive optimism does not invalidate the mission of seeking fundamental systemic transformation; indeed, the need for fundamental transformation seems now more urgent than ever, though not as originally imagined in the framework of the early liberation theology movement.

At the micro level, liberation theology called socially committed disciples of Jesus to form basic Christian communities as a way of supporting themselves spiritually in the resistance against the system's interwoven economic exploitation, political repression, and cultural seduction, and also as a way of participating in the process of transformation. Here again the contribution met an obstacle, for the modern professionalized and clericalized form of the Catholic presbyterate was not able to provide adequate grassroots pastoral leadership for the proliferation of small Christian communities. As a result, postmodern recruitment to the small community model yielded more to the advances of evangelical and pentecostal churches, which did not hesitate to set up radically decentralized, deprofessionalized, and declericalized models of pastoral leadership. This was not the fault of liberation theologians but rather of the rigid ecclesial imagination of the Catholic church's episcopal leadership.

Roots in the Lay Catholic Action Movement. Latin American liberation theology also grew out of the earlier and originally European lay Catholic Action movement by rendering it intellectually more sophisticated and prophetic and by radicalizing its famous "see, judge, act" methodology.

As is widely known, the "see, judge, act" methodology had been publicly articulated by the late Belgian Cardinal Joseph Cardijn, founder of the Young Christian Workers (YCW) movement, better known in the Romance languages as the JOC movement. Interestingly, Cardijn was always close to the international Pax Romana lay movement of Catholic Action, both before and after the 1925 foundation of YCW.

In this same vein Gustavo Gutiérrez, the acknowledged father of liberation theology, had been a chaplain for Pax Romana in Peru and still remains the official Pax Romana chaplain for Latin America. Similarly, Paulo Freire and the Basic Education movement in Brazil, out of which the first shoots of the basic Christian communities movement emerged, were all rooted in the Brazilian Catholic Action movement. One might even propose that the Brazilian Workers Party and the World Social Forum, also rooted in Brazil, were further developments of this energy, though no longer in confessionally Catholic form.

While the formula of "see, judge, act" has generally been seen as an ingenious invention of Cardijn, Stefan Gignacz, a native Australian and now Malaysian-based YCW alumnus and lay canon lawyer, points out that Cardijn himself suggested that it had earlier roots but for some reason was always reticent about these roots. Gignacz, whose doctoral thesis at Louvain focused on this very area, argues that Cardijn's "see, judge, act" method was actually a continuation of the work of the French lay Catholic democratic movement known as Le Sillon (the furrow), founded by Marc Sagnier, with even earlier roots in often marginalized Catholic lay movements and going back to the inspiration of prophetic lay figures like Fréderic Ozanam and also to the visionary but excommunicated French diocesan priest of the mid-nineteenth century Felicité de Lamennais.[2] It is interesting that Lamennais, perhaps the first person to use the phrase "Christian democracy," also spoke of "Christian socialism," albeit in a pre-Marxist sense of a general Christian commitment to the impoverished and exploited working class of early industrial capitalism.

Cardijn's reticence, Gignacz continues, was due to the fact that the Vatican had condemned Le Sillon, so Cardijn carefully and intentionally provided camouflage for continuation of its spirit within a new container. Cardijn's "see, judge, act" formula was, according to Gignacz, his shorthand way of referring to methods of democratic education pioneered by Le Sillon in its campaign to promote study circles. Even Cardijn's notion of forming elite leaders drawn from the worker masses was based on the methods of Le Sillon. Apparently what was blocked in earlier generations finally succeeded under Cardijn's shrewd clerical leadership.

Roots in Catholic Social Teaching from 1740. But the three-step model of the pastoral circle seems also to have still older roots. Much to my surprise, in doing research for two volumes on the historical, philosophical, and theological development of Catholic social teaching in the papal encyclicals, I found the three-step method employed by the popes from the beginning of this tradition in 1740.[3]

Without spending any more time on this point, suffice it to note that the structure of papal social encyclicals from 1740 forward generally follows a three-step model quite similar to Cardijn's "see, judge, act" method and to liberation theology's three moments of social analysis, theological reflection, and pastoral planning. These encyclicals typically begin with a diagnosis of the social problems confronting society and the church within it; they next move to retrieve from the faith tradition appropriate biblical and theological wisdom to evaluate these problems (generally viewed in negative terms); and finally, in light of this wisdom, they propose pastoral lines of strategy. The actual content of these three steps differs during different periods of the tradition, but the underlying methodology is constant.

Why, we might ask, do we find such commonality of method—albeit with differing contents; differing levels of sophistication; and differing sociological, theological, and pastoral orientations—across such a wide historical span of the Catholic tradition? In the next section I propose a response to that important question.

Catholic Appropriation of Aristotle's Phronesis

In a deeper philosophical sense the third and oldest source of the pastoral circle comes to Catholicism, I propose, from the African Islamic Aristotelian tradition in southern Spain, appropriated by Thomas Aquinas at the University of Paris in the thirteenth century. Up to that point the dominant philosophical tradition in Western Christian civilization had been Platonism or neo-Platonism, with Augustine of Hippo, of course, as the outstanding neo-Platonic theologian of the Christian tradition.

For Plato (at least for the traditional account of his texts[4]), truth was not discovered through investigation of the sensate material world, but rather through the rationalist intuition ("remembering" from a prior life of the soul outside the body) of abstract intellectual ideas, usually translated in English as "forms." The truth of these forms could then be ethically "applied" from higher rational heights to the lower and limited material world of the particularities of time and space. Thus, for the Platonic tradition, ethics implicitly involves two methodological moments: (1) the articulation of moral "axioms" (abstract "values" or "ideals") based on the intelligible forms; and (2) the application from above of these ideals to the less real world.

By contrast, for Aristotle the material world, known through the senses, was the only source of our knowledge, and so the search for abstract truth grew only out of concrete knowledge of the real world. In the realm of ethics Aristotle made a further distinction, not found in Plato, between theoretical reason and practical reason *(phronesis)*, with the latter involving less certitude and requiring prudential judgment. Thus, for the Aristotelian tradition, ethics implicitly involves three methodological moments: (1) rational-empirical study of reality; (2) articulation of general moral principles of right reason developed from knowledge of the reality; and (3) prudential recommendations on how to proceed in action according to right reason within reality.

There are many more dimensions of contrast between Platonic and Aristotelian ethics that could also be mentioned. For example, Aristotle proposed a communitarian understanding of the human person, claimed that the state is a natural institution rooted in the family and charged with developing virtuous citizens and with seeking the common good, and grounded ethics in the ways of nature (akin to the later Stoic tradition of natural law and today to the return to natural ecological wisdom)—all of which are found in the Catholic social-ethical tradition. By contrast, for Plato the human person was an autonomous individual who formed voluntary but rational social contacts, the state was the most powerful of these contracts and had as its purpose to enhance the economic division of labor and to restrain political evil, and the institution of the family was a concession to the masses but something elites should escape.

While the Platonic approach to social ethics is still found through Kantian variants in much of liberal Protestantism, and while in some ways the cultural project of the modern world may be seen in part as an outgrowth of a pervasive Platonic revival during the European Renaissance, the Aristotelian approach to social ethics has been dominant in Catholicism to some degree since the time of Aquinas and almost universally since the time of the Council of Trent.

Intriguing further developments in the Catholic social-ethical appropriation of Aristotle were achieved by early modern Spanish Scholastic theologians and activists as a critique of the Spanish *Conquista*. Those late Scholastics who took up the defense of the original peoples of the Americas (Native Americans) may well have planted key philosophical foundations for the subsequent legal justification of participatory democracy and for the defense of human rights. This historical period and these figures remain an important area for future research. But, to confirm the link back to liberation theology, let us at least note here that Gustavo Gutiérrez was so attracted to the greatest among the activists of this late Scholastic coalition, Bartolomé de Las Casas, that he produced a major study of his life and, like Las Casas, himself became a Dominican friar.

Conclusion

While it may have proven stimulating to reflect on the personal and historical roots of the pastoral circle, that stimulation itself grants us no fertility unless we set it against the horizon of fresh challenges in our emerging future. Elsewhere I have written more about the present global historical context and about my interpretation of the emerging postmodern era.[5] It is my sincere hope that other authors in this volume will address the issue of postmodernity, as well as other challenges for the future use of the pastoral circle, such as ethnicity, gender, and ecology.

Notes

[1] It is important to note that while Catholic social teaching has been and remains deeply critical of capitalism, it is not thereby anti-business. Capitalism as a formal system is an experiment of only a few hundred years within the modern era of the human journey, and due to its undermining of ecological, societal, and spiritual sustainability, it increasingly appears to be a failed experiment. Business, by contrast, is thousands of years old and will continue, I propose, in the post-capitalist era to flourish, albeit in a more communitarian and ecological form.

[2] Stefan Gignacz has summarized his analysis in ENEWS, the electronic journal of Pax Romana's Australian Catholic Movement for Intellectual and Cultural Affairs. Available at www.acmica.org.

[3] Only the first in this two-part series has been published: Joe Holland, *Modern Catholic Social Teaching: The Popes Confront the Industrial Era, 1740–1958* (Mahwah, NJ: Paulist Press, 2003). It is important to note that papal social encyclicals do not begin in 1891 with *Rerum novarum*, though it provides the foundation for the strategic papal response to the second stage of industrial capitalism. Rather, they begin in 1740 with the popes' first strategic responses to the European Enlightenment with its new ideology of liberalism, and then later to its embodiment in liberal democracy and liberal capitalism.

[4] There are current postmodernist readings of Plato that claim his apparent doctrines were actually the opposite of what he held and were sketched in a playful sense of paradox and irony. Whether or not these are accurate readings, and I myself have deep doubts about them, what is at stake is not Plato's actual intentions but rather the dominant appropriation of Plato within classical Christian civilization. In that appropriation Plato's words were clearly taken at face value.

[5] See Joe Holland, *The Regeneration of Ecological, Societal, and Spiritual Life: The Challenge to Humanity in the Emerging Postmodern Planetary Civilization* (Miami: Pax Romana Center for International Study of Catholic Social Teaching, 2003).

Part I

The Use in Pastoral Situations

In this first part of the book the contributors share their experiences in the use of the pastoral circle in concrete pastoral situations. Peter Henriot shows how the pastoral circle can be fruitfully applied, in a simple form, in the daily life of Small Christian Communities (SCCs) (the name given in Eastern Africa countries to base Christian communities). He also shows how the pastoral circle can be applied in a more complex way in the pastoral planning of bishops' conferences and in the dissemination of the Catholic social teaching.

Juan José Luna gives a more detailed account of how the pastoral circle was used in the preparation and process of the Inter-Regional Meeting of the Bishops of Southern Africa (IMBISA) in its planning for justice and peace. As an echo to this experience, Joseph Elsener, playing the role of devil's advocate, critically analyzes the pitfalls of the IMBISA experience and goes beyond that experience by making us aware of some possible dangers that may make the use of the pastoral circle irrelevant or illusory.

The witness of Christine Bodewes is direct and personal. She offers a full picture of the use of the pastoral circle in renewing the parish of Christ the King in the Kibera slums of Nairobi, Kenya, and outlines the main lessons she drew from the whole process.

The practical use of the pastoral circle in the cultural context of the local churches in Indonesia is presented at the end of Part I by Johannes Banawiratma. More than the chronicle of a particular experience, he stresses the need of approaching the pastoral circle not just as a technical method but as a spirituality. This spirituality is presented in ten main "agendas" that describe the fundamental interior attitude both in the individual and in the community if the use of the pastoral circle is to be successful.

1

Social Discernment
and the Pastoral Circle

PETER HENRIOT

"Please give us a workshop on discernment and the pastoral circle." That recent request, coming from a group of Zambian religious sisters, brought to my memory an incident of over twenty years ago. It was in the early 1980s, just a short time after the first edition of *Social Analysis* had appeared from the office where I then worked, the Center of Concern, in Washington D.C. Joe Holland and I had collaborated on this small booklet, which had begun to gain great popularity. I was invited to give a series of workshops in different parts of the Philippines, explaining our approach to social analysis to various audiences comprised of pastoral workers, social activists, members of religious congregations, student groups, and local popular communities.

Just a few weeks before arriving in the Philippines, I learned that the Catholic Bishops' Conference there had forbidden any church-sponsored workshops on social analysis. "Too Marxist, too provocative, too danger-ous"—these were the grounds for banning such programs in those tense days of the Marcos dictatorship. What to do? It was too late to cancel the visit altogether, and it was too important to forgo the opportunity both to share insights and to learn from others who were working on the ground.

So for one month the program went ahead, with workshops offered not as social analysis but as social discernment. Very *Jesuitical*, one friend told me! Yes, I suppose it was, in at least two senses: First, a clever turn of phrase to facilitate already designed action. Second, a more profound real-ization of the Jesuit—Ignatian—principle that God's action in history is "discernible" through carefully paying heed to one's feelings, causes of deep-est movements, desires rooted in values, and steps toward action.

Ignatius placed great emphasis on attention to the world around us, to "finding God in all things." Not simply finding the Divinity in a mystical revelation but finding God's loving involvement in the practical matters of

15

everyday life. "Contemplation on the Incarnation," a central exercise to be undertaken by retreatants during the Second Week of the *Spiritual Exercises* (see Ignatius Loyola 1992, 56), focuses on the world into which the Second Person of the Trinity is to be missioned. Ignatius asks retreatants to consider, with the same glance of the Trinity, the face of the globe with people rich and poor, black and white, living and dying, loving and killing, and so on. The spark of love ignited by this glance precipitated the incarnation event for the Trinity and, for the retreatants similarly moved, gives rise to the engaged service of humanity.

What is being addressed here, it seems to me, is the theological foundation for "reading the signs of the times." Such a "reading" is central to the church's social teaching—made explicit in John XXIII's *Pacem in terris* (1963) and Vatican II's *Gaudium et spes* (1965). This biblical concept notes that the God revealed in the Judeo-Christian tradition is a God of history, a God active in history. This God is the Yahweh who hears the cries of the oppressed people, accompanies them on a journey of liberation, establishes them as the light of the nations, chastises them for their infidelities, re-creates them in loving forgiveness. This God is the Jesus who, born of a woman, grows in ordinary village life, submits to baptism with sisters and brothers in the River Jordan, preaches good news to the poor, gathers a community of co-workers, endures persecution from the threatened powers, and experiences new life in the fullness of the resurrection.

It is the very ordinariness of God's action in history that is so extraordinary—and so compelling for us to "read," to discern, in the signs around us. This is a contextualization of experience. Discernment done with a social foundation, a social purpose, and a social consequence becomes a way of sharing in God's action in history.

But this "reading" is not simply *cognitive*, an intellectual exercise leading to understanding. It is also *affective* and *effective: Affective* in the sense of touching the deepest of our values and strongly motivating our responses. *Effective* in the sense of organizing our responses with planning, execution, and evaluation. Such a threefold description of faith has been used by theologian Avery Dulles, SJ (Dulles 1977).

How does all of this relate to the pastoral circle that Joe Holland and I drew and described in the opening section of *Social Analysis: Linking Faith and Justice*? Drawing upon my experiences of social justice work during the past fifteen years in Africa, let me offer two responses: first, examples of the use of the pastoral circle in a "discerning" fashion, and second, some lessons that can be learned from such use.

Small Christian Communities and the Pastoral Circle

The pastoral plan of the church in Zambia and in many other parts of Africa is based in the development of small Christian communities (SCCs) (see, for example, Mejía 1993). Similar in design and structure, if not always similar in purpose and action, to the base Christian communities *(communidades de base)* of Latin America, these SCCs bring together members of a local parish into different sections to deal with the pastoral and social life of the people. At its best the SCC is the church in the neighborhood, and the Sunday celebration in the larger parish is the gathering of the community of communities. I say "at its best" because the ideal is not always realized due to lack of leadership skills, weakness of commitment, and other readily understandable problems. In a very poor country like Zambia, these problems are exacerbated by the poverty struggle and cultural challenges.

To strengthen the life of the SCCs, the Jesuit Centre for Theological Reflection has in recent years developed some small pamphlets for use by these groups during their weekly meetings. The purpose of the pamphlets is to provide a resource for guided reflection that can generate faith-based action. The pastoral circle serves as the framework for the pamphlets.

One such pamphlet is entitled *What Is the Church's Social Teaching Saying about Poverty?* (JCTR 2003) In a country where 80 percent of the people live—barely survive—on less than one US dollar a day (the World Bank's definition of absolute poverty), Zambians know the issue of poverty all too well. But a Christian response to this issue is not always well understood. Hence, there is need for a guide that would sharpen the *cognitive* (better understanding), enhance the *affective* (deeper values), and strengthen the *effective* (improved response).

In four simple steps the pamphlet moves around the moments of the pastoral circle. The group members who gather for a weekday meeting of their SCC are invited *first* to listen to a story of Amai (Mrs.) Banda, who sells tomatoes by the side of the road in order to earn a little money to feed her family and meet other basic necessities. Her daily activities are described; her real-life struggle is illustrated. Then the community members are asked if they know of women like Amai Banda, or, indeed, if any of those present experience similar struggles. They are given the chance to share how they feel about such struggles in their daily lives and in the lives of the people around them. This is the moment of *contact*, the anecdotal, the asking of *what* is happening.

The *second moment* is a movement from the anecdotal to the analytical, when the group asks, "*Why* is it happening?" Simple *social analysis* stimulates a probing of causes, large and small. Some history is recounted (how long has this severe poverty existed?), some internal factors explored (what is the result of corruption?), and external factors investigated (what are the consequences of IMF and World Bank influences?). Are there cultural aspects that should be examined (such as gender determinants)? The social-analysis step helps the members of the community to see that poverty is not simply a natural phenomenon to be accepted as *inevitable,* but rather that it is the effect of human decisions taken by identifiable human actors. It can be changed.

"What does this mean to us as *Christians?*" is the question that moves the community members to the *third moment* in the pastoral circle, *reflection*. A faith reflection, a theological reflection, helps the group members identify the values that should be central to their own understanding and reaction to the issue of poverty they have contacted and analyzed. This is a critically important step, particularly in dealing with the issue of poverty. A careful scriptural study of poverty dismisses the fatalistic attitude of "the poor are always with us." And an opening of the riches of church social teaching motivates a "preferential option for the poor."

In getting the group to discuss the *fourth moment*, *response*, the pamphlet poses the question: "What do we do?" As it moves toward action, the group has to deal with two issues: Who and/or what is the church? Should the church be involved in politics? The latter question comes up when the group is challenged to see that poverty cannot be effectively responded to only through *charity* but must include a commitment to justice.

A second example of the use of the pastoral circle in materials prepared for the SCCs in Zambia is found in the pamphlet *Traditional Healing* (JCTR 2004). This pamphlet was developed by the JCTR's Inculturation Task Force in response to strong interest in help for dealing with the dilemma felt by many Zambian churchgoers: Can good Christians consult traditional healers, the *ng'anga*, herbalists, witchdoctors? As a matter of fact, good Christians do consult and in many instances are significantly helped by traditional healers. In many instances the traditional healers are themselves good Christians.

While not following with strict temporal logic the moments of the pastoral circle, this pamphlet does incorporate the four moments in its eight chapters. Storytelling about people who have consulted traditional healers, or who fear they have been bewitched, or who feel that ancestors are affecting changes in their lives, opens up the *contact* of the experience being explored. Causes for confusions about consultation come up in an *analysis* of the historical influence of European missionaries who condemned traditional healing practices as "pagan," and of the dissatisfaction of Africans with a "Westernized" medical approach that is not holistic, that is, that deals only with specific complaints and not with the whole person and his or her history, emotions, social context, and so on.

The third moment of the pastoral circle, *reflection*, is offered throughout the pamphlet in the introduction of appropriate Hebrew and Christian scripture texts that challenge the SCC members to relate biblical accounts of healings to the contemporary scene. The reflection is enriched by questions about sacramental practices in the anointing of the sick. Finally, *response* is generated through a set of guidelines that assist them to determine what is *appropriate* in consultation with traditional healers (for example, asking for good use of herbs) and what is *inappropriate* (such as seeking vengeance on alleged enemies).

I believe that these two pamphlets are instances of very creative and effective discernment through use of the pastoral circle.

Bishops' Conferences and the Pastoral Circle

In response to the call of the African Synod (1994), bishops' conferences in Africa have been more attentive to issues of justice and peace in their pastoral programs (see Africa Faith and Justice Network 1996). This is certainly true in the IMBISA and AMECEA (Association of Member Episcopal Conferences in Eastern Africa) regions. Particularly important in the struggle to promote justice and peace is an engagement of a wider group of people than just bishops, in a longer period of time than just a meeting, in discerning the best response to the challenges faced. Here the use of the pastoral circle has been particularly helpful, even if not always totally successful.

Both Juan José Luna and Josef Elsener in their contributions to this volume have described the ups and downs of IMBISA in grappling with the challenge of poverty through use of this methodology in both the preparation of a major meeting and in the actual process of that meeting (the IMBISA General Assembly of 2001). I know from my own participation in the IMBISA preparatory period that the methodology of the pastoral circle was appreciated for both its simplicity and its cogency. It helped to raise the right questions at cognitive, affective, and effective levels, even if the fullest answers were not always provided (see IMBISA 2002).

A second use of the pastoral circle by the IMBISA members was planned for the General Assembly of 2004. The topic of the meeting is a very burning issue in the churches in southern Africa—indeed throughout Africa and other developing regions—that is, *self-reliance*, or how independent a church can be in terms of meeting the necessary resources for its organization and activity (Nsanzurwimo 2003). For understandable reasons, both historical (consequences of colonial foundation) and economic (conditions of severe poverty), most churches—Catholic and Protestant—find themselves in situations of heavy dependency on outside sources. Roman congregations, European donors, North American benefactors—all these groups and many more play a disproportionately influential role in supporting the organization and activities of African churches.

Financial support is not always without "strings"—conditions either explicit or implicit. Often local bishops or church officers will look over their shoulder at the funders before taking steps that might seem to be controversial, too progressive, too "African." This could be particularly true, for example, in the area of inculturation. The African Synod of Bishops, meeting in Rome in 1994, strongly endorsed the process of inculturation, that is, making the faith more authentically Christian, more genuinely African (see Africa Faith and Justice Network 1996). But sometimes funders might be a bit nervous about this topic and transmit their nervousness to those whom they are supporting.

In its preparatory stages (and in the actual gathering of bishops) the IMBISA meeting addressed this issue of self-reliance. Utilizing the pastoral circle approach, the preparation asked the following questions:

1. *Contact:* Are there stories that we can tell about what being self-reliant means and how we have experienced this in our church over the past decade (or in a shorter time)? What have been the successes and failures? How do people—clergy and laity—react to the call to be self-reliant? Why would we bring up this topic now? What do our cooperating partners (donors) tell us about self-reliance?

2. *Analysis:* Why are we succeeding or failing in our efforts to be self-reliant? Are there any historical factors influencing our attitudes and practices about self-reliance? What are the wider social, economic, and political factors in our region that are affecting efforts at self-reliance? in our global situation? Are there cultural reasons that either promote or hinder self-reliance? Why are traditional cooperating partners (donors) raising questions about self-reliance at this time? Do these donors have a different set of values about this topic of self-reliance that influences their perceptions and responses? Will funds from outside be decreasing? Why?

3. *Reflection:* Is there anything in scripture that could guide us in our pursuit of self-reliance (for example, communities in early church; see the Acts of the Apostles and Pauline letters)? What models of church are more conducive to promoting self-reliance (such as more involvement of the laity)? What principles from the church's social teaching might guide our evaluation of the situation (for example, community, solidarity, the option for the poor)? What theological implications are there for styles of leadership within the church? Is self-reliance a realistic goal for very poor churches such as the ones in IMBISA region?

4. *Response:* How can the church as a whole in the IMBISA region work together for greater self-reliance? What is the role of the bishops, of local clergy, of laity organizations, of the faithful? What might be a strategic plan (can we set targets to be met, provide dates to be followed, and give key responsibilities to a wide group of people)? How can we be modest in our efforts and clear in our commitments? Does this topic raise questions about implications for training church leaders such as seminarians or pastoral teams?

The planning included a working paper *(instrumentum laboris)* to provide guidance around the steps of the pastoral circle. This was to be used by the small Christian communities across the countries with the request that reports should be made by many different groups in each diocese. Such a response was intended to provide a good foundation for the plenary discussions and decisions of the actual IMBISA meeting.

Preliminary planning for this important meeting brought in many interesting responses to the suggestion of again using the pastoral circle for this IMBISA meeting. One thing has been clear: reflecting the evaluations made in this volume by Luna and Elsener of the 2001 Plenary Assembly, there is clear demand for much more *theological reflection* in this process and for much stronger *response* by the way of commitments to action and calendared evaluation of what has actually happened.

The use of the pastoral circle in another regional conference of bishops, AMECEA, is also noteworthy. There the pastoral circle was used in planning for the 2002 Fourteenth Plenary Assembly and in the actual engagement in the meeting. The assembly was entitled "Deeper Evangelization in the Third Millennium—A Challenge for AMECEA." Particularly significant was the fact that clear and definitive plans and resolutions were drawn up by the end of the meeting, focusing on "holistic evangelization and integral development" (AMECEA 2002).

Another use of the pastoral circle occurred in the preparation from 1998 to 2004 for a local diocesan synod (the first ever in the Catholic church in Ethiopia) in the Apostolic Vicariate of Awasa, Ethiopia.

Formation in the Church's Social Teaching and the Pastoral Circle

Several years ago two colleagues of mine and I wrote a book to introduce the church's social teaching to a wider audience. We entitled the book *Catholic Social Teaching* (Henriot, DeBerri, and Schultheis 1992). The subtitle, *Our Best Kept Secret*, pointed to a disappointing fact in the work of both theological reflection and social action. This is the fact that the riches of the church's social teaching are very little known and very little used. This is certainly true for most churchgoers who express surprise when the pope challenges the Bush-Blair war in Iraq, when local bishops offer advice to governments about political democracy, and when parish priests express support for a trade union's struggle for living wages for its members.

Even more lamentable is the fact that many people who work for church organizations are not familiar with the church's social teaching. This is particularly regrettable if the organization is itself committed to the promotion of social issues such as peace and justice, development, human rights, and so forth. And, of course, if the church's social teaching is absent from the formation of seminarians and religious, there is not much hope that it will be known by the laity at large.

To address the problem of the church's social teaching's being a "secret" even among those who most should know about it, a network of church social teaching advocates has been set up to serve countries in eastern and southern Africa. The African Forum for Catholic Social Teachings (AFCAST) is based at Arrupe College (University of Zimbabwe) in Harare, Zimbabwe. Over the past few years the AFCAST team has pursued research and policy studies that emphasize the value-added dimension of the church's social teaching in public policy debates and decisions. Topics that have been pursued in meetings in different countries in eastern and southern Africa include electoral practices, poverty eradication, land reform, corruption, integrity of creation.

One of AFCAST's specific projects was to develop a training module that could easily be used to assist church workers to become familiar with major principles of the church's social teaching. One of the first groups to utilize the module was Catholic Relief Services (CRS), a US-based development agency working in many dioceses in Africa (and in other parts of the world).

The framework adopted for the module is the pastoral circle. The purpose is to introduce some key principles of the church's social teaching in a very practical way by assisting those engaged in the training to relate the principles to specific issues they are dealing with. Relying again on the cognitive, affective, and effective dimensions of the pastoral circle, certain principles are chosen to be explored during each moment of the pastoral circle, so that their application is seen in very concrete fashion. The placement of the principles at specific moments of the circle, as outlined below, is admittedly arbitrary. What appears at one place on the circle might very well appear at another place. But for purposes more pedagogical than logical, the principles appear where they do.

The seven principles of the church's social teaching are the option for the poor, common good, social nature, rights and responsibilities, human dignity, solidarity, subsidiarity, and stewardship. (These seven were initially chosen both because they are very central and also because they appear in other CRS educational materials.)

To illustrate how the movement around the pastoral circle can serve as an introduction to the church's social teaching, let us take as an example the issue of poor housing in a large slum in southern Africa. The community-development committee of a local parish is designing some programs to work with the residents of the slum to help them improve environmental conditions (water, sanitation, garbage collection, roads, and so on). The justice and peace committee of the local parish is training some advocacy groups to enable them to put pressure on local government officials to take actions to improve housing, security, social services (health and education), and so forth.

How can the pastoral circle be used to show the relevance—the value-added dimension—of the church's social teaching to the work of these two committees and the community with which they are cooperating?

1. *Contact:* Stories about what is happening in the slum are told from a particular value perspective, that of the *option for the poor*. This basic

principle of church social teaching places a priority on the experiences, views, needs, feelings, and stance of the poor and most vulnerable in a community. This means that when contact is made, a privileged question to be asked is: What is happening to the poor in this situation? The Latin Americans call this stance *desde los pobres*—seeing things from the side of the poor, though the lens of their experience. The knowledge of what is happening in the shanty compounds demonstrates an "accompanying" of the poor in their lived experience.

2. *Analysis:* The question of why such conditions exist will be guided by those whose *rights* are being violated and whose *responsibilities* are called upon to change the situation. The language of rights and responsibilities—rooted in the human dignity of each person in community—pushes analytical approaches beyond economic and political causes to social and cultural causes. That is, in exploring why services are not provided in the slum or why crime rates are high, the wider picture of the *social nature* of the people involved and the obligation to promote the *common good* come into focus. No analysis is value free—we are prompted to ask certain questions, to look for answers in certain places, and to be open to consequences of these answers by the value framework within which we do our analysis. Yes, we must be objective in pursuing answers, but we must not be so naive as to imagine that social research is totally value free.

3. *Reflection:* When we come to ask what it means to our faith to evaluate this situation and what is really most at stake in this situation, we can be guided by the church's social teaching about *human dignity* and *solidarity*. Every person is made in the image of God. Dignity is not earned; it is a gift. That means that those who live in the slum and those who live elsewhere are bound together in a unity that the church's social teaching refers to as *solidarity*—an interdependence that is more ethical than empirical. Reflection guided by the church's social teaching prompts a motive to act, something that naturally leads to the fourth moment of the pastoral circle.

4. *Response:* What to do is an inevitable question in the movement around the pastoral circle. Two principles of the church's social teaching orient the threefold response of planning, action, and evaluation. The first is the principle that places action at the lowest level possible—*subsidiarity*. The second is the principle that reckons the most efficient, equitable, and sustainable use of resources, *stewardship*. To implement subsidiarity demands that planning begin with involvement of those who are most affected, who are closest to the situation, and whose cooperation is most essential. Decisions and implementations of policies to address the problems should not be made at higher levels unless doing so is unavoidable. Moreover, the choice of materials to respond—for example, in the physical infrastructures within the slum

area—should recognize ecological constraints and not be wasteful or destructive of the environment—present or future.

This example of going around the circle with principles of the church's social teaching demonstrates that the pastoral circle can be a vehicle for relating the church's social teaching to practical issues facing change agents in pastoral teams, social activists, development workers, instructors, and so on. This is, in fact, real discernment.

Another module developed with the AFCAST team working with CRS is simpler and more limited. It uses the pastoral circle to deepen the living of the church's social teaching among individuals or teams. The following steps are suggested:

1. Choose a principle;
2. Identify a positive experience of that principle;
3. Go around the circle asking the following questions:
   * What happened?
   * How were you involved?
   * Why was it positive?
   * What does this tell us about the principle?
   * How do we repeat/sustain this positive experience?
4. Evaluate what you are learning about the church's social teaching.

Conclusion

When the pastoral circle has been used in the ways I have described above, the process of discernment becomes both more practical and more profound. At least this has been my personal experience. Whether used by SCCs, bishops' conferences, or development workers, the pastoral circle can enable individuals and teams to probe their own experiences in a systematic and disciplined way. The contact with experience is enriched, the analysis deepened, the reflection enhanced, and the response strengthened.

My evaluation is not intended to enshrine the pastoral circle. Certainly the other essays in this book show a variety of approaches to using the pastoral circle, all of them contributing to more effective theology, education, gender sensitivity, social action, personal growth, and so forth. But I believe that some lessons about the pastoral circle can be drawn from the examples I've sketched here.

First, genuine contact with experience is essential. By that I mean that the exercise of going around the circle will only be as rich and rewarding as is the solid foundation of experience. The first moment in the circle cannot effectively be based on book knowledge or stories of someone else's experience. If members of the SCCs shy away from sharing their own experiences, if bishops and church workers spend more time speculating about ideal situations than focusing on everyday circumstances (however disconcerting these circumstances may be), and if development agents cite scholarly reports rather than lived realities, the following stages of the circle will be very weak and unsatisfactory indeed.

Second, analysis may be simple as well as complex. The basic aim of good analysis is to discover the *why* of the *what*—the causes of the occurrences that we have described. Moving from the anecdotal to the analytical means paying attention to the many structures of reality—being especially careful not to neglect the cultural structures (see Henriot 1998). This structural analysis can be done at several levels. We saw this in the uses of the pastoral circle described above. For example, the analysis has been *economic* (Why are Amai Banda and similar Zambians suffering poverty? Why has self-reliance become a key issue for African churches?), *political* (Why have governments not designed development policies that serve all the people?), *cultural* (Why are traditional views on healing still very important in society today? Why do women especially experience problems of poverty?), *religious* (Why do the values of the church's social teaching shape a world view within which deeper explanations are possible?). It is clear that popular use of the pastoral circle may require simpler approaches in analytical methodology.

Third, reflection must be given much more prominence, especially faith-based reflection. The phrase "theological reflection" may put some people off, unless they can be shown that it is a way of shining the light of faith on the experience that has been analyzed. It is, of course, a particular kind of faith that is used as a resource. A faith-filled reading of the signs of the times is cognitive (beliefs), affective (trusts), and effective (deeds). The SCC that reflects on the story of Amai Banda does not do theology in the abstract—the scriptural and church social teachings about poverty are very concrete, very practical. I think it is noteworthy to recall that the book in which Joe Holland and I originally sketched the pastoral circle is subtitled *Linking Faith and Justice.* The moments of reflection illustrated in this chapter are indeed faith-filled moments.

Fourth, response should always be the aim of going around the pastoral circle. To the well-known phrase from the epistle of James—"Faith without works is dead!" (Jas 3:26)—I add, "The pastoral circle without response is a waste of time!" SCCs dealing with issues of poverty or of traditional healing, bishops' conferences facing the challenges of self-reliance, development workers exploring the riches of the church's social teaching—all of these groups are not engaged in academic research but in a discernment process that leads to choices. Without the planning, action, and evaluation phases of response, there is no outcome of the pastoral circle, no consequence of the efforts put in.

These four lessons can help us understand why the pastoral circle can indeed be a methodology of discernment. If I try to recall why Joe Holland and I gave the name pastoral to the circle we drew (rather than hermeneutic or some other academic phrase), I suppose it was because we recognized the need for a practical methodology that would assist people engaged in promoting a more just world in many different spheres of life. In effect, the basis for evaluating the pastoral circle—in whatever form it may take—is for me quite simple: what difference does the exercise of going around the circle make in the lives of the people whose experience we share?

If discernment is enhanced by use of the pastoral circle, then it really does become a reading of the signs of the time, with consequent engagement with the Lord of history in the movement toward the kingdom of God. *Linking faith and justice* becomes more than a subtitle of a book!

References

Africa Faith and Justice Network. 1996. *The African synod: Documents, reflections, perspectives.* Maryknoll, NY: Orbis Books.

AMECEA. 2002. The AMECEA fourteenth plenary message and resolutions. *African Ecclesial Review* 44, no. 5–6: 254–85.

Dulles, Avery, SJ. 1977. Faith in Relation to Justice. In *The faith that does justice: Examining the Christian sources for social change*, edited by John C. Haughey, SJ. New York: Paulist Press.

Henriot, Peter. 1998. Grassroots analysis: The emphasis on culture. In *Liberation theologies on shifting grounds*, edited by G. De Schrijver, 333–50. Leuven: Univ. Press.

Henriot, Peter J., Edward P. DeBerri, and Michael J. Schultheis. 1992. *Catholic social teaching: Our best kept secret.* Maryknoll, NY: Orbis Books; Washington, DC: Center of Concern.

Ignatius Loyola. 1992. *Spiritual exercises.* Translated by George Ganss. Chicago: Loyola Univ. Press.

IMBISA. 2002. *The church works to overcome poverty in southern Africa.* Harare: IMBISA.

JCTR (Jesuit Centre for Theological Reflection). 2003. *What is the church's social teaching saying about poverty?* Lusaka: JCTR.

———. 2004. *Traditional healing: A pastoral challenge for the Catholic church in Zambia.* Lusaka: JCTR.

Mejía, Rodrigo, SJ. 1993. *The church in the neighbourhood.* Nairobi: St. Paul Publications.

Nsanzurwimo, Marc. 2003. *Facing the challenge: Self-sustainability for the Catholic church in Zambia.* Ndola: Mission Press.

The Pastoral Circle

A Strategy for Justice and Peace

Juan José Luna

The challenge to promote an integral transformation process focusing on justice, development, and peace is particularly great in southern Africa. Among the many efforts to address this challenge have been the programs to introduce the use of the pastoral circle in the IMBISA (Inter-Regional Meeting of the Bishops of Southern Africa) region. It was my privilege to work in the Justice and Peace Office of the IMBISA Secretariat (Harare, Zimbabwe) from 1997 to 2002. I want to describe how we experienced the use of the pastoral circle as a powerful tool of conscientization, from the grassroots levels up to the bishops.

Personal Roots of My Interest in the Pastoral Circle

Some important factors in my personal experience help explain my attitudes and perspectives when I was appointed by IMBISA in 1997 to work for justice and peace in the southern African region.

First, as a Mexican Christian, the Guadalupe event has profoundly influenced my attitudes toward social issues. Our Lady of Guadalupe was sent to Mexico City in 1531, only ten years after the conquest of Tenochtitlán (now Mexico City) by the Spanish people. Some local tribes were defeated, and their cultural and religious values quashed. However, our Lady did not come to destroy but to bring to fullness the sparkles of light that the Aztecs already had and to build up the Mexican people—both Indians and Spaniards. She promoted a way of integration, giving a mission to the local people (represented by Juan Diego) in order to convince with words and signals the Spanish people (represented by Bishop Zumárraga). Two kinds of people,

Aztecs and Spanish, came together through the presence of the Virgin Mary in Guadalupe.

As a student of theology in Mexico (1970–72), I engaged in the building up of small Christian communities in Guerrero province, following the traditional method of see, judge, and act. In the first step (to see), we students promoted a deeper insertion in the experiences of participants through dialogue and participation, in the sense of conscientization. For the second step (to judge), we promoted a faith vision of the social problems, using the Bible as "a light on our path." It was a kind of evangelical discernment. The third step (to act) meant that decisions were taken by the community guided by their local leaders, who were chosen by the people, as the movement, enlightened by the gospel, responded to needs in communities.

After my philosophical and theological studies I was sent to study the educational sciences, with a special focus on educational methodology. Thus I am not a theologian but a Christian educator. Through his books Paulo Freire gave me important insights about a participatory method of education that are very useful for the practice of the pastoral circle. Some of those from *Education as the Practice of Freedom* (1990) that are particularly significant are:

1. Critical consciousness is the motor of cultural emancipation.
2. Education is the practice of freedom.
3. People submerged in the culture of silence have to emerge as conscious makers of their own culture.
4. The educatees are not passive recipients of knowledge.
5. The educator is not a teacher who is depositing knowledge into passive recipients. On the contrary, education is an educator-educatee in dialogue with educatee-educators. Educators can learn together with educatees.
6. Education is not an individualistic matter. It implies small groups that are able to dialogue.
7. In the problem-solving approach an expert stands some distance from reality, analyzes it into component parts, devises means for resolving difficulties in the most efficient way, and then offers a strategy or policy.
8. In the reflective group exercise all participants have to dialogue with others whose historical "vocation" is to become transforming agents of their social reality.
9. Action without critical reflection and even without gratuitous contemplation is disastrous activism. And theory or introspection in the absence of collective social action is escapist idealism or wishful thinking.
10. All people are important and merit active respect.
11. Liberating education is possible.

His book *Extension or Communication* added new insights:

1. Genuine dialogue with peasants is incompatible with simply "extending" to them technical expertise or agricultural know-how.
2. There is no room in development language for the terms *donors* and *recipients*.
3. There is an oppressive character in all nonreciprocal relationships.
4. The goal of all developmental change is to transform people, not merely to change structures.
5. The mark of a successful educator is not skill in persuasion but the ability to dialogue with educatees in a mode of reciprocity.
6. No change agent or technical expert has the right to impose personal opinions on others.
7. Authentic communication is possible.

The Challenge of Linking Faith and Justice in IMBISA

When I began work at the IMBISA Secretariat, I quickly experienced the difficulties faced in promoting justice and peace in the region. IMBISA includes nine countries (Angola, Botswana, Lesotho, Mozambique, Namibia, São Tomé e Principe, South Africa, Swaziland, and Zimbabwe) and works in two languages, English and Portuguese. IMBISA is an organ of liaison and pastoral cooperation among the episcopal conferences. The region has a total of about seventy archdioceses and dioceses. Almost every country in the region has a Catholic Commission for Justice and Peace (CCJP), working in a very difficult historical context of colonization, independence wars, conflicts, apartheid, and civil wars.

Over the years there have been efforts to raise the justice and peace agenda through IMBISA. Indeed, at its inception in 1975 the group decided that among its objectives would be work for justice and peace in the region. The First Plenary Assembly held in 1984 marked the dawn of a new era for IMBISA as it focused on the theme "The Social Teaching of the Church and Her Prophetic Mission in Southern Africa." The Second Plenary Assembly in 1988 took the theme "If you Want Peace, Work for Justice."

However, after visiting some of the CCJPs in the region in 1997 and 1998, I realized that there was a serious divide between the social, economic, and political issues and our faith. Some people dealt with issues of justice and peace without a Christian approach; others dealt with "pastoral" issues without the social dimension of faith. It was this that prompted me to promote use of the pastoral circle, precisely because it links faith and justice (for background, see McGarry 1993).

Pastoral Circle as a Strategy for IMBISA's CCJPs

As a way of introducing the pastoral circle to the region, a workshop was held in Harare in 1999 in order to train personnel of IMBISA's CCJPs in the pastoral circle method. Two Jesuit priests, Peter Henriot and Rodrigo Mejía, facilitated this workshop, which brought together bishops and diocesan justice and peace coordinators. As a fruit of the workshop, IMBISA published a booklet entitled *Pastoral Circle: A Strategy for Promoting Justice and Peace* (Henriot and Mejía 2000). The booklet, published in both English and Portuguese, was widely circulated and became very popular.

Using the lessons of the church's social teaching, the foreword of the booklet states the case clearly:

> The Second Vatican Council has said that the "split between the faith which many profess and their daily lives deserves to be counted among the more serious errors of our age" (*Gaudium et Spes*, 43). This divorce between life and faith is one of the major obstacles of a real inculturation of our faith. When faith exists in a compartment separated from our daily life, it is a faith that does not take for real the Incarnation of the Son of God in our human nature and life. Such an approach creates in a lot of people the impression that Christianity has nothing to say to history, to life. Christ is for them of no relevance, meaningless to the current human history. He does not mean anything for the human race today. . . .
>
> Evangelisation would not be complete if it did not take account of the unceasing interplay of the Gospel and of man's concrete life, both personal and social. This is why evangelisation involves an explicit message, adapted to the different situations constantly being realised, about the rights and duties of every human being, about family life without which personal growth and development is hardly possible, about life in society, about international life, peace, justice and development—a message especially energetic today about liberation" (*Evangelii Nuntiandi*, 29).
>
> In this booklet, the Pastoral Circle method is presented to a wider readership. IMBISA Justice and Peace is pleased to share with all the Christians in southern Africa this valuable method that may be an instrument to "awaken Christian communities to their evangelical responsibilities in the defence of human rights" (*Church in Africa*, 106) and to accomplish our mission of bearing "witness to Christ also by promoting justice and peace on the Continent and throughout the world" (*Church in Africa*, 105).

But preparation of a good booklet, even one that is widely circulated, is not enough to link faith and justice to pastoral action. It has been said that a parish priest is always a powerful person, not because he is able to *do* everything, but because he is able to *stop* everything. The same certainly applies to a bishop! Therefore, in order to overcome the difficulties that the IMBISA CCJPs faced in linking faith and justice, it was necessary to look for ways of strengthening the support of the IMBISA bishops for their own commissions. This was to be done by exposing the bishops to the pastoral circle. The IMBISA Justice and Peace Office took the opportunity of the 2001 IMBISA Plenary Assembly to do just this.

As a consequence, a justice and peace theme for the 2001 IMBISA Plenary Assembly was chosen: *"Poverty and Economic Justice in Southern Africa in the New Millennium: A Christian Approach."* Why did the bishops choose this theme? What was their motivation in addressing the scandal of poverty? As the entire issue of economic justice forms an integral part of human development and welfare, in the spirit of solidarity and the common good the church has an obligation to promote an authentic and substantial solution to this dehumanizing problem. It is clearly linked to the church's task of evangelization. In speaking about evangelization, Pope Paul VI said:

> For the Church, evangelizing means bringing the Good News into all the strata of humanity, and through its influence transforming humanity from within and making it new. . . . The Church evangelizes when she seeks to convert, solely through the divine power of the message she proclaims, both the personal and collective consciences of people, the activities in which they engage, and the lives and concrete milieus which are theirs. . . .
>
> For the Church it is a question not only of preaching the Gospel in ever wider geographic areas or to ever greater numbers of people, but also of affecting and as it were upsetting, through the power of the Gospel, mankind's criteria of judgment, determining values, points of interest, lines of thought, sources of inspiration and models of life, which are in contrast with the Word of God and the plan of salvation. (*Evangelium nuntiandi*, nos. 18–19)

The bishops of IMBISA were aware that millions of people were living in inhuman situations of poverty and underdevelopment in southern Africa. The same fundamental motive that inspired *Gaudium et spes,* that great document of the Second Vatican Council, inspired the bishops to choose this theme about poverty in Southern Africa: "The joys and the hopes, the griefs and the anxieties of the people of this age, especially those who are poor or in any way afflicted, these are the joys and hopes, the griefs and anxieties of the followers of Christ" (*Gaudium et spes,* no. 1).

The bishops desired that the plenary assembly would involve the whole family of God in southern Africa in solving its own problems of poverty and economic injustice in a spirit of freedom and co-responsibility. This would be necessary in order to build a better world on the solid foundation of sound ethical and spiritual principles. With this purpose in mind the following three objectives were articulated for the plenary assembly:

- Objective 1: To promote a firm commitment to economic justice and solidarity of each member of God's people.
- Objective 2: To awaken Christian communities to their evangelical responsibilities in the defense and promotion of human rights in general and economic rights in particular, avoiding the divorce between faith and life.
- Objective 3: To draw from the gospel and the social teaching of the church the ethical and spiritual principles that will guide the life and the action of the family of God in eradicating poverty and promoting economic justice.

Preparation for the 2001 Plenary Assembly

One year before the plenary assembly the method of the pastoral circle was presented to the episcopal conferences of IMBISA's region by a letter and the booklet prepared by Henriot and Mejía. This explained that the assembly would deal with the theme of poverty and economic justice by using the pastoral circle, which was presented as a tool of pastoral action that had as its aim the organizing of local and regional responses to the challenges raised by the theme. The IMBISA Secretariat stressed that the pastoral circle would be used to guarantee dialogue, participation, and ownership of the process by the whole people of God.

With the approval of IMBISA's Standing Committee, the staff at the secretariat prepared a questionnaire that was sent to all the dioceses of the region; it was to become the basis for a working paper. This working paper would then be the starting point for reflections and decisions at the plenary. Two things should be noted about the questionnaire: first, it emphasized a participatory approach coming from the people at the grassroots level; second, it followed the steps of the pastoral circle. Because it demonstrates in very concrete fashion how the pastoral circle can be used, some major details of the questionnaire are presented below:

First Step: INSERTION in order to learn about the situation of people living in poverty from themselves. What is happening?
Question No. 1. How does poverty affect your personal life, the life of your family, the life of the community in which you live? Give concrete examples.

Second Step: SOCIAL ANALYSIS in order to discover the root causes of your poverty. WHY is it happening?
Question No. 2. What is causing the described poverty?

Question No. 3. Are there any causes that come from yourself, your family, and the community?

Question No. 4. Are there any causes which come from outside? From where or whom?

Question No. 5. Why are you unable to overcome the situation of poverty?

Third step: BIBLICAL VISION AND THEOLOGICAL CRITERIA TO EVALUATE THE SITUATION in order to discover the attitudes, values that should drive the Christians in their fight for the eradication of poverty and for economic justice.

Question No. 6. In your opinion, is this situation of poverty the will of God? Please explain.

Question No. 7. In your opinion, does your Christian faith have anything to do with the promotion of a better life for all?

Question No. 8. Do you personally and your Christian community have any responsibilities coming from the Gospel to defend human and economic rights?

Fourth Step: THEOLOGICAL PRINCIPLES FOR PASTORAL PLANNING in order to get some ideas from the Family of God to plan the action for poverty eradication and economic justice.

Question No. 9. What can you do, as a person, as a Christian community to promote a better life for your family and community?

Question No. 10. What are you already doing towards this aim?

Question No. 11. What support do you expect for doing so from your parish priest, from your Christian leaders, from your Bishop?

From the responses to the questionnaire we identified eleven topics related with poverty in our region: (1) hunger, (2) shelter, (3) health, (4) employment, (5) education, (6) material resources, (7) peace, (8) transparency and good governance, (9) debt, (10) gender, and (11) youth.

In order to prepare the working paper the eleven topics were distributed among the staff of the IMBISA Secretariat with guidelines to follow the four steps of the pastoral circle in each topic. In the writing of the working paper the first step of the pastoral circle (insertion) and the second step (social analysis) were based on the replies that were received from lay people, guided by the national and diocesan CCJPs and/or by other local church structures already instituted (lay movements, catechists, social pastoral groups, Caritas, and so on) in the dioceses of IMBISA. This direct knowledge about poverty and economics and their impact on human beings, as well as the initial social analysis, was then complemented by quoting some texts relevant to the region from church documents (such as pastoral letters) and also by adding the international (regional and global) dimension of the various aspects of poverty.

2001 IMBISA Plenary Assembly

When the almost one hundred bishops gathered in Harare in September 2001 for the IMBISA Sixth Plenary Assembly, it was considered critical from the start to gain the support of everyone for use of the pastoral circle during the working sessions. This commitment was called for in a strong address delivered by Cardinal Wilfred Napier (Durban, South Africa) at the beginning of the deliberations:

> While the theme of our Assembly uses abstract terms like poverty and justice, we are talking about real men and women, youth and children. Neither poverty nor justice exists in itself. We identify and define them by comparing actual life situations with conditions considered fitting for those made in God's image and likeness. . . .
>
> Because our concern is people, we cannot deal with poverty as an objective reality divorced from people. . . .
>
> In the light of comments made about the effectiveness or rather ineffectiveness of decisions and resolutions of past plenary assemblies, one must ask whether IMBISA itself does not need to adopt the pastoral cycle for its sessions.
>
> Consider what will happen after this assembly has deliberated on poverty and economic justice in our region. What will we do to change the lives of our poor? Our message and pastoral statement will let them know that we are aware of their problems and that we want to help. But will we be able to specify what we will do? I'm sure our statement will call on our governments, the international community and our donor partners to provide us with the material resources, since we lack them.
>
> But is it true that we are so lacking in resources? What about the skills and talents in our communities? What about the poor themselves? Don't they have the most necessary resource, namely, their strong sense of dignity and self-belief, which can make all the difference?
>
> This challenges us to enable the poor to regain if necessary, but otherwise to reassert, their self-belief and dignity by giving them the knowledge and skills to question and analyze the causes of their poverty, to reflect on them from God's point of view, and to take the steps to climb out of the pit of poverty and especially hopelessness. . . .
>
> That is the reason for my proposal that the pastoral cycle become the ordinary way for IMBISA to conduct its plenary assembly, especially when dealing with socioeconomic, political or justice issues.

At the plenary assembly an introduction to the pastoral circle was given, followed by short talks on each of the four steps of the circle. This oriented the group discussions. The bishops were divided into five English groups and four Portuguese groups in order to discuss some topics of poverty according to the four steps of the pastoral circle. At that moment it was considered more important to facilitate the experience of use of the pastoral circle by the bishops themselves rather than discussing all the responses organized under the headings of the working paper.

While all the steps were very important, the most crucial steps for the bishops at the plenary were the third step of *theological reflection* (Is this situation of economic and human poverty the will of God?) and the fourth step (decisions on the pastoral principles that should guide every *pastoral action plan* related to promoting poverty eradication and economic justice in the region. Through their pastors the people in the region expected a light from God that could guide and empower them so that they themselves could participate fully in their poverty eradication and in the promotion of economic justice for all.

After the Plenary Assembly

At the end of the plenary assembly all the bishops wanted to have a guiding pastoral (action) plan for the region. They asked the newly elected IMBISA Standing Committee to prepare that publication. The task was assigned to the IMBISA Secretariat in general and to the new Justice and Peace Desk in particular.

The secretaries of the nine groups of bishops and priests turned over to the IMBISA Justice and Peace Desk all the material collected during the assembly's small-group discussions. The materials were compiled and presented to the Standing Committee in November 2001. The secretariat was then asked to prepare a pastoral document to guide the action of the church in the region to fight poverty. In April 2002 such a document was presented at a meeting of the Standing Committee. The committee approved the pastoral plan (chapter 4) and asked that the other three chapters—which corresponded to the three initial steps of the pastoral circle—be shortened.

With the participation of almost all the bishops in charge of CCJPs in the region, the national coordinators and some specialists in the church's social teaching (Peter Henriot, SJ, and Sister Carol Schommer, RSHM) facilitated a workshop in Harare (September 2002). The purpose of the workshop was to inform the participants about the approved IMBISA Pastoral Plan for Poverty Eradication and to gain their support and involvement for national implementation of the plan. (Other chapters that supported the regional plan were not yet ready.)

In early 2003 the final document was published in two languages under the title *A Pastoral Document for Poverty Eradication: "That They May Have Life" (John 10:10): The Church Works to Overcome Poverty in Southern Africa* (IMBISA 2002). But an amazing thing had occurred during the editing process: the all-important chapter 5, the pastoral plan (correspond-ing to the fourth step of the pastoral circle), was omitted! This extremely important section had been discussed in the September 2002 workshop. It was to guide the effective implementation of the pastoral assembly. I will return to this omission after some other observations.

Briefly, here is an outline of the final publication:

Chapter 1: "That They May Have Life (John 10:10)—The Church Works to Overcome Poverty in Southern Africa" provides a summary of the assembly's preparation and actual time together.

Chapter 2: "The Griefs and Anxieties of the Peoples of Southern Africa" corresponds to the first step of the pastoral circle, insertion. It notes that God has richly blessed Africa as a whole in human, cultural, and natural resources. But it goes on to state in very sharp words the problem of Africa as expressed by Africans themselves in the process of using the pastoral circle.

> However, Africa has the world's poorest people. We have witnessed declines in life expectancy and individual income, collapsing social services and a steady rise in infant and maternal mortality. Never end-ing conflicts, repressive regimes, crumbling infrastructure and low rates of new infrastructure development, and fragile economies remain the characteristic features of the Southern African social, political, and economic landscape.
>
> Behind the statistics lies a reality that is fraught with human suffer-ing and poverty. The dimensions of this suffering encompass not only the physical well being of our societies, but also the basic human rights and dignity of individuals and communities throughout the continent. The marginalized population of this continent has repeatedly been denied the right to participate in the decisions that directly affect them. Their basic human rights have been trampled over repeatedly and de-cisions regarding their lives have been made without seeking their opinion or input. Such injustices levied upon the people of Africa are prime examples of how, through no fault of their own, the peoples of Southern Africa are suffering from extreme impoverishment.

This section puts out a strong challenge by asking why the people in southern Africa are so impoverished amid such great human and natural resources and what we as the family of God in southern Africa can do in response to the severe poverty afflicting our sisters and brothers. This moves the document on to social analysis.

Chapter 3: "The Root Causes of Our Griefs and Anxieties" corresponds to the second step of the pastoral circle, the social analysis of the situation that was presented in chapter 2. Several key causes are identified as factors influencing the situation in southern Africa. They are summarized under the following headings:

- "Human Decisions—The Ethical Dimension of Poverty": poverty is not a necessary state but a consequence of conscious decisions made by some humans.
- "Right Economic Decisions—Wrong Ethical Decisions": an increase in wealth and material riches for some causes immense suffering for millions.
- "The Global Dimension of Poverty and Underdevelopment": globalization is increasing in influence and means that efforts to address poverty in southern Africa depend more and more on factors beyond the boundaries of the region.
- "A New Culture Shaped by a Market Fundamentalist Economic Ideology": the maximization of profit and consolidation of power are cultural norms that ignore the values of solidarity, common good and spiritual well-being.

Chapter 4: "The Church's Vision for Life in All Its Fullness" presents the third step of the pastoral circle, theological reflection. Drawing upon the understanding of integral evangelization found in the church's social teaching, the document emphasizes that the concern of the church in the southern Africa region "is to overcome poverty by being a living sign and instrument of universal solidarity, so as to build a new global human community of justice, peace, and respect for the integrity of creation."

As for a pastoral plan for action, it is at this point that the booklet prepared as a followup to the plenary assembly departed dramatically from the process of the pastoral circle used in the preparation and actual experience of the assembly. Only a few brief remarks, in rather general terms, are made about a designed followup to the assembly. It is not clear why this omission occurred, but its consequences have been indeed unfortunate. What had been offered in the original text for this final chapter—the text discussed at earlier follow-up sessions of IMBISA described above—emphasized in some detail the need to develop common goals, strategies, and objectives to implement the vision and mission. The proposed action plan was based on the principles of the church's social teaching, found especially in the African Synod of 1994. Indeed, there was a clear emphasis on the strategy to build "the capacity of our national and regional structures for reflection and social action inspired by Gospel values and CST [Catholic social teaching] principles."

That this all-important chapter outlining a pastoral plan for action could be omitted is something that requires reflection when we draw up lessons that can be learned from IMBISA's use of the pastoral circle.

Conclusions

The commitment of IMBISA to use the pastoral circle as a process to strengthen its role of evangelization through a focus on poverty and economic justice in the region is important, not only for what was actually done—or not done—but also for what can be learned. By way of conclusion, let me briefly highlight a few important lessons and directions for the future:

- The pastoral circle is becoming a very important tool for justice and peace in IMBISA region.
- It was necessary to train (not by *teaching* but by *training*) bishops and members of the CCJPs in order to convince them that the pastoral circle is a very important method to link faith and justice in the region.
- People in the small Christian communities are able to use the pastoral circle if they have leaders who ask the correct questions, promoting dialogue and participation. We realized this by the replies that we received to the questionnaire.
- Insertion and analysis, the first and second steps of the pastoral circle, should not be done by someone coming from outside the situation, but by the people who are living in the situation. Paulo Freire's method of dialogue and conscientization is crucial to allow people to become subjects—transforming agents of their social reality and of their own history—instead of objects of study by others.
- In the second step (social analysis) it is very important to look for the quality of the human decisions that are root causes of the situation.
- In the third step (theological reflection) it is very important to enlighten the situation with the social teaching of the church, which is the social teaching of Jesus Christ.
- Also in the third step, an excellent approach might be the *lectio divina,* which starts by reading the word of God and finishes by looking for planned action for transformation according to the word of God.
- The fourth step (planning for response) must never be omitted or the pastoral circle becomes merely a theoretical exercise unrelated to the transformation of society and/or church.
- The pastoral circle might be used to deal with global issues as well as regional issues, national issues, and local issues.

References

Freire, Paulo. 1974. *Extension or communication.* Translated by Louise Bigwood and Margaret Marshall. London: Sheed & Ward.

———. 1976. *Education as the practice of freedom.* Translated and edited by Myra Bergman Ramos. London: Writers and Readers Publishing Cooperative.

Henriot, Peter, and Rodrigo Mejía. 2000. *Pastoral circle: A strategy for promoting justice and peace.* IMBISA Occasional Papers No. 5. Harare: IMBISA.

IMBISA. 2002. Sixth Plenary Assembly. *A pastoral document for poverty eradication: "That they may have life" (John 10:10): The church works to overcome poverty in Southern Africa.* Harare: IMBISA.

McGarry, C., et al., eds. 1993. *A light on our path.* Nairobi: Paulines Publications.

3

Pitfalls in the Use
of the Pastoral Circle

Josef Elsener

The *Advocatus Diaboli*, the devil's advocate as he is popularly known, has a long tradition in the church. Pope Benedict XIV occupied this position for twenty years (1708–28) and carried it out faithfully and successfully before he was elected pope. This institution has helped the church to avoid a pitfall in the process of canonization, namely, that somebody is declared a saint of the church who is not worthy of it. The *Promoter Fidei*, which is the official name of the devil's advocate, has the task to go in detail through the report on the life and virtues of the person to be canonized. He scrutinizes all his or her writings and looks painstakingly for any reason why this person should not be declared a saint. His task is to counterbalance the popular opinion of those who want a person to be declared a saint. By this formal system of presentation of the less popular opinion, the church tries to avoid the damage that would be caused if an unworthy person is canonized.

By and large the church has done well with this centuries-old institution. Other processes and approaches in the church would need a similar institution of the devil's advocate in order to save the church from some embarrassments and possible failures in its activities.

In recent years business and management circles have discovered the importance of the role of the *Advocatus Diaboli*. His role is not be confused with the function of problem solver, teacher, or consultor; nor is that of an *ombudsman*, whose job is to deal with complaints received from the general public. The devil's advocate, rather, plays the role of the one who "spoils the game." When ideas, plans, and programs are represented, he "shoots them down": he attacks them, dramatizes them, shows the weaknesses of the arguments, and points to where they lead if carried out to the last. He presents "the other side of the story"; in other words, he offers a critical

40

opposition. He forces the presenters of ideas and programs to think logically and analytically in order to strengthen and clarify their arguments and plans.

This essay examines the pastoral circle approach with the eyes of a devil's advocate and intends to point out some pitfalls the pastoral circle approach should avoid if it wants to make a successful contribution to the pastoral activities of the church. The essay takes its examples mainly from the use of the approach in the church of southern Africa.

The purpose of introducing the figure of the devil's advocate goes, however, beyond this essay. The pastoral circle approach would do well if it made use of the role of a modern devil's advocate, and not merely in order to see that the steps or phases of the pastoral circle are faithfully and properly applied. The pastoral circle approach aims at transformation, at change of an existing situation. As the use of the devil's advocate in business and management circles shows, he or she is not there to ensure the status quo. He or she needs the ability to step aside and to look from the outside at the situation and to develop a critical attitude. Transformation agents, men or women who can initiate change, are needed.

In the analysis phase of the circle, the psychological, social, organizational factors involved in the situation being analyzed for the purpose of transformation should be looked at: the factors favoring and hindering change, possible resistance to change, leadership needed for transformation and change. It should be asked whether the particular situation and culture under analysis produce people with a critical attitude, and where they can be found. Individuals and groups of people who have a critical attitude and can act as transformation or change agents should be identified.

In the action phase of the circle use should be made of such individuals and groups with a critical attitude for introducing and promoting transformation and change.

The First Pitfall: The Starting Point of the Analysis

In our pastoral work and when planning a new church program, we usually behave as if we were starting from zero and as if nothing had been done before. Our point of departure is usually "Where are we going?" and we forget to ask ourselves "Where do we come from?" Rather than plunging immediately into the insertion or contact phase of the pastoral circle, it would be much better if we started with a short evaluation of what has been done before. A Chinese proverb says, "Before correcting others, first make the round of your own house three times."

The pastoral circle tool should therefore first of all be applied to the relevant local church organization (regional, national, diocesan, parish) itself with its departments or commissions before turning to the wider socioeconomic situation in the country or the region. It seems to be a difficult task in terms of both time and energy, but it may save us from other pitfalls down the road.

Before applying the pastoral circle as a tool of pastoral planning (such as for the justice and peace work of a diocese), we should look first at whether any pastoral planning is being done here and now and in what ways. Has social analysis already been done in one way or another? Who has done it and at what level? What is the place of justice and peace work within the present-day understanding of the mission of the church and its pastoral work? How does that work in fact fit into the overall pastoral planning of the local church?

Some reflections and questions might be useful in this very first step of the insertion or contact stage.

The Climate in the Universal Church

The Hermeneutic Question

The analytical approach of the "see, judge, and act" method that was recommended by Pope John XXIII in *Mater et magistra* was used successfully by the Second Vatican Council in its analysis of the church in the modern world *(Gaudium et spes)*. It was the Latin American bishops at their CELAM conferences of Medellín (1968) and Puebla (1979) who took up this method most systematically in their deliberations and documents. As a starting point they looked at reality as a "sign of the times" in which God's plan of salvation was revealed. They went on to analyze and interpret this reality in the light of the gospel.

In preparation for the fourth CELAM conference a number of national bishops' conferences recommended that this method should once again be used because they considered it to be in conformity with the principle of incarnation: "In its task of evangelizing the church had to remain in the service of the word of God so that it could assume flesh and blood in the human reality under changing circumstances" *(Secunda relatio)*. When the bishops eventually gathered for the conference in Santo Domingo from October 12 to October 18, 1992, they were forced under difficult working conditions to accept a draft of a final document that departed from the three steps of "see, judge, and act" and replaced it with the deductive method (Klein 1992, 261). The first part of the document, entitled "Jesus Christ, the Gospel of the Father," starts with a confession of faith that is followed by a very short summary of the five hundred years of evangelization. The second part is entitled "Jesus Christ Lives On in His Church as the Announcer of the Gospel." Each part and the chapters in them first present the doctrine and then draw pastoral conclusions from the doctrine. This presentation constitutes a radical departure from the theological and pastoral approach of the previous two conferences.

An international symposium that focused, among other topics, on this hermeneutical shift was held from November 21 to November 23, 1996, at the Center for Liberation Theology of the Faculty of Theology, Katholieke Universiteit, Leuven, Belgium. De Schrijver (1998) argued that this process of setting aside social analysis had already begun at Puebla. In his initial discussion paper he

> called attention to the fact that, starting from Puebla and under the impulse of López Trujillo, an open confrontation was mounted against liberationists acting in the style of Medellín. . . . The renewed interest in culture was launched to provide a solely sacrosanct alternative to the initial liberationist analysis—which in terms of ecclesiastical politics implied the invalidation or even the condemnation of the movement that was in favour of this analysis. . . . The same countertrend was one of the potent undercurrents in Santo Domingo, and was reinforced by the "Romanizers" in that conference. (De Schrijver 1998, 417)

Under the guise of an apparently universal Catholic culture, the need for a closer look and analysis of diverse cultural situations was considered to be superfluous. An emphasis on (Christian) culture was to replace the option for the poor.

The history of the church in Latin America since Santo Domingo has shown that its final document with its switch from the inductive to the deductive method has not had the same impact on the pastoral reality as the documents of Medellín and Puebla. But unfortunately, the pastoral approach has received a severe setback since there has been a tendency to return to that deductive approach in church documents and pronouncements since then at the universal and continental and even national level.

The Celebration of the New Millennium and the Continental Synods of Bishops

The preparation and celebration of the new millennium took center place in the Catholic church worldwide in the last years before the new millennium. It meant that everything else had to take second (or even third) place, and it promoted a triumphalistic image of church. One gets the impression that the church exhausted all its energies in these celebrations and that there have hardly been any new initiatives since then.

The series of five continental sessions of the synod of bishops that were held between 1994 and 1999 (for Africa, America, Asia, Europe, and Oceania) and that were meant to be preparations for the millennium followed a similar line. Their preparations, the sessions, and the documents promulgated after these special assemblies, as they are officially called, can hardly be considered to be documents that look at the full reality of the continent in question, judge it in the light of the gospel, and bring out forward-looking pastoral conclusions and recommendations.

Catholic Social Teaching

The church is proud of its social teaching and of its past history—more than one hundred years old. Such an attitude is prone to the following dangers:

- It creates the false impression that Catholic social teaching is a "fixed deposit" and ready made, and that it needs only to be applied.
- It behaves as if Catholic social teaching has already solved all the issues that might arise. Is it open to new issues and how are they being developed in the church?
- It overemphasizes the teaching function of the church in socioeconomic issues, stressing the need for more sociological research and theological reflection and thus not getting to the action program based on them. It is not without reason that Catholic social teaching is called "the best kept secret of the church."

The Church in Africa

The Church in Africa, the post-synodal document published after the Special Assembly for Africa of the Synod of Bishops in 1994, has been called the model document for the post-synodal exhortations of the other continents (John Paul II 1995). Comparing the many social and economic questions that were the subject of the interventions in the synod hall and those that are taken up in this exhortation, one can ask oneself whether the following facts and trends of the church in Africa are sufficiently reflected in the document:

Is the Church in Africa a Receiving Church, a Dependent Church?

Is there a true partnership within the universal church, or is the church in Africa still being treated as a receiving church? Although there is much talk about self-reliance of the church and much lip service is given to self-reliance, the church in Africa remains a dependent church. False forms of self-reliance are being promoted, for example, the false gospel that the church is an "income-generating project."

Have the Present Trends in the Church in Africa Found Sufficient Reflection?

- The influence of charismatic and pentecostal movements of other Christian churches on the pentecostal movement in the Catholic church.

- The existence of apocalyptic and end-of the world movements and tendencies relying on pseudo-prophetic revelations in some African countries (such as Uganda).
- The growing number of healing churches responding to the day-to-day needs of the people: diseases, physical and psychological "blockages"; Jesus is presented as "my personal savior."
- Poverty and the so-called prosperity churches; the mushrooming of African churches that present wealth and prosperity as a sign of God's blessing.
- The influence in Africa of international lay movements such as Focolari, Opus Dei, the New Catechumenate, and the St. Egidio Community.
- The ecumenical approach: the character of the relationship of the Catholic church to the national councils of churches (full or associate membership, observer status), to other churches, and to national church and church-like organizations.

The Issue of Inculturation

Inculturation has been one of the main themes of the African Synod. It would be interesting to identify the reasons why this topic has received such prominence. Several bishops referred to the double loyalty of many African Christians; they are torn between the world of Christian beliefs and values and the world of African traditions and beliefs. The South African Bishops' Conference indicated still another aspect, namely, the "existing deep wound caused when the local culture was neglected or even despised for many years. We have to work for the healing of such wounds. We begin our task of inculturation by asking pardon for having hurt others by not respecting their culture in the church for many years" (SACBC 1995).

Although inculturation remains a legitimate aim of all missionary and pastoral activity, there appears to be a shift toward a more dialectic approach. Even if positive elements of African traditional religion are accepted, more importance is given to the break with the past that Christ has brought. There are frequent warnings against syncretism.

The Situation in the Local Church

Here are some questions that dioceses and parishes should ask themselves when looking at themselves and where they come from:

- Are small Christian communities (SCC) functioning? How do they function? What are their priorities? Is there a national or diocesan policy on SCCs? Are they fostered or left on their own? Are SCCs merely charismatic prayer groups or are they also action groups?

- Are there any Bible study groups? Are they active? To what extent? What are their priorities? What are the methods of Bible study used in their sessions? Do they start their Bible study sessions with a life situation to which they apply a suitable Bible text, or do they start with a Bible text that they then try to apply to their life situation? In what ways are these methods similar or dissimilar to the pastoral circle method?

In a February 9, 1998, letter to the IMBISA (Inter-Regional Meeting of the Bishops of Southern Africa) Secretariat, Bishop Fritz Lobinger of Aliwal North, South Africa, wrote:

> It has been acknowledged frequently that the biblical reflection in SCC was the single most effective cause for the dramatic upsurge in Catholics having and reading the bible. In many parts of Africa Catholics now equal the other churches in bible reading because of these SCCs.
>
> It has, however, also been repeatedly noted that this communal biblical reflection lacks social relevance. The reflections are never purely individualistic and are never supernaturalistic but they hardly ever go beyond neighbourhood issues. They are repetitive and confine themselves to sickness, concern for the lapsed, and for petty offences among neighbours. They fail to touch social issues of wider implications and are therefore often considered irrelevant.
>
> The difference between the biblical reflection in the SCCs of Africa and that in other continents is that the SCCs of Africa base themselves only on the biblical text, while in other areas the communities use reflection outlines as well.
>
> It is these reflection outlines that help the small communities to find the courage to mention the pressing social problems in the light of the gospel. The members of the communities are of course aware of the immense social problems but without a reflection guide they find it too threatening to mention them. Without reflection guides they also lack the terminology and the simple methods of linking the biblical text and the pressing social issues.

Examples of these reflections are given.

- What church lay associations exist? Are they based on sex and age: men, women, youth? Are they engaged in particular works such as justice and peace, charitable work (Caritas, St. Vincent de Paul), development projects? What place do they have within the diocese? the parish?
- What are the functions of pastoral and parish councils: consultative, deliberative? How are the members chosen? What is the position of the priests on the councils?
- What channels are used by the local church to communicate and to inform? internally? to the outside? How are pastoral statements composed?

Is there any prior consultation? Are they translated into the vernacular languages? How are they disseminated? Is there any follow up? Does this local church have access to public media? In what ways? Are they being used?

• What is the relationship to the political bodies that form the national, regional, and local governments? Access? formally? informally? Influence on policy? Participation in advisory structures, such as economic forums, education? Relationship to political parties? Cooperation with other NGOs and in particular projects?

• How is the justice and peace work organized at the diocesan and parish levels? How is it structured? What are its powers, aims, objectives, and functions? What is its relationship to the bishop, with the pastoral department, to other departments and commissions? What is the procedure it must follow when making statements on issues of justice and peace? What work is it actually doing? Does it have any impact? What are the difficulties in achieving the aims and objectives?

What has been said so far can be summarized as the need for an analysis of the church's resources. Jesus said, "For which of you, intending to build a tower, would not first sit down and estimate the cost to see whether he has enough to complete it? Otherwise, when he has laid a foundation and is unable to finish, all who see it will ridicule him, saying, 'This fellow began to build and was not able to finish'" (Lk 14:28–29).

Thus, the church should at the outset of any pastoral-action planning do an analysis of its resources and also its weaknesses. These are some points to consider:

• The greatest strength of the church lies in its grassroots, in the SCCs.
• In countries with a long history of civil wars and social upheavals, the church is sometimes the only social organization whose structures are still somewhat functioning and whose moral and ethical voice is being heard beyond the traditional family structure.
• The church has a long tradition of humanitarian work and emergency assistance in times of hunger and natural disasters.
• The church has a worldwide network beyond local, regional, and national boundaries.

The Second Pitfall:
The Missing Link between Social Analysis
and Theological Reflection

Once the existing social situation has been studied and the root causes of the present situation analyzed, the pastoral circle method is supposed to proceed to a theological reflection of the gathered facts and underlying values and norms. This reflection should be based on the teachings of the gospel and systematized in Catholic social teaching. It appears that this move from social analysis to theological reflection is not easy. It seems to be beset and bedeviled by two different but related departures or aberrations from the accepted path or circle.

Not Separating Social Analysis and Theological Reflection Hermeneutically

Social analysis should not be mixed with value judgments. The two should be treated separately. This does not mean that the social analysis should not look at the values and norms that affect the situation or shape the issue. They are even necessary in order to "understand" particular facts or situations in their wider social and cultural context. But at the social analysis stage we should not mix in our own value judgments—whatever they are and originate from—as outside or even as participant observers. As it is not possible to dissociate oneself completely from one's own value judgments, even in the contact and social analysis stage, it is necessary to become aware of them and to make them transparent. A useful hint is to go through the facts and descriptions gathered in the social analysis so see when and where qualifying adjectives such as *good, bad, right, wrong, positive, negative, appropriate, inappropriate, proper, improper, moral, immoral,* and so on appear.

The SECAM (Symposium of Episcopal Conferences of Africa and Madagascar) pastoral letter *Christ Our Peace (Eph 2:14): Church-as-Family-of-God, Place and Sacrament of Pardon, Reconciliation, and Peace in Africa* offers several examples of this mixture of social analysis with value judgments. At its Eleventh Plenary Assembly at Midrand (Johannesburg) in 1997, SECAM began its deliberations on the pastoral consequences of the church-as-family-of-God in the situation of conflicts, violence, and war that prevailed at that time in Africa. The Twelfth Assembly at Rocca di Papa (Rome), October 1–8, 2000, discussed a revised draft of the document. It was published in 2001 by mandate of the assembly under the signatures of Archbishop L. Monsengwo Pasinya, president, and Fr. Peter Lwaminda, secretary general of SECAM. The document begins its first chapter with an analysis of the state of the world and Africa, concentrating on the conflicts and wars and their causes (ethnic antagonism and wars, wars by proxy, structural violence, socioeconomic inequality). It then discusses the efforts of humanity to find lasting peace (the silence of arms, the principle of reciprocity, respect of human rights, the rule of law). The analysis of the root causes of the problems, conflicts, and struggles in Africa concentrates almost entirely on historical causes and on external factors. Internal factors are either hardly mentioned at all (such as "the risky management of national resources, characterized by squandering of money, excessive corruption, a disastrous confusion of the public and private property of leaders, bad governance, consisting of casualness and carelessness, of lack of attention to the common good and to the conditions of the poorest," no. 30) or reduced to and explained away by external factors (ethnic antagonism and rivalry, ethnic wars, racism and apartheid, slavery, nos. 16–23), or lack of diversification in the economies (no. 30). Such an approach is not helpful to an objective and factual analysis. It instinctively shies away from looking at one's own weaknesses and its internal causes, whether psychological, political, cultural, or religious.

More serious is the mixing of the analysis with value judgments without mentioning on which values these judgments are based. For example, when dealing with racism and apartheid (no. 21), it states: "We should . . . denounce racist attitudes based on pigmentation and cultural diversity" and "no discrimination based on sex, color, race, religion or political conviction is tolerable in a world without frontiers, where the other should always be seen as a partner in interaction and enrichment." The section "Give and Be Given" (nos. 36–39) goes beyond simply explaining that this is in Africa one of the bases of conflict resolution but judges that "the common good and the greater interest of the nation are part of the ethical basis of social justice" and could thus form a basis of any "give and be given" solution. On the rule of law (nos. 41–42) the document says that it "is an absolute necessity . . . a necessity for democracy." Nowhere is it said from where this "necessity" is derived.

By issuing value judgments on some aspects of the social situation, the SECAM pastoral letter anticipates the next step of the pastoral circle in its chapter 2, which is entitled "A Theological Discussion of That Peace That Christ Alone Offers Mankind." In this theological discussion or reflection the letter falls into a second trap.

Moving to a Level Completely Dissociated from the Facts of the Social Analysis

Instead of asking how the situation described in the social analysis is to be seen and reflected in the light of the message of the gospel, the SECAM pastoral letter of 2001 draws a picture or vision of peace that has hardly any connection with the problems, conflicts and struggles of Africa presented in the previous section or stage. One gets the impression that this almost celestial vision seems to forget the men and women of flesh and blood who are struggling with the realities described in chapter 1.

It is therefore not surprising that "the peace offered by Christ to men" is judged to be "basically spiritual" and that "for Africans and African states, here is a perspective which should unite them at the level of their deepest religious convictions" (no. 52), thus completely ignoring the serious conflicts in Africa that are based on religious beliefs, such as those in Nigeria or Uganda.

The church is presented as a community of human beings who seem not to be touched at all by the ethnic antagonism and rivalry that "predominate" in Africa (no. 16). The church as the reconciled and united family of God is described in words that sound almost cynical when one has in mind the tragic realities of Rwanda, where Christians killed each other in the thousands: "The church is, both for the world and for Africa, the place and the sacrament of pardon, reconciliation and peace" (no. 59).

Setting one's vision too high, or, to put it in terms of sports, putting the bar too high, and not relating it to stark reality will discourage people from acting. This brings us to the next step after the theological reflection, the action planning, and with it the third pitfall.

The Third Pitfall: Avoiding Detailed Pastoral Planning

Chapter 3 of the SECAM letter develops the demands on the church if it is to become a place and sacrament of reconciliation, peace, and forgiveness for Africa. In view of all the problems highlighted by social analysis and seen in the light of lofty ideals, it is understandable that there is the tendency to remain with some general recommendations and to shy away from concrete and detailed action plans. Such an attitude is all the more logical if the impression exists that all these problems have to be tackled at the same time. This is an impossible task because of limited human, financial, and technical resources. But how does one arrive at a realistic action plan?

Here another example from Africa might be appropriate. When IMBISA prepared for its Sixth Plenary Assembly to be held in August 2001, it decided to look at the reality of poverty and economic injustice in southern Africa in the new millennium and to give a Christian response to it. The bishops chose the pastoral circle approach for the preparatory stage. They involved the whole family of God in the member bishops' conferences and dioceses, and they followed the same method during the assembly itself. The results have been published in *That We May Have Life (John 10:10): The Church Works to Overcome Poverty in Southern Africa: A Pastoral Document for Poverty Eradication.* (For a more detailed discussion of this event, see Chapter 2 herein.)

The fourth phase of the pastoral circle, the application of the ethical and spiritual principles from the gospel and Catholic social teaching to the situation of poverty and economic injustice, is unfortunately missing in the final publication of the IMBISA document. Without this fourth phase the rest remains very much in the air. Various draft stages of the document had a chapter on strategic pastoral planning. It defined several elements of such planning (mission statement, goals, strategies, objectives) and outlined four strategies and several respective objectives. It is unfortunate that this chapter was left out of the final document, particularly since Cardinal Wilfrid Napier had proposed in his opening address "that the pastoral circle become the ordinary way for IMBISA to conduct its plenary assembly, especially when dealing with socioeconomic, political or justice issues." Even the original intention of training people in the pastoral circle method receives no additional comment. One is left with the impression that the mission of the church ends with proclaiming the social teaching of the church or that the authors of the document merely wanted to provide the pastoral principles by which action would be guided, arguing that it was not possible to provide common practical solutions since the church was facing very different situations in the nine countries of IMBISA.

The preamble of the IMBISA document enumerates the following three objectives of the plenary:

1. To promote a firm commitment to economic justice and solidarity;
2. To overcome the divorce between faith and life in the Christian communities; and
3. To provide the ethical and spiritual principles to guide the family of God.

In place of an action program, the document ends with a general appeal to all church commissions and church structures. But even the best of plans are not achieved by mere appeals. To succeed requires qualified persons who can be trained for this task, particularly if the poor themselves are to participate in the whole process, and finances. In the address to the IMBISA Plenary of 2001, Cardinal Napier challenged the church "to enable the poor to regain if necessary, but otherwise to reassert, their self-belief and dignity by giving them the knowledge and skills to question and analyze the causes of their poverty, to reflect on them from God's point of view, and to take the steps to climb out of the pit of poverty and especially hopelessness." Therefore, the above three objectives of the document should have been augmented by a fourth, envisaging an action plan and dealing with the required resources for the implementation of such a plan.

Here are some points to be considered for any plan of implementation:

Guiding Principles of Implementation

To distinguish between awakening people to the pastoral principles and implementing these principles in action. Bringing the good news and the principles of social teaching to the people, particularly the poor, is one thing; implementing them in concrete situations is another. There is a tendency in the church to believe that by making the principles known, one automatically has also implemented them. Both actions need distinguishable and concrete steps in order to be effective.

To select priorities. In order not to overtax oneself in the action planning, it is necessary to select priorities. Courage is needed to focus on some particular objectives, because choosing priorities necessarily means that certain goals and actions might have to be postponed or left out altogether, while others receive greater urgency.

To express objectives in quantifiable results and benefits and within a given time frame. Quantifying the expected results and benefits makes it possible to evaluate the planned actions. It also enables the planners to compare the objectives with the available resources of the church. In this way the limited means can be applied and used in the most efficient way.

Capacity Building or Empowerment

Any pastoral plan should have as one of the objectives to allocate the human and financial resources in order to implement the objectives of the pastoral plan. The individuals or groups that are to be trained for action have to be identified, and they need different forms of assistance and training to empower them for action. An appeal to the "family of God" or to the "Christian communities" is much too vague. Priests, social workers, single mothers, HIV-infected persons, and so on need different forms of assistance to empower them in their fight against poverty. When it comes to the question of who is going to do it, any planning in the church has to keep in mind the various role players in the church and the specific roles they are playing and at what level they are acting. For example, when considering what the bishops have to do, their roles as teachers, as pastors, and as advocates have to be looked at separately. Furthermore, bishops exercise their roles in their own diocese, in national bishops' conferences, in regional and continental conferences, and as partners of the churches in the North.

Likewise, the laity in the church has to distinguish the roles it has to play on its own and the clergy, other Christian churches, other faith communities, and within the political community.

A consideration of the needed and available human and financial resources should help to avoid an action plan that is too general, too ambitious, and that strains the resources of the church.

Organizational Tools

The pastoral circle approach is an organizational tool. But it is the contention of this essay that its fourth phase is the weakest link in the method and remains much too general, usually getting lost in generalities such as "something ought to be done about . . . " or merely enumerating some questions to which the plan of action has to respond. In view of this weakness, it was all the more important for the IMBISA document to go into details of action planning.

Sound principles and methods of project organization as practiced by management should be applied. In a publication of the Pastoral Institute of Eastern Africa entitled *Pastoral Planning: A Process for Discernment* (1975) the author, Father Edward R. Killackey, MM, provided some of the organizational tools needed to create an operational plan that outlines what an organization is expected to accomplish in order of priority and within given time periods. He describes planning as an anticipatory decision-making process. An organization decides what to do in order to realize the organization's purpose. Planning has to be carried out before action is taken. Planning requires not just one decision but a whole range of interdependent decisions. There are no independent decisions. Planning is done in stages or phases; decisions made in an earlier phase have to be taken into account when making decisions in a later phase (Killackey 1975).

Financial planning is part of the operational plan. Although budgeting is not to be equated with planning, it nevertheless has a place even within pastoral planning.

The definitions of the elements of every plan of action may vary according to different authors, but they have in common that they lead from the more general to the more specific. Killackey gives the following definitions:

- Objectives are broad, long-range but realizable aims, not ideals.
- Goals are shorter-term specifications of objectives.
- Targets are specific, individual commitments to action, indicating who will do what, when and where to assist in achieving one of the goals and thereby, advancing towards an objective. (Killackey 1975, 2)

Anthony D'Souza, in his trilogy on leadership and effective management (1995), has some useful hints for leading and planning effectively, particularly in planning change. *Training for Transformation* by Anne Hope and Sally Timmel (1995) has proved very helpful for the training of community leaders in Africa and contains practical guidance on making decisions and planning action.

The Fourth Pitfall: The Lack of Evaluation

One cannot stress enough the need for evaluation. Church conferences and meetings usually end up with a number of resolutions and recommendations but without deciding who is going to monitor and evaluate the implementation of these decisions. For example, the IMBISA Plenary Assembly of 1998 in Manzini had as its theme "The Powerful Word of God," and it adopted a number of recommendations, but nowhere was there any evaluation of whether these recommendations had been carried out or not. Likewise, the Plenary Assembly of 2001 on the subject "Poverty and Economic Justice" had no mechanisms for how the implementation of its three objectives could be evaluated.

The lack of evaluation is also one of the root causes of the complaints that church meetings are particularly ineffective and mere "talk shops."

Evaluation is not the final step of a project; rather, it should accompany the whole process through its different stages in the form of controlling or monitoring. In addition, it creates possibilities of adjusting the action plan to changed situations and conditions.

Again, handbooks and guides on project planning and management give valuable information on how evaluation can be organized and carried out.

Conclusion

The pastoral circle approach is presented as a circle with a number of steps to be taken or as a spiral that has as its permanent center the human experience but that never returns to exactly the same starting point. Moving along the path of this circle or spiral there are certain steps to be taken that help one to climb further and further. This essay has shown that this path is also strewn with stumbling blocks or pocked with potholes that have to be avoided in order to proceed. While these potential pitfalls should not prevent one from walking the path, one should proceed with caution.

In this contribution I have acted as a devil's advocate, pointing at some of the potential pitfalls in using the pastoral circle. But it is also important to note that, when applied in a proper way, the pastoral circle can itself act as a devil's advocate.

References

De Schrijver, G., ed. 1998. *Liberation theologies on shifting grounds: A clash of socio-economic and cultural paradigms.* Leuven: University Press.

D'Souza, Anthony. 1995. *Leadership: A trilogy on leadership and effective management.* Nairobi: Paulines Publications.

Hope, Anne, and Sally Timmel. 1995. *Training for transformation: A handbook for community workers.* Rev. ed. Books I, II, III. Gweru, Zimbabwe: Mambo Press.

IMBISA. 2002. Sixth Plenary Assembly. *A pastoral document for poverty eradication: "That they may have life" (John 10:10): The church works to overcome poverty in Southern Africa.* Harare: IMBISA.

John Paul II. 1995. *The church in Africa: Post-synodal exhortation ecclesia in Africa.* Nairobi: Paulines Publications.

Killackey, Edward R. 1975. *Pastoral planning: A process for discernment.* Gaba Pastoral Papers No. 40. Kampala: Gaba Publications.

Klein, Nikolaus. 1992. Die Konferenz von Santo Domingo 1992. *Orientierung* 56, no. 1, 229–32; no. 2, 259–62.

Monsengwo Pasinya, L., and P. Lwaminda. 2001. *"Christ our peace" (Eph 2:14): The church-as-family-of God, place and sacrament of pardon, reconciliation, and peace in Africa.* Pastoral letter of SECAM. Accra, November 6.

SACBC (Southern African Catholic Bishops' Conference). 1995. *Pastoral statement on inculturation.* Pretoria, November 16.

4

Can the Pastoral Circle Transform a Parish?

CHRISTINE BODEWES

This essay is about one parish's experience using the pastoral circle to develop a pastoral plan in a large African urban parish. It was a participatory process in which the parishioners were involved in a reflective sharing about the reality of their lives, their faith, and how the church could become an agent of change both in their spiritual and social lives.

The parish's use of the pastoral circle has led to a remarkable transformation in the church and the community. The parish has changed from a *duka*, or shop, where people came "when they needed to get something," to a community where people come together to listen to different views and adopt innovative ways of solving their problems. According to the parish priest, "Before they were coming to the parish asking for onions and we were giving them tomatoes. Now we are talking the same language."

Christ the King Catholic Church, Kibera

Christ the King Catholic Church is located in the heart of Kibera in Nairobi, Kenya. Kibera has the notorious distinction of being the largest and most densely populated slum in all of sub-Saharan Africa, with over 700,000 people squeezed onto less than 550 acres.

The parishioners of Christ the King live on the very margins of economic and social boundaries where mere survival is the major focus of their day-to-day life. Houses are made of mud and tin. Typically, four to five people stay in a room that averages ten by twenty feet. The only walkways are narrow dirt paths that frequently flood and are impassable during the rainy seasons.

Residents of Kibera have little or no access to electricity, garbage pickup, or proper sanitation or toilets. Potable water is sold on the black market at prices three times higher than normal city rates. Due to the scarcity of pit latrines, most people use "flying toilets" to dispose of human waste. This means depositing the waste in a plastic bag and throwing it onto the roofs or garbage heaps. In addition to the abysmal living conditions, there are no government health facilities and only one government school in Kibera. More than half of the children do not even attend primary school.

The level of poverty is extremely high. While many people are unemployed, those who manage to find work generally earn less than US$2 a day selling fruits and vegetables or working as casual unskilled laborers. In the absence of viable income activities many are forced to resort to theft, prostitution, and illegal brewing of alcohol to survive.

The parish boundaries include seven of the thirteen villages in Kibera, which are home to 340,000 people. Christ the King is the only parish in the Archdiocese of Nairobi whose boundaries fall completely inside a slum and can be accessed only by foot. The parish is administered by the Guadalupe Fathers with assistance from a pastoral team that caters to the pastoral, physical, and emotional needs of over four thousand Catholics.[1]

The parish is organized around the model of small Christian communities or *jumuiya* that meet regularly to pray and undertake church-related activities. The twenty-two *jumuiyas* are clustered into five sub-parishes. In addition to the main parish compound, there are four chapels located in the different sub-parishes. Each *jumuiya* and sub-parish has a leadership structure and these leaders are also part of the parish pastoral council, an advisory board that coordinates with the parish priest to oversee all pastoral action.[2]

The *jumuiyas* that are in existence are very active and play a key role in the life of the parish. However, the total number of parishioners who are *jumuiya* members (less than 10 percent) is relatively low. There are several reasons for this. First, many people do not consider Kibera to be their home. Many prefer their rural homestead and move back and forth to Kibera only when they can find work in Nairobi. For others, Kibera is merely a stopover residence while they are looking for a job in the city. The transitory lifestyle in Kibera is not conducive to joining *jumuiyas* or other groups. Second, the parish is only five years old. Until very recently faith formation was not a priority, and as a result, many Christians are simply not adequately informed about the faith communities.

The Pastoral Circle

In 2001 the parish undertook an evaluation whose major findings showed that the parish had responded well in meeting the parishioners' spiritual needs by offering Mass and sacraments but had not responded adequately in addressing their social needs. The pastoral team members also recognized that because they knew very little of the reality of Kibera, they were unable to respond to the myriad social issues facing parishioners. They also recognized the limitations of the traditional planning processes in which a handful of priests and leaders determined parish activities. Father Gerry Whelan, SJ, who was assisting with the final evaluation for the years 1998–2001, suggested the parish use the pastoral circle, which was consistent with a decision by the Guadalupe Fathers in the late 1990s to use the pastoral circle in all of their parishes.

As a result, in June of 2002 the parish priest assembled a four-member team to oversee the implementation of the pastoral circle.[3] The parish priest also arranged for Father Francesco Pierli, MCCJ, the director of the Social Ministry Research Network Centre, and his colleague Reginald Nalugala to assist the team in designing a pastoral circle methodology appropriate for a very poor slum parish. The parish used and adapted the pastoral circle methodology popularized by Joe Holland and Peter Henriot, SJ, as described in the revised and expanded edition of *Social Analysis: Linking Faith and Justice* published in 1983.

First Step of the Pastoral Circle: Insertion

There was not a formal moment of insertion because the pastoral circle team was composed of experienced members of the pastoral team and well acquainted with Kibera. However, in order to ascertain the capacity and interest of the parishioners to participate in the pastoral circle, the team distributed a simple questionnaire that asked the *jumuiyas* about their membership, levels of participation, and activities. Although a high percentage responded (about 70 percent), the information provided was vague and incomplete; much of this can be attributed to low levels of literacy. As a result, the team decided that they would forgo using any written questionnaires and instead would facilitate participatory discussions in the individual *jumuiyas*.

The team also talked with a sampling of Sunday Christians (Catholics whose interaction with the parish is strictly limited to Sunday Mass) and learned that both their interest and availability were very low. Consequently, the team decided to work primarily with the *jumuiyas* and other parish groups like the choirs, women's group, youth members, and to include the Sunday Christians when possible.[4]

Second Step of the Pastoral Circle: Social/Cultural Analysis

The social/cultural analysis step lasted ten months, during which the team facilitated approximately ninety meetings with the different *jumuiyas* and parish groups. During these meetings there were discussions about six distinct topics: (1) the demographics of Kibera, (2) African traditions and values, (3) socioeconomic and political issues, (4) a review of the parish ministries, (5) parish structures, and (6) parish feedback.

Demographics of Kibera

The aim of the first section of the social/cultural analysis was to learn more about the living conditions in Kibera. Using a framework of fifty guided questions, the team facilitated informal discussions on a broad range of demographic-related issues such as population, housing conditions, incomes and expenses, employment, migration patterns, infrastructure quality, education levels, and health standards.[5]

Jumuiya members were invited to relate their own experiences and were encouraged to offer their own views and opinions. The *jumuiya* members were very open and willing to share their stories.[6] This was particularly true when the group was made up of only women. For example, while discussing marriage and family issues including taboo topics like abortion and birth control, many women shared very personal experiences.

African Traditions and Values

The objective of this section was to evaluate the influence of traditional beliefs and Christian values in the day-to-day lives of the parishioners. The *jumuiyas* discussed what, if any, traditional tribal practices they were still following and the reasons many African customs have been lost in the urban slum environment. The *jumuiya* members also talked about which Christian teachings and values they follow, those they have not fully accepted, and the link between traditional culture and Christianity.

The team modified its approach to this topic in a number of ways. First, the discussions were much less guided and allowed for more expansive responses. This phase of the discussions was very emotive, with many parishioners expressing strong feelings and emotions about their cultural practices, topics very close to their hearts. For example, there were many heated discussions on the tension between Christian marriage and the widespread practice of polygamy in Kibera.

Second, the team specifically involved youth in this section, particularly young people who had been born and raised in Kibera. This was done to compare and analyze the reasons for the different generational views about traditional customs. In stark contrast to their parents, many youth expressed very little interest in their traditions and customs.

Socioeconomic and Political Issues

The aim of this section was to help the parishioners identify and better understand the myriad social problems in Kibera and the complex social, economic, and political structures and players that influence the Kibera community. The team chose fifteen specific issues that had been highlighted in earlier sections and delved deeper into them. The issues discussed included

unemployment, idle youth, drugs and alcohol, prostitution, crime, tribalism, environment, housing, literacy, land, women, the elderly, money, politics, and abortion. During the discussions the *jumuiyas* reflected more deeply
on the root causes and effects of these fundamental problems.

These discussions took on a unique dimension because they happened
during the campaign for the 2002 Kenyan national election. Because political campaigns in Kibera often become violent, people were reluctant to walk
in the community in the evening. As a result, the team met with the *jumuiya*
members for discussions only on weekend afternoons, which significantly
lowered the participation levels. However, on the positive side, there was an
attitude of growing hope and optimism. The team observed the parishioners shift from complaining and casting blame to offering positive and concrete alternatives with the hope that a new government would bring dramatic political and economic changes to Kenya.

Review of Parish Ministries

When the pastoral circle started, the parish was actively engaged in fourteen ministries: catechesis, liturgy, evangelization, human rights, women's
ministry, dispensary, the primary school, pro-life, communications, cultural
center, Sunday school, Biblical center, nursery school and pre-school unit,
and development center (microfinance and vocational training).

In early sections of the social/cultural analysis the parishioners were given
many opportunities to identify their needs and expectations. In order to
enhance this information, the team evaluated the needs of the Christian
community through the eyes of the pastoral team members, who were already serving the parish in the different ministries. The team interviewed
each ministry coordinator about how the ministry came to exist, the history
of its activities, its successes and challenges, and the perceived needs of the
parishioners.

Parish Structures

The team added this section on parish structures in the social/cultural
analysis because of the number and intensity of views expressed about these
structures in the prior four sections. There was a great deal of criticism of
the power structures and the roles of the parish priest, parish pastoral council, and the pastoral team. Many people openly stated that they felt disconnected from or even abandoned by the parish.

Given the intensity of feelings on these issues, the team decided to give all
jumuiya members a chance to voice their views on parish structures and
what they expected from the parish. These discussions were more evaluative in nature and were directed at eliciting specific suggestions that would

allow for more participation by the parishioners, especially in the area of decision making. During these discussions there were repeated requests for more faith formation and leadership training. These discussions generated the largest turnout of all five sections and clearly demonstrated the universal concern over these issues in the parish.

Parish Feedback

After the interviews for the first five sections were finished, the team summarized and translated the findings into Kiswahili. Copies were made for all of the *jumuiya* members and taken back to each *jumuiya* for a feedback session. In each of these sessions the *jumuiya* members were asked to take turns reading the results aloud to make sure that even those with limited literacy skills could participate. Each group was then given the opportunity to correct the findings and to make any additions.

For the team facilitating the pastoral circle, this part of the social/cultural analysis was the most satisfying. There was a spontaneous and visible transformation in the people as they recognized their own ideas and suggestions and realized they had been listened to. For the first time they were able to identify what they could do, both individually and collectively as a church, to respond to the problems they had identified. At the end of these sessions each *jumuiya* was asked to rank the top three socioeconomic problems facing it and the three biggest problem areas in the parish.

Third Step of the Pastoral Circle: Theological Reflection

During this process the people questioned the structures and circumstances that created and perpetuated the problems in Kibera and reflected on how the Christian community at Christ the King could be an agent of transformation in the environment of Kibera. The starting point for the theological reflection was the African synod and its call to build the church as the family of God.

The parish priest formed a new team to facilitate the theological reflection step.[7] Together with the parish priest this team grouped the fifteen socioeconomic issues into three themes (family, social, and political structures) and identified relevant references from the Bible for each theme. The team visited each *jumuiya* several times, focusing on a different theme each time.[8] In each session one member of the *jumuiya* read aloud the summarized findings on the relevant socioeconomic issues and another member read related scripture verses. After a time of reflective prayer the groups discussed the relevance of the scripture to the specific problems in Kibera.

The process of theological reflection was very successful in uncovering a number of important dynamics in Kibera, of which tribalism is key. Tribal affiliation influences every aspect of life in Kibera—which neighborhood people choose to live in, from whom one buys vegetables, and which person is supported in local elections. It is also the source of considerable conflict and violence in the community. In December 2001 tribal clashes took the lives of twenty-five people, including some of our parishioners, and destroyed thousands of dollars worth of property.

During the theological reflection people identified why they rely so heavily on tribal affiliation and reflected on the teachings of Jesus in the parable of the Good Samaritan.[9] Many participants identified themselves with the priest in the parable and described how they also avoid a sick person lying in the path because it is too expensive to hire a wheelbarrow to carry the sick person to the hospital. *Jumuiya* members admitted that they would only help a sick person who was known to them or who was a member of their tribe. In reflecting on the question "Who is your neighbor?" parishioners were challenged to view people from other ethnic groups as their neighbors.

Fourth Step of the Pastoral Circle: Pastoral Planning

The objective of the pastoral planning step was to use the information gathered and reflected upon in the social/cultural analysis and theological reflection to develop a five-year parish plan that could realistically bring about spiritual and social transformation in the parish and in the larger Kibera community. The planning comprised two separate prongs—socioeconomic issues and spiritual issues.

With respect to the first prong, the first step in the planning process was to call each sub-parish together to meet as a group and democratically select one socioeconomic issue as that region's priority issue.[10] The parish brought in trained facilitators to facilitate this process in a one-day reflection in each sub-parish.[11] The sub-parishes chose abortion, alcohol and drugs, HIV/AIDS, and unemployment as the priority socioeconomic issues.

It should be noted that the team decided to add HIV/AIDS as a possible priority issue for every sub-parish to choose, even though it was not one of the original fifteen socioeconomic problems. The team observed early on that the mere mention of HIV/AIDS "shut down" the group and ended the discussion. People simply refused to discuss this topic.

In the African culture HIV/AIDS is still highly stigmatized because it is associated with sexual promiscuity. The stigma is so great that many people are embarrassed and ashamed to even say the word aloud. And yet, it is the most serious problem facing the parish. Thus, the team insisted that AIDS be included as a possible priority issue.

The facilitators helped the sub-parishes not only to choose a priority issue but also to start formulating a plan on how to respond to that issue as a sub-parish by first identifying the causes and the effects of that issue in the community. This process was done by "building a tree." Using the information provided by participants, the facilitator wrote the name of the priority issue on the "tree trunk." As the discussion progressed, the facilitator labeled the tree roots as the root causes of the problems and added separate leaves on the branches as the effects were identified. In some of the sub-parishes a list of possible solutions was also generated.

This tree-building method, used widely in community-development circles, was used to give the participants, many of whom are illiterate, a visual image that would relate the priority issue to their daily lives. The process also allowed them to participate in making the tree, root by root and leaf by leaf, as they went deeper and deeper into the problem.

As an example, in Soweto sub-parish the trunk of the tree (major issue) was alcohol and drug abuse along with the sale of illegal alcohol by Catholics. The tree's roots (causes) included hunger, peer pressure, inherited alcoholism, depression and stress due to unemployment, and the need to numb feelings in order to practice prostitution. One of the most powerful root causes of the problem was the silence of the church, especially about the sale of illegal alcohol by church members.

The alcohol and drug-abuse tree had many leaves (effects), including greater unemployment, increased poverty, more street kids, illness and death, increased incidence of HIV/AIDS, domestic abuse, crime, prostitution, unsafe sexual behaviors, poor role modeling for children, and the tarnished reputation of the church. After this analysis the sub-parish members prepared a list of actions to fight the problem, including educating and raising awareness about alcohol, organizing as a church and demanding that illegal brew not be brought into Kibera illegally by the police, forming support groups for people addicted to alcohol and drugs, helping the sellers of illegal brew to find alternative businesses, and lobbying the government to dismiss local officials and police who refuse to enforce the laws banning the illegal brews.

With respect to the second prong, it was not necessary to ask the *jumuiya* members to choose a spiritual issue because the overwhelming response in the feedback phase had been a call for more faith formation at all levels in the parish. This issue was addressed separately at a parish-level meeting of all the sub-parish leaders. After building the faith formation tree, parish leaders identified training and formation in the following areas as priorities: (1) the role and responsibility of the *jumuiya;* (2) basic teachings of the Catholic church, especially on the sacraments; and (3) leadership training and formation.

The next activity in the pastoral planning was to develop specific plans in each of the sub-parishes to address the chosen priority issue. The parish priest assembled a planning group that was trained on the terminology and steps in the planning process. This group then trained leaders from each sub-parish.

The planning group met with each *jumuiya* to brainstorm what could be done on its priority issues. The use of a systematic planning process with goals, objectives, and so forth was not practical at the *jumuiya* level because many people were unable to understand these concepts or the complex language of planning. Therefore, the information from each brainstorming session at the *jumuiya* level was summarized and added to by the sub-parish leaders.

Finally, a smaller parish-wide team was created to take all the ideas and information from the *jumuiyas* and sub-parishes and write a systematic pastoral plan.[12] These plans were then taken to the parish pastoral council and ministry coordinators for review and harmonization. This planning team also formulated a new vision, mission, and general objective for the whole parish.

After completing the pastoral plan, a process that took almost two years, the participants wanted to celebrate their achievement and share it with the whole parish community. In a Mass held outside to accommodate over two thousand people, the parish priest offered up the social/cultural analysis and the parish plans at the offertory in a colorful and excited celebration. This Mass was a historical moment of true communion in the parish. The plan of each sub-parish was painted onto a large white sheet, and during the Mass each sheet was presented to the priest in the traditional African way; that is, the parish priest sat on a wooden stool and held a cane representing his position as elder as he received the plans. The plans were then read aloud, and each plan was hung on the parish church wall. In addition, each sub-parish acted out a short drama to illustrate the priority issue in its area and its approach to solving it. The sheets were taken to the sub-parish chapels where they are hanging now as a reminder and source of motivation to work on the priority issues.

Parish Transformation

Christ the King parish was transformed as a result of the pastoral circle activities in several key ways, including (1) power, decision making, and parish activities were decentralized; (2) parish ministries were changed to better meet community needs; (3) parish spirit and participation increased; and (4) attitudes and viewpoints were transformed.

Power, Decision Making, and Parish Activities Were Decentralized

From the beginning of the pastoral circle process it was evident that the power structure in the parish was an issue of contention. Historically, the parish priest and the parish pastoral council had made decisions with little to no participation by the parishioners. After reviewing the findings of the pastoral circle, the parish priest, in consultation with the parish leaders, made fundamental changes to this top-down structure of the parish by decentralizing power. The parish structure essentially changed from a triangle, with the parish priest at the top and the Christians at the bottom, to a circle, with the parish priest, leaders, and Christians interacting more equitably.

A small but very powerful symbol of this transformation was that the parish priest, who had previously kept the keys to every door in the parish, gave the keys to the parish leaders in the sub-parishes. Despite fears of theft and vandalism, no incidents have occurred. Another change occurred when the parish priest, who used to have complete control over parish finances, distributed funds to the sub-parishes; the leaders now decide how to spend these funds. An unanticipated result is that costs have been reduced, and the parish is now saving more money than before.

In the past the parish pastoral council met frequently and made nearly all of the decisions for the parish. These decisions ranged from important policy issues to minor issues such as how the altar should be arranged. As a group, the Pastoral Parish Council was not representative of the parishioners because most of the members were from a single ethnic group. Now the council, which is much smaller and more representative, meets only six times a year and makes decisions only at the policy level. The newly elected sub-parish leaders, who come directly from the regions, make most of the day-to-day decisions at the regional level. Similarly, the pastoral team, made up of coordinators of each ministry, now has been reduced in number and plays only an advisory role.

Previously, ministries operated as small organizations independent of the parish pastoral council and of one another. Now, ministry coordinators participate in all of the council meetings. They plan together and work on events that emphasize the priority issues. This new structure encourages innovation, sharing of resources, greater networking, and more participation. For example, all of the ministries and the parish pastoral council were actively involved in planning and implementing the African Bible on the Ground initiative (described below).

There has even been a physical shift in the power base. Many pastoral activities have been moved from the central parish compound to the sub-parishes. There are three new priests, who are taking on a more pastoral approach to the community. For example, Sunday Masses and regular liturgies are now being held in each sub-parish as well as in the main parish. Each priest has been assigned to a sub-parish on a monthly rotation to respond to the specific needs of the Christians living in that neighborhood. Spending significant amounts of time in the sub-parishes, the priests make home visits, celebrate Mass in homes, and try to become part of the daily life of their parishioners. In fact, one of the new priests has moved into a house in a sub-parish in order to better respond to the social and sacramental needs of his neighbors. In response, new youth groups and choirs have come up spontaneously and regularly participate in the liturgy in the sub-parishes.

Changed Parish Ministries to Better Meet Community Needs

The social/cultural analysis showed that the existing ministries were limited in their relevance and effectiveness. Over the years each new parish priest had changed the structures, personnel, and priorities according to his own views. New departments were created without consultation or input from community; as a result, they could not sustain themselves because of lack of participation. The depth of this problem was illustrated by the fact that some ministry coordinators had other interpretations of their jobs or the ministries they were supposed to be leading. For example, in the women's ministry the parish priest wanted to focus on building solidarity among women and advocacy issues, while the ministry coordinator thought that the objective was to help women start income-generating projects.

In response to the voices heard during the process using the pastoral circle, the parish phased out some of the ministries and amalgamated others. The women's ministry was phased out completely. This phasing out provided an opportunity for a new initiative to arise. A group of single mothers in the parish spontaneously came together to form the Saint Magdalene women's group as a support group to help one another. The group is already registered with the government. One example of its activities is raising money to buy flour for destitute members.

Another example of how the pastoral circle has transformed the way ministries work is in addressing the priority needs in neighborhoods and sub-parish regions. The self-reliance ministry focuses its skills training and job searching in the two sub-parishes that identified unemployment as the priority issue. With this new focus the ministry has become more efficient and effective in the way it serves the parish.

The activities of many ministries were also decentralized, and the coordinators and staff are now physically more often in the community. For example, rather than offering workshops in the main parish compound, the human rights ministry trained a team of parishioners in civic education. This team, in turn, visits the *jumuiyas* in the evenings to teach the parishioners about their legal and human rights.

Increased Parish Spirit

The dynamics of the pastoral circle process gave the parishioners new hope and energy, manifest as increased involvement and the responsibility of parishioners in the day-to-day activities of the parish. The number of parishioners has grown by 20 percent; the main church, as well as the sub-parish chapels, is now full on Sundays. Weekly Mass collections have increased by 100 percent. In addition, six new *jumuiyas* were started spontaneously last year.

There is clearly a new sense of belonging and unity in the parish. Not only has the number of *jumuiyas* increased, but the nature of the membership has also been transformed. In the past many people were excluded from decision-making processes because of unspoken rules of exclusion. For example, a woman who was a second wife, or not married in the church, would be excluded from many parish activities, especially decision making. Because the pastoral circle process included everyone, previously excluded people are now accustomed to participate in meetings and share their views.

In the past there was one salaried catechist to visit all of the *jumuiyas* and offer spiritual support. Now the faith-formation ministry has trained thirty-four volunteer catechists; each is assigned to a specific *jumuiya* to teach religion and to respond to sacramental needs. Similarly, a call for volunteer home-based care workers to visit the sick, particularly those with HIV/AIDS, put out by the health ministry was answered by a number of new volunteers from the sub-parishes. The parish is now training these volunteers—the Good Samaritans.

The quality of communication with the parish priest has also improved. In the past a visit to the parish usually meant a complaint over petty issues such as who should read the weekly announcements. In the new spirit the number of squabbles has decreased. Parish members have started to visit the parish priest with an attitude of reconciliation and often with offers to help. This new spirit is also seen in the liturgies, celebrations, and social activities in the sub-parishes that focus on "their" priority issue from the pastoral planning.

Another illustration of this transformation of spirit is the number of successful creative events addressing priority issues. Arising from the call from all levels for more faith formation, a number of ministries, along with the thirty-four new catechists and youth groups, worked together to host the African Bible on the Ground initiative. This event puts theological reflection in action; its aim is to help Christians understand the Bible in their daily lives and within their particular African culture. Leaders attended a one-week retreat during which they engaged in deeper theological reflection on the findings of the social/cultural analysis, focusing on the fifteen socioeconomic and political issues.

When the catechists came back to the parish, they built small huts to represent each of the fifteen issues. The huts were built with plastic and paper materials that are similar to the homes of the Kibera people. They were filled with pictures, diagrams, and scripture verses designed to help the Christians understand the issue in the context of the Bible and of Kibera and African cultures. For three days, while parishioners walked through the huts, the catechists helped them to interpret issues like crime, prostitution, and unemployment in light of the teachings of Christ. The parish subsequently took the Bible on the Ground to all of Kibera, with over two thousand people attending from all religious denominations.

Transformed Attitudes and Viewpoints

As the social/cultural analysis data were reviewed again during the pastoral planning, it was clear that it was taboo to discuss openly many of the priority issues such as alcohol abuse, HIV/AIDS, and abortion. Moreover, parishioners lacked fundamental understanding of the root causes of these problems. As a result, there was a consensus that the parish needed to focus on sensitization, awareness, and education before taking on projects or actions to address these problems.

One of the areas in which transformation of viewpoint was addressed in a very visible way was alcohol abuse. Many aspects of the alcohol problem had been raised, such as production of home brew by single women for economic survival, abuse and domestic violence by unemployed men, and the impact on youth of the growing number of local bars. *Chang'aa* is an illegal alcoholic brew that is widely distributed and consumed in Kibera. It is very toxic and can be lethal, yet it is consumed in large amounts by both men and women of all ages. It is seen as a cheap way to escape problems for a while.

The human rights ministry in conjunction with the youth groups organized an advocacy campaign called Kibera United Against *Chang'aa*. The aim was to raise awareness about the effects of *chang'aa* and to reduce the stigma associated with openly opposing *chang'aa*. A talent show was organized, and the people of Kibera were invited to write original music about *chang'aa*. The winners were featured in the first rock concert ever held in Kibera. Several internationally and nationally known Kenyan musicians volunteered their time and participated.

In contrast to alcohol abuse, HIV/AIDS was glaringly absent in the whole social/cultural analysis. However, one sub-parish had the courage to identify it as a priority issue in the pastoral planning moment. In response, the youth of the parish organized a Mr. and Miss Kibera beauty contest with the theme "Beauty to Demolish AIDS." Thousands of young and old alike participated in the day-long event as young people walked the catwalk and shared their talents. While the crowd enjoyed the music, dancing, and singing, the most important result was that the youth were able to sensitize the community and break the silence that surrounds AIDS in the parish and in Kibera as a whole.

The Way Forward

The pastoral circle did not end with the celebration liturgy in the compound of Christ the King parish. The parish scheduled an evaluation of the progress made for November of each year. This will be accompanied by a liturgical celebration to celebrate the successes and failures of that year. Then a planning activity will be held for the upcoming year on the priority issues in the parish.

To ensure that the voices of the people are heard, the parish is currently working on a popular publication in Kiswahili about the process and some of the major findings of the social/cultural analysis. The parish intends to acknowledge the contributions of each person by presenting a booklet in the context of a liturgical celebration.

Many people outside the parish are also concerned about the same issues that surfaced in the pastoral circle exercise. Many churches and development organizations have heard about the process and trust in the reliability of the information gathered. Also, the information is in Kiswahili and in a format that is easy to understand and distribute. The parish is planning to link up with some of the other churches in Kibera and choose one issue, like education or AIDS, and use the pastoral circle to develop a joint action plan that could influence all of Kibera.

Conclusions

Several major conclusions can be drawn. First, the parish was not sufficiently prepared for the pastoral circle. Most people, including the ministry coordinators, had never heard of social analysis or taken part in any systematic parish planning activity. Too, the parishioners had minimal experience in giving their views, particularly views that might be perceived as critical of the church.

In hindsight the team realized that the parish should have organized day-long participatory workshops with all *jumuiyas* before starting to explain the whole process and particularly the methods and length of time it would take. A liturgical celebration to launch the pastoral circle would also have given it greater credibility and support. Participation would also have been strengthened if the team had provided periodic progress reports, perhaps in the Sunday liturgies. These could have updated the parish on the progress made and announced the next phase in the circle, clarified issues and problems, and invited additional input from the parish on the overall process. Another omission was not involving any parishioners in the initial planning process.

Second, the team was very sensitive to the fact that many researchers and NGO representatives in Kibera over the years had used the community to gather information and then disappeared. This created an environment of resentment and suspicion in the community. In order to avoid being viewed in this vein, we introduced a feedback phase at the end of the social/cultural analysis. We gave all the participants copies of their documented responses and asked them to take turns reading aloud their prior views.

The feedback was helpful for several reasons. First, parishioners were able to recognize their own words and ideas, which made them feel listened to. Second, it gave the team an opportunity to confirm the accuracy of what had been written. Finally, participants were given an opportunity to make additional comments. We found that they used this phase to go deeper into the topic. Because of this, the level of participation increased dramatically. People would actually stop discussions to make sure we were writing down everything that was being said.

Third, three practical factors influenced participation in the pastoral circle: parishioners' working hours, weather, and the national election. In the beginning the team met the *jumuiyas* in the daytime, but it found that many people were unavailable because they were working or looking for jobs. When meetings were scheduled in the evening hours, the participation levels rose dramatically and many more men participated. The team continued some of the day meetings when discussing issues especially sensitive to women, such as abortion, birth control, and marriage.

Weather was also a major factor. During the rainy seasons mud and refuse flooded the footpaths, which discouraged people from attending. The third factor that influenced the number of people participating was the national election. People feared violence, and participation was low. On weekends trucks of youth organizations of political parties were brought in by politicians, given alcohol, and sent around the villages to buy people's voter cards, hold rallies, and give handouts. Many Christians chose to attend those events rather than to participate in the pastoral circle activities.

A more fundamental factor influenced the participation in the theological reflection and pastoral planning moments. What we called "pastoral circle fatigue" was experienced by both parishioners and the facilitating team. After a year of meetings people simply did not have the enthusiasm to attend or to engage as actively in discussion and reflection. Nor did the team members always have the energy to inspire participants. Were we to do it again, we would shorten or omit the demographic section of the social/cultural analysis and hold only a small number of focus groups to verify and enrich the secondary demographic data. We would also increase the size of the team and insist that the priests in the parish be involved in order to distribute the tasks more evenly.

Fourth, the theological reflection moment, which suffered the effect of the fatigue, was also influenced by difficulties in planning and methodology. Because of other commitments, only two members of the core pastoral circle team were available to lead this moment. The new team, which lacked familiarity with the parishioners, had limited rapport and spontaneous discussion with the *jumuiya* members suffered. Further, the new team faced difficulties connecting the theological reflection discussions to previous steps of the pastoral circle.

The use of "stand alone" Old Testament verses also proved to be challenging. Often these verses were taken too literally, and the discussion could not be related easily to the current experience in Kibera. For example, in some discussions the Old Testament Bible verses were used to justify oppression and abuse of women within the church and home. The use of a single parable, which was discussed in depth with parishioners, was much more fruitful. Parishioners would easily identify themselves as characters, which allowed them to connect the scriptural reading to their lives.

Theological reflection was done only on the socioeconomic issues. It would have been helpful to extend the theological reflection to the issues of traditional African culture and issues related to the structure and function of the parish. The reason this was not done was because of time pressure to finish the pastoral circle.

Fifth, at the outset the parish had no idea how enormous this process would be and how demanding on both the team and the *jumuiya* members. If the pastoral team had agreed on specific roles, time tables, and resources needed and where they would come from, the process would have been strengthened. In addition, the core team members were interested in different steps of the pastoral circle. These issues should have been discussed at the beginning so that consensus could have been reached about how and why the parish was doing the pastoral circle.[13]

Notes

[1] The pastoral team includes three sisters working full time and a number of sisters working part time in the school, faith formation, and health clinic, two full-time lay missioners, and a salaried staff of five local lay people from the parish.

[2] In addition to the *jumuiyas*, the parish has other ministries that are part of the parish family, including catechists, choirs, youth, single mothers, and a civic-education group.

[3] The four designated members were Father Raul Nava Trujillo (the current parish priest), Sister Jennifer Simwa (a Sacred Heart sister and social worker with many years of experience in schools and parishes in Kenya and Uganda who was hired to coordinate the social analysis); Christine Bodewes (a Maryknoll lay missioner and coordinator of the human rights ministry), and Lillian Mwangi (the coordinator of the social communications ministry and lifelong resident of Kibera).

[4] About three hundred parishioners participated on a consistent basis in the pastoral cycle process.

[5] Examples of the guided questions used to facilitate the discussions: How much is your rent? What ethnic group does your landlord come from, and does he or she live in Kibera? How much do you spend for breakfast, lunch, and dinner? Why did you come to Kibera, and why do you stay? Do you use birth control? How do you relate with your neighbors?

[6] It is noteworthy that during these discussions the team only prompted questions and documented the responses. It did not offer answers or opinions, even when asked, in order to avoid biasing the outcome.

[7] The team included two Augustinian seminarians, Brother Henry Ngwala Opondo and Brother Jacob Ariek; a Cannosian sister, Sister Sarah Nampeera; a Franciscan sister, Sister Concepta Mangana; and Lillian Mwangi.

[8] The thirty-five visits that made up this process took about six weeks to complete.

[9] This parable was selected because of its particular affinity to the reality of Kibera. It is a common occurrence to see people lying either sick or drunk on the

pathways in Kibera. It is equally common to see hundreds of people pass that person by without offering help.

[10] For example, in the sub-parish of Soweto, *jumuiya* members identified a number of issues including alcohol, land ownership, employment, old age, tribalism, and crime. However, the four *jumuiyas* chose alcohol as a priority problem because much of the illegal alcoholic production and sales is located in their neighborhood.

[11] The team chose to invite trained facilitators, as opposed to training local parish leaders to facilitate these meetings, primarily because of time constraints. The pressure to finish the parish planning was very high because parish elections had been suspended until its completion. Also, the meetings were difficult to facilitate given the large numbers of participants and the complexity and sensitivity of the issues.

[12] This team was called the pastoral planning team; it included selected people from the pastoral team, the sub-parish council, and an executive member of the parish pastoral council.

[13] The parish would like to recognize and give thanks to the many people who had the faith and the courage to participate in the pastoral circle, especially the members of the *jumuiyas*, choirs, and youth, who made great sacrifices of their time to share their ideas and were committed to building an authentic family of God in Christ the King Catholic Church. The parish could not have succeeded in this endeavor without the untiring commitment of Father Raul Nava, Sister Jennifer Simwa, Lillian Mwangi, Father Robert Jalbert, Father Javier Gonzalez, Father Francesco Pierlii, and Mr. Reginald Nalugala. Special thanks also go to Laura and Doug Krefting for their assistance in distilling and editing the whole experience.

5

The Pastoral Circle as Spirituality

Toward an Open and Contextual Church

JOHANNES BANAWIRATMA

The pastoral circle, sometimes called pastoral cycle or spiral, has been helping Christian communities to live contextually for the past twenty-five years. It continues to help activists and theologians serve their communities. The pastoral circle is not just a method to be applied in practice; it needs a spirituality of openness. Only open communities can apply the pastoral circle. The following ten agenda, meant to name important conditions for being an open church and practicing contextual theology, are based on my experience as a theologian in Indonesia. All agenda are interconnected and need to be understood as a whole. These reflections are focused on an understanding of the pastoral circle as a spirituality of openness.

Being Open Church: Communion of Contextual Communities

Christian faith is contextually experienced, and the encounter with Jesus Christ needs to be communicated contextually. Another way of encountering Christ would only offer a Christ of colonialism. A new way of being church that is more helpful to practice our Christian faith and to be more flexible to face current challenges can be described as an open church, which is church as *a communion of contextual communities* that are living a spirituality of openness. Only this kind of community can become a subject that can apply the pastoral circle in a way that is helpful.

The Federation of Asian Bishops' Conferences (FABC) envisioned being a new church as a "participatory Church," which will have to be "a communion of communities." Its concrete forms are basic ecclesial (Christian) communities—neighborhood groups gathered together by the word of God to pray and share the gospel of Jesus, living their daily lives, and in one mind and heart realizing their mission (Rosales and Arévalo 1992). We can say that this is the way of transforming the life of the church "from below." A similar reflection has occurred in Europe, where the future of the church is envisioned as base communities (Hebblethwaite 1993; Hebblethwaite 1994).

A basic Christian community is not exclusive. Christ's gospel invites us to develop brotherhood and sisterhood with all people. Therefore, a basic Christian community is open to the development of becoming a basic *human* community that shows concerns for the struggles for the common good and integral human liberation. A basic human community can be described as a small community involved in social activities to eliminate suffering, to struggle for a just society, and to sustain the development of the people and the environment. Basic human communities are *primarily* groups of powerless people empowering themselves; *secondarily,* they can be facilitators for other groups in solidarity with them.

From a Christian perspective the struggle of basic human communities is fundamentally related to Christian orthopraxis. The basic human community is a response to the demands of the Christian faith in the midst of identity claims within our multicultural and multireligious context. In our Christian language it is the struggle for God's reign. The basic human community is a community of God's reign (Pieris 1988; Banawiratma and Mueller 1999; Singgih 1999; Mangunwijaya 1999).

Crossing the boundaries of their religions and beliefs, these communities are united in real life situations and actual concerns. Based on the values of God's reign, the Christian and human community is open to interreligious or interfaith community. People of different faiths and religions can mutually enrich and help each other to come closer to the Ultimate Mystery (Panikkar 1978; Dunne 1978).

It is important to reflect further on a new way of being church that the FABC, in its meetings in Bangkok in 1982 (FABC III) and Bandung 1990 (FABC V) called "a communion of communities." It is not just a sum of many communities. The first letter of Paul to the Corinthians can help us to deepen our understanding of this new way of being church.

> When you meet together, it is not really to eat the Lord's supper. For when the time comes to eat, each of you goes ahead with your own supper, and one goes hungry and another becomes drunk. . . . Whoever, therefore, eats the bread or drinks the cup of the Lord in an unworthy manner will be answerable for the body and blood of the Lord. Examine yourselves, and only then eat of the bread and drink of the cup. For all who eat and drink without discerning the body, eat and drink judgment against themselves. For this reason, many of you are weak and ill, and some have died. (1 Cor 11:20–21, 27–30)

There is no communion of communities in the body and blood of the Lord if "one goes hungry and another becomes drunk," if there is a separation between the rich and the poor. A new way of being church cannot happen without solidarity with the poor (Mangunwijaya 1999). People with successful businesses who come to the Sunday liturgy or to the Lord's supper and offer big donations but who avoid creating just relationships, ones that don't exploit others, are violating the body and blood of the Lord. The communion in the Lord should be the communion of communities of liberation from weakness, illness, and death.

Threefold Dialogue: The Poor, Cultures, and Religions

As a communion of communities the Asian church undergoes three interrelated dialogues—with the poor, with the cultures, and with the religions—as expressed in 1974 by FABC I (Rosales and Arévalo 1992). In terms of the pastoral circle, these dialogues are the first moment, the moment of inscription or contact. They are indispensable for the church's preferential option for the poor, as well as for a spirituality of openness toward cultures and religions.

The pastoral circle should become a means of linking faith and justice, a means of making a serious option for and with the poor. God has an agreement with the poor to ally against mammon, against the accumulation and absolutization of wealth and power. In his life, his words, his deeds, and his death Jesus revealed himself as the Liberator of life. Witnessing the kinship of God, Jesus is the symbol of the conflict between God and mammon. Like Jesus himself, the church cannot avoid facing the conflict between the power of God and the power of mammon (Pieris 1999; Krueger 1997). The church's preferential option for and with the poor and the oppressed cannot achieve its goal without listening and learning from them through dialogue.

Contextualization means the effort of a community of faith to live out the gospel of Christ. In this effort there are at least two cultural contexts involved, that of the community and that of the gospel. Therefore the effort of contextualization always includes intercultural or intercontextual encounters (Samartha 1996).

Contextualization never means isolating a community from its own context, which is impossible in our world today. Every culture has its own richness and limit. Through cultural encounters the communities can share values. The way of being contextual communities is not a way of exclusivism or elitism. Gospel values need to be found through critical communication and brought out within the cultural process. For example, nowadays the secular culture learns from the cosmic-holistic one, but the cosmic-holistic culture needs to learn from the secular in order to avoid a discriminative way of living in the community. Through critical dialogue the community can learn to celebrate different charisms and to be open to the participation of all in the service of the community.

In our present-day world the Christian community has to be aware of the globalizing process that marginalizes poor people. Imperialistic globalization should be opposed by a counter strategy, a globalization of solidarity or globalization from below, namely, a culture of networking among contextual communities in view of globalization without marginalization, building a worldwide community of justice and peace that recognizes the integrity of creation. In our pluralistic world our spirituality needs to enter into interreligious and intercultural dialogue and collaboration. Experiences have taught us that the movements for liberation need to be supported by as many people as possible. In a holistic framework the participation of all is important.

It is only since Vatican II that the church explicitly accepts and promotes religious freedom. "Let Christians, while witnessing to their own faith and way of life, acknowledge, preserve and encourage the *spiritual* and *moral truths* found among non-Christians, also their *social life* and *cultures*" (*Nostra aetate,* no. 2). The church not only respects human dignity and human rights but recognizes spiritual and moral truth in other religions.

Every religion has its own historical experience and its own values. It is not just a preparation for the gospel or a deviation from the gospel. Christianity is not meant to promote a ghetto or a "Christian tribe." Christians are called to discern and to follow the presence and the work of the Spirit blowing within and outside the church. The historical limit of revelation and of human condition brings an obligation to be open to others. *To be religious today is to be interreligious; to be faithful is to practice interfaith dialogue.*

During the last decade Indonesia has been marked by massive unrest and collective violence. This collective violence, in which religions were involved, destroyed houses, markets, shops, factories, banks, cars, police outposts, government offices, court buildings, churches, mosques, and orphanages. More than that, people were cruelly treated, tortured, and killed. Almost all the unrest and collective violence were marked by a religious dimension. The history of Indonesia has shown that people of various religions united when they became agents fighting against colonialism, exploitation, and oppression. When the common (vertical) enemy disappeared, there were tendencies toward (horizontal) conflicts among people of various religions. Religious people are called to be committed to the common good. Interreligious harmony without common concern and struggle for social justice would issue in a false and unjust harmony.

Rooted in the Gospel of Christ: Christian Resources

Contextual faith and reflection upon faith are not disconnected from Christian traditions. These are the sources of the third moment in the pastoral circle. The crux of the matter is not rejecting or accepting the traditions. We need to respect traditions in critical dialogue in order to be able to touch their inner core or constants (see Chapter 6 herein). It might happen that the critical and dialogical reflection uncovers what is hidden in Christian witness and tradition as well as rediscovers what is forgotten. Contextual faith and theology should be rooted in the gospel of Jesus Christ, which has been always interpreted and will always be interpreted by the faith community.

Contextualization is not an application of abstract truth within the concrete reality of life. It is to accept the concrete reality, namely, the Jesus event, as meaningful or even decisive for all cultures. The tension between particularity and universality cannot be overcome by abstract formulation, but only by dialectical and continuous communication.

Moreover, the decisive element of the Jesus event is not only expressed in verbal language but also and more particularly in the language of action. Aloysius Pieris's distinction of two categories of the poor is very helpful to see the decisive element in following the gospel of Jesus Christ. The first category of the poor are those who are the victims of mammon; they are vicars of Christ:

> These are the victims of nations who act as the eschatological judge of nations (Mt. 25:36ff.). They are the least sisters and brothers of Jesus who receive our love in Christ's name and thus open the gate of the Kingdom for us. . . . Their poverty is forced upon them because of a wrong "house-management" *(oiko-nomia)* of the world by mammon-worshippers. . . . The poor are . . . sinners as much as the rich. . . . Their victimhood is therefore the sole basis of their election. . . . Their holiness consists . . . in responding to their calling to be God's covenant partners, to be liberating force in the world. (Pieris 1999, 59)

The second category of the poor includes the renouncers of mammon as followers of Christ:

> These have voluntarily made themselves poor for the sake of entering the Kingdom as demanded by Jesus. Their poverty is known as evangelical, as it is undertaken for the sake of the gospel. They alone are *qualified* to preach the Good News of the kingdom to the (first category of the) poor. . . . The old formula "no salvation outside the church" is now replaced by "no salvation outside God's covenant with the poor." . . . The evangelically poor receive their mission through their solidarity with the socially poor. (Pieris 1999, 60)

To follow Christ means to be poor evangelically (second category), that is in solidarity with the physical poor (first category).

Love in Action

The pastoral circle leads to action. To be Christian means to follow the Way in orthopraxis. "Not everyone who says to me, 'Lord, Lord,' will enter the kingdom of heaven, but only the one who does the will of my Father in heaven." From orthopraxis the truth of the gospel proclamation gains its credibility. "Today more than ever, the Church is aware that her social message will gain credibility more immediately from the witness of actions than as a result of its internal logic and consistency" (*Centesimus annus*, no. 57). By living so, the church becomes more and more the community of Christ's disciples who are "not from this world" but "in this world" and thus become a "sacrament of salvation" (*Lumen gentium*, no. 1).

Most Asian churches might still be too liturgically oriented. The return to the value of God's reign implies the return to a genuine liturgy that is a source and summit of the living faith. Personal prayer interiorizes the love of God personally, and liturgical celebrations kindle our faith and hope in God's promise. But if they are not genuine, they cannot become the source and the summit; they can even become illusive (1 Jn 4:20). True liturgy comes out of and flows back to the liturgy of life. The return to the value of God's reign with the liturgy of life as source and summit means to shift the orientation and activities of our churches from internally oriented to externally oriented (Pieris 1999).

The church finds Christ in the poor as the vicars of Christ. What we do to them, we do to Christ; what we do not do to them, we do not do to Christ (Mt 25:31–46). The poor are not objects of Christian charity. They are subjects and agents of social change. Therefore, the most appreciative service to them is companionship in such a way that they themselves are able to control their lives.

Their poverty is rooted especially in structural injustice, where the unjust power of the dominating system affects different areas of life. Thus economic, political, and cultural injustices are interconnected. Women suffer not only because of social injustice; they are also subordinated and discriminated against as women. The minority and the weak, in the case of race, ethnic group, religion, or age, can be treated unjustly by the majority and the strong. Here the human rights issue comes up. In addition, we should remember the ecological aspect, because the poor have no choice but to live with the destruction of environment.

Therefore, within the existing context of the conflicts between God and mammon, between God's reign and anti-God's reign, orthopraxis means to struggle for justice, to empower the poor with the perspective of gender justice, human rights, and ecojustice. Many experiences show that empowering movements need to include all. This means not only men, but also women and the environment. To include all means also defending and promoting the participation of all, human responsibility, and human rights regardless of gender, race, age, majority-minority relations, or other factors. In being faithful to Jesus Christ, Christians cannot avoid the conflicts against the victimizers embodying the power of anti-God's reign.

Prayer and Contemplation

The whole process of the pastoral circle needs prayer and contemplation. Through human witness and by the work of the Holy Spirit, Jesus Christ (historical-glorified) is encountered, so that we can say, "It is no longer because of what you said that we believe, for we have heard for ourselves, and we know that this is truly the Savior of the world" (Jn 4:42). This encounter or mystical experience is expressed and deepened through prayer and contemplation that help us to be with Christ and to participate in the mysteries of his life. "I am the vine, you are the branches. Those who abide in me and I in them bear much fruit, because apart from me you can do nothing" (Jn 15:5). Our faith reflection or our doing of theology is moved by the faith and love experience. It is an effort of *intellectus fidei* as well as *intellectus amoris*.

The way of being church from below is not only in accordance with concrete brotherhood/sisterhood and social commitments. It is also facilitating the disciples of Christ to share their faith experiences with others and to help one another to develop mystical experience and personal contact with Jesus Christ. Thus, all the community members will increasingly experience the church's mystery, namely, their participation in God's plan and actions.

The question is how far personal and communal prayer can help to internalize and socialize the experience of encounter with Christ. Many young people enjoy the way of contemplative prayer of the Taizé community. An ecumenical recollection in a Taizé style of praying has helped Catholic and Protestant communities to enter into a deeper ecumenical experience rooted in the same Christ. *Mystical Theology* by William Johnston (2000) is an example of books that help to reflect this aspect of faith.

Contextual Analysis and Reflection

Contextual analysis and reflection come up in the second and third moment of the pastoral circle. Contextual analysis and reflection exercise their functions within the community by reading the signs of the time: hearing, interpreting, and announcing the *Logos* (Word) and the *Sophia* (Wisdom) of life. They address the community of faith, and as a part of the community, they address different groups and societies as well as their interrelations. Socio-theological reflection tries to offer deeper understanding of the actual situation (the hermeneutical dimension) and concrete direction or impetus for further actions (the ethical dimension). It might happen that critical and dialogical reflection uncovers what is hidden in Christian witness and rediscovers what is forgotten. We have tried to do this kind of reflection in *Contextual Social Theology: An Indonesian Model* (Banawiratma and Mueller 1999).

Critical reflection is not neutral. It is negatively or positively related to the community's involvement. Contextual reflection tries consciously to immerse itself in praxis; it is praxis based and praxis oriented. Theological reflection is not only *fides quaerens intellectum*, faith that seeks understanding, but it is first of all *fides sperans liberationem*, faith that hopes for liberation (Pieris). Theological reflection is becoming *intellectus amoris et misericordiae* (Sobrino), understanding of love and mercy, a compassionate understanding.

Epistemologically the relation among the knower, the process of knowing, and the knowledge (the known) is very close. Most academic theologians are not social activists (although they can be). However, a minimum of contact with the actions of a community is required to develop a contextual theology, which needs not only brain but also heart and hands. By having contact with community, theology follows the priority of orthopraxis.

Intertextual and Intercontextual Dialogue

Intertextual and intercontextual dialogue belongs to the third moment of the pastoral circle. The community of faith puts efforts to live the gospel in a certain context. It deals with interpretation of the reality related to the resources of faith that also have text and context. Contextual analysis and reflection are always intertextual and intercontextual, since they are done in communication among communities with their own texts and contexts. The way of living contextually is the way of critical dialogue and communication. By sharing and witnessing, we can become more conscious that our interpretation is limited, that we always need a continuous process of dialogue and reinterpretation. By sharing and witnessing we are open to coming closer to the core of faith and its responsible manifestation here and now.

An example is our interreligious context in Indonesia. Our Muslim sisters and brothers have difficulty in understanding our sharing of faith experience and doctrine on Christ and the Trinity. In fact, the same difficulty occurs within our Christian community. The difficulty touches not only the field of doctrine but also the field of prayer. Our belief in Christ and the Trinity is based on the paschal mystery, on the death and resurrection of Jesus as well as on the gift of the Holy Spirit. Exactly on this point we have difficulty with the Muslim interpretation, although a Muslim theologian such as Mahmoud Mustafa Ayoub (1980, 1993) opens a closer interpretation.

According to Ayoub the text of the Qur'an (4:157–58) that says that Jesus did not really die crucified is not a historical statement but a *theological* statement.

Instead of taking the cross and resurrection, we can have the word of God as point of entrance for our sharing of faith with Muslim sisters and brothers. The word of God, which has divine and human qualities, mediates the encounter between God and human beings. God is the Creator, the greatest and compassionate God, the almighty and merciful One, who creates, sustains, and cares for the whole creation. The God of Christians and Muslims is the same God of Abraham. We Christians address the same God as Abba, the motherly father of Jesus and our motherly father.

Interdisciplinary Approach

Being a contextual community relates to various and complex realities. The multifaceted analysis and reflection of faith that take seriously social reality are very important for a spirituality of openness. For this purpose the spirituality of the pastoral circle needs interdisciplinary dialogue and cooperation. Contextual theology as an academic enterprise needs to fulfill academic accountability, just as do other disciplines.

The interdisciplinary approach, particularly in cooperation with the social sciences, helps the reflection of faith make relevant interpretations and give an orientation to the community (Banawiratma and Mueller 1999; Boff and Pixley 1989). Through this dialogue, the understanding of Christ's gospel will be fertilized. The critical dialogue between theological reflection and social analysis aims at actions that change the reality into new social situations dreamed of in the life of faith. The dialogue with other disciplines can also bring new vision and a new articulation of faith as, for example, in Diarmuid O'Murchu's *Quantum Theology* (1997).

Kenotic Spirituality

Spirituality can be understood as a way to respond to experience. It is related to what is experienced, whether human beings, the world, or God. Jesus lived a deep spirituality of solidarity with the world. He was born in solidarity with the homeless. His words and actions delighted the sick, the hungry, and the suffering. Jesus' spirituality is a *kenosis* spirituality, a self-emptying spirituality, until the last consequence.

We are used to the conception of "the Word became flesh" (Jn 1:14), forgetting the fact that the Word became servant, washing the feet of the disciples (Jn 13:1–17). The letter to the Philippians says, "Christ Jesus . . . emptied himself, taking form of a slave. . . . He humbled himself and became obedient to the point of death—even death on the cross" (Phil 2:10). Incarnation is only the beginning of the kenotic way of Christ.

Following the self-emptying spirituality, Jesus' disciples are transformed to become more like Jesus. Such is a spirituality of powerlessness and continuous conversion, of renewal to be more open to others and to God. The self-transformation of Jesus' disciples makes an impact on their social solidarity and stimulates wider transformation, namely, the transformation of societal life. Without kenotic spirituality the process of pastoral circle would not be a road of following the kenotic Christ.

Transformation through Affirmation and Confrontation

Transformation of social reality is the ultimate aim of the pastoral circle process. The cultural, political, and economic realities are ambivalent. They express not only positive values but also anti-values. Therefore, we need a critical interpretation of the data, and the contextual response can be affirmation or confrontation in view of a positive transformation. There is no blueprint for this attitude; the way to go is critical dialogue. To escape from the critical attitude might mean to support imperialist interests and to refuse an evangelical mission.

The ambivalence touches not only the reality outside the church but also within the church, within our tradition. Our openness requires from us respect and self-criticism. Contextualization needs to be open to the richness of history and variety of traditions. Thus we avoid sticking to a certain tradition or moment of history as well as to the actual form (status quo). The transformation of our particularity can bring further transformations of us as individuals and as societies.

The primacy of the gospel's orthopraxis demands the transformation of the churches from below, which is already begun in basic Christian (ecclesial) communities and the basic human communities as well as the basic interfaith community. It is a new way of being church that is a communion of contextual communities. Such a way involves critical dialogues toward social transformation. As a human and limited reality the church can only exercise its mission and become a dynamic community of faith if it becomes a community of dialogue and transformation. The demands of developing contextual communities are ultimately the demands of truly encountering and following Christ as well as the response to embody the contextual Christ as the medium that transforms life in God, who is always greater, until God becomes all in all (1 Cor 15:28).

The proposed ten agenda for the pastoral circle as a spirituality of openness can be summarized and presented schematically in Figure 5–1, which also shows how the different agenda are interrelated.

Figure 5–1. The Pastoral Circle: Contextualized Spirituality

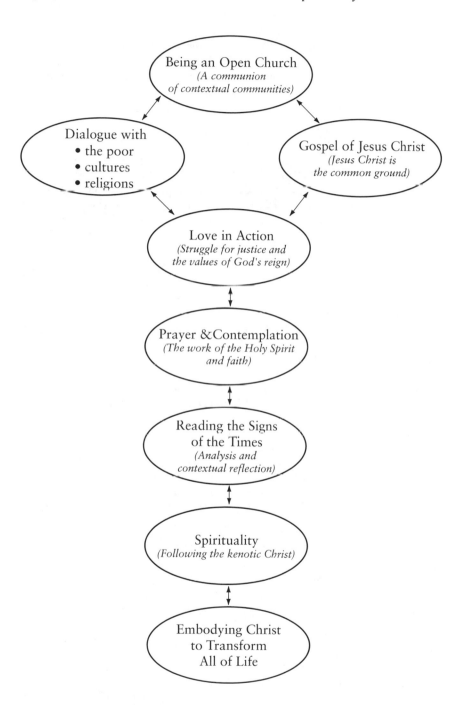

Conclusion

In this contribution I have elaborated on the pastoral circle, not so much as a method or strategy, but as spirituality, a spirituality of openness, a way of being an open church. It is my contention that only an open church can be a contextual church or a church from below. In the context of Indonesia this means a church open to and in dialogue with the poor, the cultures of our country, and the religions. Therefore, a contextual church must be intercultural, interreligious, and intercontextual. That is why in the Indonesian context we prefer to speak about the basic human community instead of basic Christian communities. Through a spirituality of openness—not only openness to other believers but also openness to the Mystery—in prayer and contemplation, our theology will be transformed to be more open, more contextual, and thus more liberative.

References

Ayoub, Mahmoud Mustafa. 1980. The death of Jesus: Reality or delusion? A study of the death of Jesus in Tafsir literature. *The Muslim World* 70:91–121.
———. 1993. The miracle of Jesus: Muslim reflections on the divine Word. In *Christology in dialogue*, edited by Robert F. Berkey and Sarah A. Edwards, 221–28. Cleveland, OH: Pilgrim Press.
Banawiratma, J. B., and J. Mueller. 1999. Contextual social theology: An Indonesian model. *EAPR* [East Asian Pastoral Review] 36, no. 1–2.
Boff, Clodovis, and George V. Pixley. 1989. *The Bible, the church, and the poor.* Maryknoll, NY: Orbis Books.
Dunne, John. 1978. *The way of all the earth: Experiments in truth and religion.* New York: Macmillan Publishing.
Hebblethwaite, Margaret. 1993. *Basic is beautiful: Basic ecclesial communities from Third World to First World.* London: Fount, Harper-Collins.
———. 1994. *Base communities: An introduction.* Mahwah, NJ: Paulist Press.
Johnston, William. 2000. *Mystical theology: Science of love.* Maryknoll, NY: Orbis Books.
Krueger, Rene. 1997. *Gott oder mammon: Das Lukasevangelium und die Oekonomie.* Luzern: Edition Exodus.
Mangunwijaya, Y. B. 1999. *Gereja diapora.* Yogyakarta: Kanisius.
O'Murchu, Diarmuid. 1997. *Quantum theology.* New York: Crossroad.
Panikkar, Raimundo. 1978. *The intrareligious dialogue.* New York: Paulist Press.
Pieris, Aloysius. 1988. *An Asian theology of liberation.* Maryknoll, NY: Orbis Books; Edinburgh: T&T Clark.
———. 1999. *God's reign for the poor: A return to the Jesus formula.* Gonawila-Kelaniya: Tulana Research Centre.
Rosales, Gaudencio, and C. G. Arévalo, eds. 1992. *For all the peoples of Asia: Federation of Asian Bishops' Conferences.* Vol. 1, *Documents from 1970 to 1991.* Maryknoll, NY: Orbis Books; Quezon City, Manila: Claretian Publications.

————. 1997. *For all the peoples of Asia: Federation of Asian Bishops' Conferences.* Vol. 2, *Documents from 1992 to 1996.* Quezon City, Manila: Claretian Publications.

Samartha, Stanley J. 1996. *Between two cultures: Ecumenical ministry in a pluralist world.* Geneva: WCC Publications.

Singgih, E. G. 1999. Gereja diaspora dan basic human communities. In *Tinjauan Kritis atas gereja diaspora Romo mangunwijaya,* edited by A. Sudiardja, 95–111. Yogyakarta: Kanisius.

Part II

The Use in Academic Settings

The second part of this book puts together the contributions that concern the use of the pastoral circle in academic settings, that is, the teaching of theology at major seminary levels or on faculties of theology. It is, therefore, the use of the pastoral circle as a pedagogical tool for theological and ministerial formation.

The contribution of José de Mesa familiarizes the reader with the notion of theological constants in order to explain how the truth, which is always the purpose of theological reflection, is not just a socially or culturally relevant truth but also a truth that is faithful to the constants of the living tradition of the church. The author warns against a too superficial understanding of the pastoral circle as a "theological shortcut." The reflection is enriched by the concrete case study of his Filipino experience.

Frans Wijsen delivers his reflections, which are the fruit of his long experience in Africa, Indonesia, and as a professor on the faculty of theology at Radboud University, Nijmegen, the Netherlands. He shares his concerns about the isolation of theologians in Europe and about theology becoming a purely theoretical science disconnected from social realities. This disconnection leads to a gap between applied theology and academic theology. In the second part of his contribution he describes what he considers the major shifts in the pastoral circle.

Rodrigo Mejía, based on his experience as a pastoral-theology lecturer for more than twenty-five years in Africa, proposes a new paradigm for the teaching of pastoral theology inspired by the four stages of the pastoral circle. The most practical aspect of this paradigm is the involvement of the student in the skills of pastoral fieldwork, which maintains a link between the classroom and the daily life of people.

In a similar vein, Madge Karecki shares her experience of teaching in the Department of Christian Spirituality, Church History and Missiology of the University of South Africa (Unisa). She describes the efforts to bridge the rift between theology and social life by using a praxis-based approach. She shows how the pastoral circle, used in three modules, has helped the students to "do" missiology rather than simply to "study" missiology.

At the end of this part Gerrit Singgih shares how the people at the Theological Faculty of Duta Wacana, a Protestant University in Yogyakarta, Java, Indonesia, understand the pastoral circle. His main contribution, however, concerns the dialogical dimension of the pastoral circle and its transformative effect. The pastoral circle leads not only to the transformation of communities but also to the personal transformation of the lecturer.

6

Theological Constants
and Theological Reflections

The Question of Truth in the Pastoral Circle

JOSÉ DE MESA

Arising from a renewed interest in theological reflection (Bevans 1992; Whitehead and Whitehead 1995), a valid concern related to the pastoral circle is the enhancement of its "theological reflection" component.[1] The pastoral circle through social analysis had already brought to the fore the realization that context significantly affects understanding, including the way we comprehend the Christian faith. It makes us conscious of how rooted such theology is in the context being analyzed.[2] This much is implied in inquiring after methodological assumptions and the connection a given theology has with the existing social situation (Holland and Henriot 1983, 10).

Meaningfulness of Theological Reflection

Underscored in this approach to theological reflection is the question of relevance, one that is admittedly legitimate and needs to be asked and asked first. Whether as an affirmation, a correction, or an alternative to the existing theology, the meaningfulness of any theological reflection has, as it were, chronological priority over the question of its truthfulness. For however "true" or coherent any existing theology is, it is likely to be ignored if it does not make any sense in people's lives.

Theological reflection in general arises from or is a result of the *mutual* interaction of the Judeo-Christian tradition and contemporary experience (Küng 1980; Bevans 1992). Both are essential and constitutive elements of a theology. From this general principle comes the requirement that a given theological reflection be rooted not only in experience, but in the tradition as well. Both poles of realities refer to experience, the setting of God's gracious and transforming offer of life and love. The Judeo-Christian tradition is constituted by the communally recognized, discerned, and accepted experiences of believers past and present that collectively represent this community's life and acquired wisdom and that serve as a continuing source of guidance and inspiration. It enables us to discern ambiguous situations in the light of faith and to see the divinely charged depths of our experiences today in the societies in which we live. Contemporary experiences, on the other hand, equally matter, not only because they make up life today in which God is actively present, but also because they throw light on the meaning and importance of the tradition for our times as well as our situations.

The Question of Truth in Theological Reflection

At some given point after so much rightfully placed focus on the question of relevance, the question of truth (meaning fidelity to the tradition) must be faced squarely. The criterion of meaningfulness of a given theology is not the only measure of Christian theological reflection. In the pastoral circle there is an insistence that "the Word of God (be) brought to bear upon the situation" and analyzed experience be understood "in the light of living faith, scripture, church social teaching, and the resources of the tradition" (Holland and Henriot 1983, 9). Developing an approach to the multifaceted question of truth would, to be sure, add to the usefulness of the pastoral circle. We cannot assume that a theology is necessarily true or faithful to the Judeo-Christian tradition when it is relevant to people's experience.[3] A theology that makes sense may not automatically be in harmony with the gospel. It may be that the importance of this question of truth is not yet felt by groups or communities whose major preoccupation is yet to give life to meaningful theologies. After all, the general predominance of Western theologies had both prevented and discouraged creative theologizing in the church. But with the development of contextual theologies, this concern will certainly surface, like it or not. This cannot be tackled in a facile way, as if the truth is easily determined. The challenge of the question of truth comes from two sides, each of which exhibits a situation of diversity:[4] One, the diversity of contexts and, therefore, of corresponding theological articulations as particular contextualizations. The other, the diversity in the testimony of the tradition that indicates that theological truth is expressed in a pluriform manner.

The first Christian communities attended to this question of truth as the number of theologies grew, all claiming to be true. This gave birth to the various gospels that were written and which are now apocryphal rather than canonical. These might have somehow resonated in certain settings, attesting to their meaningfulness, but all had eventually been subjected to the probing question of truthfulness or fidelity to the Judeo-Christian tradition. Hence, some were judged to be faithful to it and others not. The gospels of Matthew, Luke, Mark, and John merited recognition as true faith testimonies. But the gospels of Thomas and of Peter were communally evaluated in the light of the tradition and found wanting. Truth is not settled only by meaningfulness. Otherwise, we would run into problems concerning the "relevance" of the medieval theology of the Crusades legitimizing war and plunder, or the Christian sentiment in Nazi Germany that Jews could justifiably be eliminated because they were responsible for the death of Jesus Christ.

Gauging the Truth of Theological Reflection

Such truth of theology is gauged in terms of its fidelity to the Judeo-Christian tradition.[5] Determining its correctness, however, is not straightforward. First of all, it is a given that truth in this sense can never be verified by a theoretical consideration alone. One would need to take into account also the actual practice of Christian life and the *consensus fidelium* as corequisites for such verification. Truth needs to be done, not just contemplated. This is the criterion of orthopraxis so underscored in the evangelical sign for discipleship. Experience of the "fruit of the Spirit" (Gal 5:22) in Christian life is important in making judgments about what is true. Truth, too, is revealed when the entire community, through the inspiration of the Spirit, comes to a consensus about a particular interpretation of the gospel (cf. *Lumen gentium*, no. 12). As a result, such accepted interpretation can neither be made light of nor totally ignored.

Without suggesting in any way that these two accompanying and indispensable criteria for discerning the truth are of less importance, I wish to focus and limit my attention at this juncture on the element of theological verification of faith statements. Theological verification has a role to play, albeit limited, in judging what is or is not true about what we express in language regarding the faith. Discerning the true faith, as far as Vincent of Lerins was concerned, means knowing "that faith which has been believed everywhere, always, and by all."[6] It is possible to read this formula in terms of sameness and to resolve differences by insisting on uniformity.[7] But in a pluralistic situation we have come to recognize today even in theology, we are entitled to ask just how we can determine that the faith is believed everywhere, always, and by all while respecting genuine diversity.

We remember that truth can never be possessed but only "aimed at" *(attingere veritatem)*. Human formulations are very fragile indications of truth, especially when we heed the wisdom found in apophatic theology (McKim 1996, 15). Human statements concerning our faith experience are really a paradoxical combination of the absolute, "the Truth," and the relative, the historical cultural. They do in a sense possess absoluteness within relativity. These formulations combine God's gracious influence as well as limited human grasp and articulation.[8] They are not the truth, but they are reliable signs of the truth. Still they are important because language is a human way of making sense of our experiences and acknowledging the truth.

A purely wordless profession of faith simply does not exist. Religious speech, with its strange logic, consists of speaking about the inexpressible. What is peculiar about the inexpressible, by comparison with mere "nothing," is that it is in fact spoken about. One may say that revelation becomes precisely revelation when it is expressed and spoken about, just as in the whole of human life it is only through language that things become publicly revealed and enter the sphere of "revelation." But any absolutizing of our language would be an objectification of the mystery, and by that very fact its denial. On the other hand, we have also to recognize that truth, albeit as promise, is somehow reached in language; otherwise we have to deny all possibility of being addressed by the *faithful* God.[9] So truth must also be recognized *to some extent* in any particular expression of faith.

In addition, the reliability of a given theological reflection as indicative of the truth is made manifest through time and experience. History is a witness to orthodoxies that were eventually considered heterodoxies, and heterodoxies that were subsequently judged to be orthodoxies (Principe 1987, 70–73; Noonan 1993, 662–77). Caution is needed when encountering claims that a theology is automatically faithful to the tradition or orthodox if it is the official theology of a given church, say the Roman Catholic Church through its Vatican agencies. Historical awareness has made us realize that even official church teaching can be mistaken. There is, for instance, the solemnly declared doctrine of *extra ecclesiam nulla salus* of the Council of Florence-Ferrara, which has been revised in Vatican II (see *Lumen gentium*, no. 16; Neuner and Dupuis 1996, 285). The church's earlier teaching that owning slaves was moral changed when Vatican II explicitly condemned it as evil (see *Gaudium et spes*, nos. 27, 29). And would the church still cling to the Aristotelian and Thomistic view that females are misbegotten males (Ranke-Heinemann 1990, 74–75)? There is also Augustine's opposition to the natural-family-planning's endorsement today of the so-called natural means of birth control (Ranke-Heinemann 1990, 85–86, 95–96). The test of time is a must in gauging the truthfulness of a theological reflection, as the Spirit works within the processes of history, not outside it. But how do we factor this element of time into theological reflection? Or, more generally, how can we tackle this question of truth without diminishing the meaningfulness of a different theological reflection?

Access to the Tradition

The relevance of theological reflection need not overshadow the importance of its being true to the tradition. But a practical difficulty arises from the way many practitioners who are not professional theologians relate to the tradition as a source for theologizing. Access to the riches of the Christian heritage does not seem to be easy. A certain form of alienation, so think Whitehead and Whitehead, arises from "a pervasive sense of distance" brought about by "great respect for their religious heritage" and by being "intimidated by its weight." While they may have "an appreciation of the complexity and sacredness of the tradition," these practitioners also do not have "the skills of access" appropriate to their needs. They need tools "to engage the tradition as a resource for practical decision making." We are, then, confronted with the challenge to develop methods of access to the tradition suitable for those working directly within the community of faith. "For both minister and faithful," suggest the Whiteheads, "the goal is not mastery but befriending—an increase in intimacy with the tradition. The image of *befriending* suggests a more-than-intellectual grasp, a familiarity that includes both *appreciative awareness of the tradition and comfort with its diversity and contradictions* (emphasis mine)" (Whitehead and Whitehead 1995, 9, emphasis added).

In this connection can the experience of the past be of assistance? Are there signposts for recognizing truth in a theological formulation? Is it possible to factor in the element of the test of time in an approach to the question of truth? I would like to suggest a procedure, one of many, I am sure, to discern whether a specific theological reflection is true to the tradition or not, without downplaying its significance to contemporary experience. The use of constant theological elements, or simply *constants,* discovered in the diversity of faith expressions at different times and different places as guide may provide an answer to our inquiry. This would be a positive step in befriending the tradition, a coming to an "appreciative awareness" of it as well as a becoming "comfortable with its diversity and contradictions."

Constants in Theology

Pluriformity is so much part of our tradition that one may even argue for its being characteristic of our theology. Yet for all the differences that are present, there is unanimity in the claim that it is the one and the same faith. The one recognizable tradition is shown to be dynamic through a diversity of expressions. From this perspective neither mere uniformity nor sheer diversity can be the measure of theological truth. What holds unity and diversity together in relation to truth, I think, is the existence of theological constants in the tradition, especially those found in scripture.

Constants, because they are deemed essential, are the underlying, interrelated elements always found in the differing expressions of the faith. They are the common elemental themes discerned in different theological expressions, but they are not identical to specific contextualized articulations. It would be a mistake to consider them as fixed content that can be applied anytime or anywhere regardless of the situation. Nevertheless, it must be borne in mind that these constants are never discovered apart from their contextual expressions.[10] They keep recurring in the many different local formulations of faith, whether the recurrence is expressed at different historical periods in one locality or, more or less at the same time, in different contemporaneous communities. In new situations they can be regarded as if they were "questions" (Bevans and Schroeder 2004, 34) awaiting particular answers vis-à-vis the specific context, whether cultural, historical, religious, or gender related. As a term, *constants* suggests both steadiness and adaptability, resoluteness and flexibility, commonality and differentiation as exemplified in the very same faith in Jesus Christ but with truly different historical and cultural expressions. Constants point to the truth yet allow that truth to be understood and expressed contextually. They assure continuity even in what may appear (to some) as "discontinuous" interpretations. They make possible a theological unity without rigid theological uniformity. They thus serve as indicators of harmony with the tradition, but they do so in a manner suitable to a particular context.

The Function of Constants in Theological Reflection

Constants are discovered post factum rather than a priori, and they require the test of time. Constants already presume a de facto situation of theological pluriformity, unlike sameness, which presupposes a condition of uniformity. It may be said, perhaps, that the development of contextual theological reflection made the discovery of constants imperative. Constants so discerned appear to have two related functions: (1) they can assist in evaluating the truthfulness of a theology, and (2) they can also serve as guide in articulating a fresh interpretation of the gospel. Together as interrelated elements, constants serve as continuing indispensable reference points that we can consult and ground our doing of theology. It can easily happen that as we assess our theology with the use of constants, we are at the same time articulating a new one by structuring it according to them. I shall illustrate this later.

Without minimizing social relevance and cultural meaningfulness of faith expressions, constants may be looked upon as bases of and signposts for inculturated or contextualized theological reflections that are rooted in and faithful to the Judeo-Christian tradition. They also enable cross-historical and cross-cultural comparisons thereby serving as reminders of which aspects of the faith (as represented by particular constants) need to be attended to in a new formulation by a local community. It may well be that a set of constants discovered in one local church may alert other local churches to certain aspects of the faith that they have not quite paid attention to but recognize as essential. After all, every contextualization of the gospel brings certain aspects of it to the foreground, while others are relegated to the background. This implies that use of constants in gauging the truthfulness of a given theological reflection requires dialogue with other communities of faith, whether of the past or of the present. Openness and willingness to learn is an imperative within this framework and procedure because constants are discovered precisely in a communally oriented theologizing.

Unity in the true faith in the midst of diversity may be made possible because communities subscribe to the same constants. Despite the "wild profusion of the varying statements of these differing groups" as they respond to differing contexts, maintains Walls (1996, 6–7), there is in Christianity an "essential continuity" by which it remains itself as it transforms itself in missionary outreach. Even as we recognize differences in language, culture, and context, we also detect certain constants that define Christianity. This is already true for the foundational constant of the Christian faith itself, which is Jesus Christ. Rather than just state that Jesus Christ is the main fact or content of Christian belief, it may be more helpful to express this as a constant, a common element, or a unifying strand, because even the interpretation of who Jesus is had been diverse right from the very beginning. It is for this reason that Dunn (1990, 11–32) prefers not to speak of a single *kerygma* but rather of *kerygmata*. Indeed, nowhere can one find the basic proclamation except in specific cultural forms, unless one thinks that an uninterpreted core can exist independently of its expressions.

The primary witness to Jesus' significance is expressed by four gospels instead of just one, not to mention the various letters that, together with the gospels, constitute the New Testament of Christians. This pluriformity in scripture finds parallels in sacraments and ministries, which are expressive of different needs and of cultures involved (Dunn 1990, 103–23, 150–73). But there are limits to the ways constants can be interpreted and expressed. We know that there are theological formulations which had been judged to be unfaithful to the tradition and are, therefore, unacceptable within the faith community. Still, constants can be of significant help in discerning whether a theological expression is in accord with the gospel or is moving away from it.

The Structural Constants according to Schillebeeckx

Illustrative of how these are discovered, Schillebeeckx thinks that four structural constants emerge when the various New Testament theologies are *compared* (1981, 51–55). As we go through this foundational testimony of the first disciples carefully, we discover that there are many different explanations regarding the salvific event that is Jesus. It may come as a surprise for some that the explanations are divergent and incapable of being harmonized. This, of course, is not necessarily disadvantageous. It goes to show that Christians in different places and at different times have always attempted to give expression to the significance of their faith in God in ways intelligible to their cultures (religion included) and histories (with its different dimensions).

The study of the New Testament does not stop when the divergent explanations are uncovered. Once charted, Schillebeeckx maintains, it becomes possible to compare them with one another and to look for *constant structures* in each of the New Testament writings. These constants hold the divergent explanations together. This basic experience, interpreted in a variety of ways but nevertheless the same, then reveals the recurring common elements that have structured the one New Testament experience. In his analysis there are four such constants: (1) a basic theological and anthropological principle: God wills the salvation of human beings in and through history and people find their fulfillment through this divine action; (2) a christological mediation: it is Jesus of Nazareth who reveals definitely who God is and who human beings are before God; (3) the message and lifestyle of the church, the following of Jesus, and the embodiment of his Spirit in today's world; and (4) eschatological fulfillment: God's salvific will, though already operative in our world ("already"), cannot be confined within the boundaries of our history and therefore looks toward a future ("not yet"). This New Testament structuring (constants in relationship to one another) serves as a creative model pointing out the major directions rather than as a blueprint to be reproduced or adapted for a particular culture and history. With the use of constants in gauging the truthfulness of a given theology or working out a new one with an eye to its rootedness in the gospel, we can determine which aspects of the tradition we have already attended to and which ones we still need to consider.[11]

Constants in Theological Themes

So far we have indicated the presence of constants in Christianity as a whole (Jesus as the Christ) and in the New Testament experience (four structural constants). These are wide areas of theological reflection, ones that may not immediately appeal to or be useful for practitioners of the pastoral circle. To be sure, they will eventually have to be thought about and expressed in any given theology. But local theological reflections like those found among the peasants of Solentiname or base communities initially may simply attend to more limited or simpler theological (doctrinal) themes or topics already found in popularized or folk Catholicism, such as providence, grace, sin, church, sacrament, justice, liberation, and salvation.[12]

In *Constants in Context: A Theology of Mission for Today* constants are utilized in both the analysis of what has been articulated in the past regarding mission and the construction of a contemporary theology of mission (Bevans and Schroeder 2004).[13] What we find here in terms of constants bridges, as it were, the broader constants that Dunn and Schillebeeckx had named and the more limited constants found in themes such as sacrament, providence, grace, sin, justice, liberation, or salvation that we may fruit-fully start with. To Bevans and Schroeder, the church is "missionary by its very nature" (*Ad gentes*, no. 2) and becomes so by attending to each and every *context* in which it finds itself. In analyzing the rich diversity of theo-logical traditions regarding mission, they discern recurrent patterns. These are six constants—six doctrinal themes to which the church must be faith-ful at every boundary crossing, and in every context. The interaction and articulation of these six constants—Christology, ecclesiology, eschatology, salvation, anthropology, and culture—will determine the way that the church's missionary practice is lived out in the various periods of its his-tory.[14] These are like theological questions, which need to be answered in the concrete cultural and historical contexts. Mission is seen as "a story of constants in context." It needs to "preserve, defend and proclaim the con-stants of the church's traditions," while "[responding] creatively and boldly to the contexts in which it finds itself." And indeed, the church has been basically faithful to the constants that make up its mission and bestow it its identity throughout varying and conflictive contexts (Bevans and Schroeder 2004, 9).

If we take our cue from the work of Bevans and Schroeder, can we, by way of example, do something similar with *sacrament* or *sacramentality*? Can we discover constants in the Greek, Roman, and Tridentine formula-tions of what *sacrament* means within Catholicism and use these, in con-junction with the primary witness of scripture, as a set of interrelated ele-ments either to assess a theological reflection about sacrament or, looking to the future, to construct an inculturated theological reflection on this very same reality? Whether our task is that of evaluation or that of construction, the constants function as reference points that can guide the assessment or their enfleshments according to a given context. In this way constants pro-vide "regulation" and "impetus." They gauge and stimulate theology at the same time. Questions such as the following may then be asked: What faith elements (constants) have to be present in the theological reflection one is articulating, without which it would not be a Christian theological reflec-tion on sacrament? Have all the theological constants been taken into ac-count in the theological reflection one is already evaluating or still formu-lating?

Discovering the Constants
in Western Theologies of Sacrament

The sacramental manner of feeling, thinking, and acting within the Chris-tian praxis of the faith identifies and characterizes Catholicism (McBrien 1995, 257). Underlying the sacramental principle and attitude is the convic-tion that "all reality, both animate and inanimate, is potentially or in fact the bearer of God's presence and the instrument of God's saving activity on humanity's behalf" (Francis 1995, 1148). There is no question here of whether we ought to talk about sacrament or not, but of *how* to speak of it. It had earlier been spoken of as *mysterion* (Greek) and *sacramentum* (Latin) in early Christianity and not necessarily in only one sense (see Ganoczy 1984, 7–30; Martos 1991; Francis 1995, 1146–47). Can it be spoken of in a different way without being untrue to the tradition (Osborne 1995, 16–17)?

Comparative Theological Analysis

Mysterion, as an interpretative model for *sacrament,* arises from the language of mystery religions existent since the seventh century B.C.E.; their rituals were kept secret from the uninitiated.[15] Entering into this religious-cultural thought-world, the church began to speak of God's action, particularly in Jesus Christ, as *mysteria* and Jesus as "the great Mystagogue."[16] The "hidden" or "secret" plan of God for the salvation of the whole world was "revealed" in the person, life, and ministry of Jesus. The early theologians of the church, seeing a potent force to hand on the faith to their world at home with ritual and philosophical *mysteria* (Ganoczy 1984, 15–17), utilized the *mysterion* language,[17] albeit critically.

Tertullian, the African lawyer and son of a Roman officer, introduced a significant change in Christian theology when he chose to render the Greek term *mysterion* by the Latin word *sacramentum.* Meanings associated with *sacramentum* resonated with the Roman cultural world, and the concept brought with it an ethical dimension, that of human responsibility. Tertullian's use of the term was primarily in reference to adult baptism, in which converts freely and solemnly committed themselves to the service of Christ. Just as soldiers pronounced total allegiance to the emperor by an oath and thereby were initiated to service, so Christians dedicate themselves to the Lord by baptism and are initiated into Christian life and service (Martos 1991, 21; Macquarrie 1999, 4). Tertullian's approach to baptism (and to some degree to the eucharist) provides an ethical dimension to sacramentality as part of the relationship between God and the baptized.

Understanding of sacrament in the light of mystery cults as well as Roman oaths was synthesized and enriched by Augustine of Hippo, who employed a neo-Platonic philosophical framework, taking care not to devalue visible material signs (Ganoczy 1984, 20). He regarded every object as consisting of "a purely spiritual, timeless, unchanging part, and a material, temporal, transitory part" (Ganoczy 1984, 21). The latter served to make visible and symbolize the former. To him, a *sacramentum* was "a sign of a sacred thing," which makes the number of possible sacraments virtually infinite.[18]

A thorough reshaping of this Augustinian heritage, which remained the basis for subsequent approaches in sacramentology, occurred when Aristotelian rather than Platonic philosophy was utilized as the interpretative model.

This development culminated in the work of Thomas Aquinas (d.1274), who synthesized the understanding of *sacramentum* while emphasizing the empirical and the effective.[19] In working out the effective causality of God as expressed in and through the instrumental causality, he utilized the Aristotelian vocabulary related to physical substances—*matter*, the component that is capable of being shaped in a number of ways, and *form*, the determining, shaping element. Matter refers to visible elements, like water in baptism or bread and wine in the eucharist. Form points to the words that the one administering the sacrament uses to indicate the meaning or intent of the action (Ganoczy 1984, 26–27; see also Wuellner 1966). When correctly combined, sacraments effect grace *ex opere operato* (literally, "by the work worked" or "from the doing of the thing done").

Much of the Tridentine understanding and formulation of sacrament(s) (Osborne 1995, 24–34) that Filipinos inherited from the West arose from the Aristotelian-influenced theology of Thomas Aquinas.[20] Emphasis on ritual—its structure, function, and effectivity—drew attention away from what is expected of the believer. It overshadowed the symbolic aspect of the sacraments and their aspect as appeals to the person (Koch 1995, 606–7). As a result, meticulous attention had to be given to the administering of the signs to ensure their effectivity. Thomas Aquinas's "insistence on the causal nature of the sacraments," notes Martos, "led canonists to insist on proper performance of the rituals" (1991, 66–67). Careful enactment had become more important than meaningfulness to people (Cooke 1990, 181–82).

Theological Constants of Sacrament

We have seen how the Greek term *mysterion* and the Latin word *sacramentum* express the reality of sacrament in their own respective culturally and historically conditioned ways. If we were to determine which theological elements recur in these different interpretations of sacrament, we would be able tentatively to indicate five theological constants: revelation, the element of faith, its salvific effect, the ethical consequences arising from the God-human relationship, and the pattern of the invisible becoming manifest in what is visible. These constantly recurring elements together constitute the "building blocks," as it were, of what sacrament is.

In the Greek *mysterion*, revelation stands for the saving deeds of God in Jesus Christ referred to as *mysteria*. These, within the Platonic philosophical scheme of interpretation, are invisible, eternal, and spiritual realities. By virtue of our faith we participate in these divine mysteries through visible rituals, which are temporal and material, and so become "divinized." "Imitation" is the consequence of such participation. Through a process of perception and assimilation, one becomes a living and perfect replica of the Redeemer.

Revelation has virtually the same meaning in the Latin term *sacramentum,* namely, the life, passion, and death of Jesus Christ. What is interesting, however, is that faith is defined as "an oath of fidelity" to the Lord Jesus in baptism after the pattern of the Roman soldier's oath to his emperor. This makes the baptized person a member of the community of salvation. The faithful owe Jesus Christ the loyalty befitting him, an allegiance that is freely undertaken. But this visible "oath" is preceded, inspired, and founded on the self-initiated, invisible loyalty of God to human beings.

When we come to the Tridentine definition of *sacrament* as "an outward sign instituted by Christ to give grace," we find the same theological elements. Again, revelation is seen as the self-initiated action of God, but now formulated as Christ instituting the sacraments that give grace. But for that grace to be received, it is necessary for the human being responding to God's action in and through the sacrament not to put any obstacle to it *(non ponentibus obicem).* While we may object to this minimalist notion of faith, it nevertheless includes human involvement in the sacramental relation. And because sacraments, which are visible signs, work *ex opere operato,* we are "justified" by the invisible grace working through them. In this outlook it is the responsibility of the recipient of the sacraments to remain and grow in sanctifying grace by frequenting them, especially penance and the eucharist (see *Catechism of the Council of Trent,* no. 160).

The above comparative analysis of three different formulations of *sacrament* has allowed us to discover and make explicit the theological constants operative in them. As scripture functions as *norma normans non normata*[21] in theological reflection, it is necessary to compare these constants with the primary witness of the Bible regarding the nature of the presence of God in our world. Revelation is God coming to liberate Israel from bondage in Egypt. Revelation is saving action, and saving action is revelatory. For Israel, God's invisible saving deeds occur and are experienced in the visibility of history. Israel's faith is expressed by its sense of awe and wonder of the ineffability of God's unmerited and liberating presence in its history as well as by its resolve, as a consequence, not to take God's name in vain.

Constants and the Filipino Theological Reflection on Bakas

Keeping in mind the above constants, we now explore the viability of a newly formulated theological reflection on sacrament in terms of relevance and fidelity to the tradition, namely, the Filipino notion of *bakas* (see Figure 6–1). *Bakas* (visible trace, mark, print, indication) is a familiar category of Filipino sensory experience, unlike the strange, Western-derived, and transliterated terms *misterio* or *sakramento*. As an experiential concept, it is capable of expressing or evoking meanings related to past, present, and future events or phenomena (Boff 1987, 13). This is useful when we recall that the Christian understanding of sacrament remembers the past, recalling the memory of Jesus and all that it stands for in the Christian community; it celebrates the continued presence of the Spirit as grace made visible; and it anticipates the future of definitive salvation promised by God in Jesus Christ.

Bakas, moving on its own cultural trajectory, indicates the visibility of something that transcends it, thereby suggesting the presence of something not visible or palpable. We only have a glimpse of the reality through its trace *(bakas)* (Richter 1990, 13–14). Precisely for this reason, *bakas* is an appropriate term for sacrament. *Bakas* as *bakas* is not full experience of reality to those who perceive it. The term itself helps us avoid total identification of a reality with the traces we experience of that reality. Hence, *bakas* not only recognizes mystery but actually expresses it to be so (Guzie 1981, 17). The invisible-visible combination has a wider basis in the Filipino understanding of the human person expressed in the concepts *loob* (literally, "inside" or "within") and *labas* (literally, "outside" or "without"). *Loob*, the inner self, is one of the richest concepts, content and value-wise, in the Filipino way of thinking which was, curiously, not explored by local theology until recently (Alejo 1993). *Loob* is a holistic understanding of the most authentic self of a person in relation to God, others and the world. Thought, feeling, and behavior are all situated in the *loob*. This is the source of freedom, initiative, reflection, gut feeling, and decision.

The *loob* of a person is not visible, as such, but through relationships we can come to know it, albeit imperfectly. In the complementarity of the within *(loob)* and the without *(labas)*, every element found "inside" normally has a counterpart located "outside" and vice versa (Covar 1993, 3–12). *Loob* and *labas* are two sides of the total reality, complementary but not identical. In this *loob-labas* (inside-outside) relationship and complementarity, the culture is inclined to value the former as more important than the latter. That which emanates from the *loob* (the inner self) is regarded as authentic or true, while that which is perceived as the *labas* (outer self) can be ambivalent; it can disclose or conceal the *loob*. *Bakas*, thus, allows for an alternative reading of history, community, persons, and the material world (from the Christian perspective, for instance), where *palatandáan* (a sign in contrast to symbol) would not. *Bakas* is capable of seeing through the historical fiasco that was the life of Jesus as he hung on the cross in utter shame and failure. To most of his contemporaries this was a clear sign *(palatandáan)* of defeat. Yet as a symbol *(bakas)* the disciples saw in it the triumph of goodness over evil.

The presence of a *bakas* spontaneously also implies that someone or something is behind and responsible for it. *Bakas* is not an existing reality that stands on its own. Otherwise, it would not be a *bakas* or trace of reality, but rather the very reality itself. *Bakas* is a *bakas* of someone or something that caused it to be. The very concept of *bakas* asks for "authorship" or "cause" and its recognition. One needs an "eye" (sight) or "feeling" (touch) to recognize a *bakas* as *bakas,* just as a hunter needs to recognize something as a *bakas* of the animal he is after *(pamamakas).* From the Christian Filipino perspective, this *loob* is God's *kagandahang-loob.* According to John, "God is *agape*" (1 Jn 4:8, 16). Within the Filipino relational point of view, *agape* can be meaningfully and truthfully rendered as *kagandahang-loob* (gracious goodness aimed at the well-being of others) because it is that kind of love that is inclusive and focused on the interest of the other (see Barclay 1964, 17–30). As an essentially relational concept, *kagandahang-loob* denotes kindheartedness, benevolence, goodness (as a specific act), helpfulness, and generosity of the whole person. But it connotes gracious initiative, focus on the well-being of the other, goodness that is not self-seeking, and generosity beyond compare. Thus, God can rightly be imaged as *kagandahang-loob* itself.

A clear advantage of the concept and term *bakás* is seen in its verbal form *(pamamakas)* suggesting both *discernment* of God's presence in life and *discipleship* in following Jesus in the world. If God's *kagandahang-loob* represents divine action in *bakas, pamamakas* stands for the faith response as it is lived out personally, communally, and socially. *Pamamakas* denotes action and connotes action commensurate to the task at hand, whether this is expressed as ethical living or as prayerful celebration. After all, "sacraments are actions, not things" (Guzie 1981, 31–37). Part of the genius of Filipino language is in its use of prefixes, infixes, and suffixes to enable a word to perform different functions within a sentence. Thus *bakás* as noun can be transposed into its verbal form by adding a prefix. *Pamamakas* (or *bakasín, bumakás, magbakás*) means "to trace, track or follow by means of marks, tracks or signs." Our Christian vocation is to follow Jesus by tracing, as it were, the indications or signs of his Spirit in the world and in the church. We are alert to the signs *(bakas)* of his active presence in our midst, ever observant for any indication, particularly in the only trace he left by which we can be known as his disciples: love for one another. As church we highlight and celebrate through our sacramental worship what we experience, discover, and recognize of the divinely initiated activity in the world. One can easily translate *pamamakas* in this sense as *discernment* of God's gracious and transforming presence in history and in the world.[22]

But because *pamamakas* also means "to follow," it can be interpreted in a metaphorical sense as "following Jesus." Following the footsteps of Jesus is a popular expression of living in the Spirit of Jesus, not in the sense of literal imitation of his life, but with the meaning of allowing his spirit to so permeate our lives that we live as he lived.[23] In this sense *pamamakas* is discipleship from a sacramental perspective, a view reminiscent of the connotation that Tertullian saw in his adoption of the term *sacramentum,* the soldier's oath of loyalty. This is fundamentally done by "[striving] first for the reign of God and God's righteousness" (Mt 6:33) and living out the mandate that Jesus gave—"This is my commandment, that you love one another as I have loved you" (Jn 15:12).

Figure 6–1. Comparison of Cultural Interpretations of Sacramentality with the Theological Constants

Theological constants	Mysterion	Sacramentum	Council of Trent	Filipino "Bakas"
Revelation	The *mysteria* that were the saving deeds of God in Jesus Christ (ontological view)	The *mysteria* of the life, passion, and death of Jesus Christ	Sacraments as instituted by Christ	*Pagmamagandangloob ng Diyos* as presence
Faith	Participation through initiation	Oath of allegiance	*Non ponentibus obicem* (By not putting an obstacle)	*Pamamakas* as active tracing of God's presence in the world and experiences
Salvific effect	Participation (divinization)	Membership in the community of salvation	"For our justification" (*ex opere operato*)	*Pagbabago ng loob*
Ethical consequences	"Imitation," through a process of perception and assimilation, one becomes a living and perfect replica of the Redeemer	Allegiance, being loyal, a self-undertaken commitment tc Jesus Christ	Remain and grow in sanctifying grace by frequenting the sacraments, espeically penance and eucharist	*Pamamankas* as discipleship
Sacramental pattern (visible/invisible)	The eternal, spiritual reality/the temporal and material realties	Loyalty or fidelity/oath	Invisible grace/visible sign	*Ang nababakas/ang bakas*

Conclusion

Our treatment of constants here does not pretend in any way to have answered all the related questions on the matter, but we hope that it has shown the importance of truth in the theological reflection of the pastoral circle process. Following the constants does not totally guarantee the truth of a theology in context, but it does provide a reasonably strong indication of at least wanting to stand with the tradition on this matter. Hopefully, though, this discussion on constants has made a small contribution on how both the imperative of relevance and the question of truth in theological reflection should be seriously taken into account.

As there is no easy way to learning social analysis in the pastoral circle, there is also no easy way to learning serious theological reflection within it.[24] It has been noted that reflecting theologically with social analysis in mind does not come automatically. One needs to be trained in it. By the same token, doing theology with the question of truth in mind will require some learning and practice. The pastoral circle is not a proposed "easy way" or a theological shortcut. We cannot afford a concern for pure theoretical truth without any social relevance or an exclusive concern for social relevance without the basis of a theological truth faithful to the tradition of the church. Such is the challenge of a proper use of the pastoral circle: only genuine truth will set us free (Jn 8:32).

Notes

[1] Holland and Henriot concentrate on "social analysis, the second moment of the pastoral circle" (1983, 13–14). But while this analysis is done in a theological context, "more extended reflections on the third and fourth moments of the circle, namely, theological reflection and pastoral planning," are still needed.

[2] The document *Mysterium ecclesiae* provides a clear official example of the historical and cultural conditioning of any theology, as cited in Neuner and Dupuis (1996, 63–64).

[3] For a discussion of a relational understanding of *truth* in contrast to the ontological reading of it, see De Mesa (1998).

[4] Pontifical Biblical Commission, "Unity and Diversity in the Church," April 11–15, 1988, in Neuner and Dupuis 1998, 323–24.

[5] *Truth* in scripture is relational rather than ontological or metaphysical. It also cannot be reduced to the correctness of a particular theological interpretation. "Truthfulness (is) a demand of the message of Jesus" and is a challenge to the way the church lives today (Küng 1968).

[6] Vincent of Lerins, *Commonitory* (fifth century), in McKim 1996, 299.

[7] There have been interpretations of the Vincentian canon in this sense (see Crowley 1997, 38–49).

[8] "What theological pluralism claims as a matter of principle is that, not simply because of cultural and other differences in the perceiving subject, but also because

of the inexhaustible nature of the divine 'object,' it is impossible to comprehend God from one viewpoint or to express that comprehension in only one manner" (Mahoney 1987, 272).

⁹ The promise that the Christian community would remain in the truth would be an empty one if this community cannot speak out at certain crucial moments of its history about what really belongs to the content of its faith.

¹⁰ The core of the gospel message in relation to its specific cultural formulation is not one of the kernel and its husk. It is much more like the layers of the onion to the onion itself. Peeling away each layer will not bring us to the core of the onion but to disappearance of the onion itself (Bevans 1992, 33–36).

¹¹ Schillebeeckx also points out that the "four structural elements" are what "Christians must take into account of in any contemporary reinterpretation in which an echo of the gospel of Jesus Christ can be detected, if they want to preserve this gospel in its wholeness while at the same time making it speak to their own age in word and deed" (1981, 638).

¹² By way of examples, see reflections on the sacrament of the eucharist by peasants in Cardenal (1982, 121–36), and the "theologizing" of the Maasai on the church in Donovan (1982, 81–98).

¹³ Chapter 1 focuses on *context* and the church's mission; chapter 2 focuses on the *constants* to which the church must be faithful in carrying out its mission (Bevans and Schroeder 2004).

¹⁴ "The answers to these questions about Jesus, about the church, about the future, about salvation, about the human nature and human culture have certainly varied through the two millennia of Christianity's existence, as the church has lived out its missionary nature in various contexts. As *questions*, however, they remain ever present and ever urgent, because how they are answered is how Christianity finds its concrete identity as it constitutes itself in fidelity to Jesus' mission" (Bevans and Schroeder 2004, 34).

¹⁵ *Mysteria* primarily refers to a whole group of secret cults that had developed among the Greeks and in the Hellenic Orient, usually on the periphery of the commonly practiced religions (Ganoczy 1984, 8). *Disciplina arcani* refers to the rule of secrecy practiced by some pagan religions and Christianity. It stipulates that some elements of religion should not be made available to the uninitiated (Kelly 1992, 46).

¹⁶ Justin, Irenaeus, Clement of Alexandria, and Tertullian were among those who used the *mysterion* category (Kelly 1992, 15).

¹⁷ "For the early Christian faith it was not its dissimilarity with the religions of the environment that was the problem, but its similarity" (Bosch 1991, 193; cf. Macquarrie 1999, 5).

¹⁸ Martos 1991, 43. Among the many sacraments in Augustine's mind were the Lord's Prayer and the Nicene Creed, the Easter liturgy and the sign of the cross, the baptismal font and its water, the ashes of penitence, and the oil of anointing.

¹⁹ For a discussion of the development and nuances of the term *sacramentum* in the Middle Ages of Europe, see Martos 1991, 47–76.

²⁰ Thomas Aquinas depended heavily on Augustine's thought on this matter (Schulte 1970, 378–79).

²¹ "Norming norm that is not normed," or simply, primary norm in the sense of being principal guide and inspiration.

²² "God, in all that is most living and incarnate in him, is not far away from us, altogether apart from the world we see, touch, hear, smell and taste about us" (Teilhard de Chardin 1962, 64).

²³ "Are we to understand the 'imitation of Christ,'" Jung asks, "in the sense that we should copy his life and, if I may use the expression, ape his stigmata; or in the deeper sense that we are to live our own proper lives as truly as he lived his in all its implications? It is no easy matter to live a life that is modeled on Christ's, but it is unspeakably harder to live one's own life as truly as Christ lived his" (Jung 1933, 236, cited in Guzie 1981, 78).

²⁴ In the introduction to *Social Analysis*, Holland and Henriot state that they "do not offer a simple 'how to' approach to social analysis, a manual of 'ten easy steps' for application to [our] local situation. Rather, [they] explore the development of the new interest in social analysis and demonstrate its usefulness in approaching social justice action" (1983, 5).

References

Alejo, A. 1993. *Tao po! Tuloy!: Isang landas ng pag-unawa sa loob ng tao*. Quezon City: Office for Research and Development, Ateneo de Manila Univ.

Barclay, William. 1964. *New testament words*. London: SCM Press.

Bevans, Stephen B. 1992. *Models of contextual theology*. Maryknoll, NY: Orbis Books.

Bevans Stephen B., and Roger P. Schroeder. 2004. *Constants in context: A theology of mission for today*. Maryknoll, NY: Orbis Books.

Boff, Leonardo. 1987. *Sacraments of life, life of sacraments*. Portland, OR: Pastoral Press.

Bosch, David. 1991. *Transforming mission*. Maryknoll, NY: Orbis Books.

Cardenal, Ernesto. 1982. *The gospel in Solentiname*. 4 vols. Maryknoll, NY: Orbis Books.

Catechism of the Council of Trent for parish priests. 1970. Translated by John A. McHugh and Charles J. Callan. Manila: Sinag-tala Publishers.

Cooke, Berard J. 1990. *Distancing of God: The ambiguity of symbol in history and theology*. Minneapolis: Fortress Press.

Covar, P. 1993. *Kaalamang bayang dalumat ng pagkataong Pilipino*. Quezon City: Dr. Jose Cuyegkeng Memorial Library and Information Center.

Crowley, Paul. 1997. *In ten thousand places: Dogma in a pluralistic church*. New York: Crossroad.

De Mesa, José. 1998. The quest for "truth" in Asia. *East Asian Pastoral Review* 35, no. 3/4.

Donovan, Vincent J. 1982. *Christianity rediscovered*. Maryknoll, NY: Orbis Books.

Dunn, J. 1990. *Unity and diversity in the New Testament: An inquiry into the character of earliest Christianity*. 2nd ed. London: SCM Press.

Francis, M. 1995. Sacrament. In *Encyclopedia of Catholicism*, edited by Richard McBrien. San Francisco: HarperSanFrancisco.

Ganoczy, A. 1984. *An introduction to Catholic sacramental theology*. New York: Paulist Press.

Guzie, T. 1981. *The book of sacramental basics*. New York: Paulist Press.

Holland, Joe, and Peter Henriot. 1983. *Social analysis: Linking faith and justice*. Rev. ed. Maryknoll, NY: Orbis Books; Washington, DC: Center of Concern.

Jung, Carl. 1933. Psychotherapists or clergy. In Carl Jung, *In search of a soul*, translated by W. S. Dell and Carry F. Baynes. New York: Harcourt Brace Jovanovich.

Kelly, J. 1992. *The concise dictionary of early Christianity*. Collegeville, MN: Liturgical Press.

Koch, G. 1995. Sacrament. In *Handbook of Catholic theology*, edited by W. Beinert and Francis Schüssler Fiorenza. New York: Crossroad.

Küng, Hans. 1968. *Truthfulness: The future of the church*. New York: Sheed and Ward.

————. 1980. Toward a new consensus in Catholic and ecumenical theology. *Journal of Ecumenical Studies* 17, no. 1.

Macquarrie, J. 1999. *A guide to the sacraments*. New York: Continuum.

Mahoney, J. 1987. *The making of moral theology: A study of the Roman Catholic tradition*. Oxford: Clarendon.

Martos, J. 1991. *Doors to the sacred: A historical introduction to sacraments in the Catholic Church*. Rev. ed. Tarrytown, NY: Triumph Books, 1991.

McBrien, Richard. 1995. Catholicism. In *Encyclopedia of Catholicism*, edited by Richard McBrien. San Francisco: HarperSanFrancisco.

McKim, D. 1996. *Westminster dictionary of theological terms*. Louisville, KY: Westminster John Knox Press.

Neuner, J., and J. Dupuis, eds. 1996. *The Christian faith in the doctrinal documents of the Catholic Church*. Bangalore: Theological Publications in India.

Noonan, J., Jr. 1993. Development in moral doctrine. *Theological Studies* 54, 662–77.

Osborne, K. 1995. *Sacramental guidelines: A companion to the new catechism for religious educators*. New York: Paulist Press.

Principe, W. 1987. When "authentic teachings change." *The Ecumenist* 25/26.

Rahner, Karl, et al., eds. 1970. *Sacramentum mundi 5*. London: Search Press.

Ranke-Heinemann, U. 1990. *Eunuchs for the kingdom of heaven*. New York: Doubleday.

Richter, K. 1990. *The meaning of the sacramental symbols*. Collegeville, MN: Liturgical Press.

Schillebeeckx, Edward 1981. *Interim report on the books "Jesus" and "Christ."* New York: Crossroad.

Schulte, R. 1970. Sacraments. In *Sacramentum Mundi 5*, edited by Karl Rahner, 378–79. London: Search Press.

Teilhard de Chardin, Pierre. 1962. *The divine milieu: An essay on the interior life*. London: Collins.

Walls, A. 1996. The gospel as prisoner and liberator of culture. *The missionary movement in Christian history: Studies in the transmission of faith*. Maryknoll, NY: Orbis Books.

Whitehead, D., and E. Whitehead. 1995. *Method in ministry: Theological reflection and Christian ministry*. Rev. ed. Kansas City: Sheed and Ward.

Wuellner, B. 1966. *A dictionary of Scholastic philosophy*. Milwaukee: Bruce Publishing.

7

The Practical-Theological Spiral

Bridging Theology in the West
and the Rest of the World

FRANS WIJSEN

Within the Ecumenical Association of Third World Theologians (EATWOT) there has been a long debate about the different ways of practicing theology; in fact, dissatisfaction with European theological epistemology and methodology was the main reason for starting this association. At its inaugural meeting in Dar es Salaam in 1976 the participants stated: "We reject as irrelevant an academic type of theology that is divorced from action. We are prepared for a radical break in epistemology which makes commitment the first act of theology and engages in critical reflection on the reality of the Third World" (Fabella and Torres 1977, 269). In general European theology is said to be theoretical, abstract, and context free, whereas third-world theology is practical, concrete, and contextual. There is a divide between "academic" theology and "applied" theology, and between the practitioners of the two forms of theology, academics and activists.

As a lecturer in various institutions in Africa and Asia and one who also works with third-world students in Europe, I am always struck by the fact that the research proposals and papers of these students are mostly aimed at promoting the transformation of church and society. This is understandable, of course, as the contexts in which they do theology are often marked by poverty, injustice, war, and ecological and medical disasters. In Europe, on the other hand, theological practice is growing more and more detached from practical problems and has become more of a "pure science." This, too, is understandable in the context of highly secularized societies, where health and wealth are catered for by governments, and churches are being largely marginalized. In Europe theology tries to justify itself by joining in academic debates and to compensate for its seeming irrelevance by using unquestioned scientific methods.

Often the divide leads to tacit misunderstandings and even open conflict between theologians in the West and their counterparts in "the Rest" of the world (Becker 1999). It appears that the gulf between the two ways of doing theology and their practitioners has widened over the past few decades. Some twenty or thirty years ago it was quite fashionable to deal with third-world theologies in European faculties of theology. The bibliographies of modules in Christology and ecclesiology often included authors from the Southern hemisphere. This accorded with the critical climate that prevailed in Europe after the student revolts and the broad acceptance of an emancipatory view of science (Habermas 1968) in the 1970s and 1980s. There was lively interaction between "political" theologians in Europe and "liberation" theologians in the Third World. Some of them knew each other personally and had studied together, mostly at European universities. On the whole, presuppositions were shared, although contexts differed. But the emancipatory interest at European universities fizzled out and science has once more become—to a large extent—positivist. By and large this applies to theology as well, with the possible exceptions of feminist theology and my own discipline of missiology.

The objective of this contribution is to help bridge the gap between European and third-world theologians with a view to better understand and possibly to collaborate on common concerns, such as globalization and the marginalization of groups on the underside of societies worldwide (Amaladoss 1999). Following, but also broadening, the basic intuition of Holland and Henriot (1983, 8; Henriot 1998, 340) concerning the dialectical relation between experience and reflection, it will be argued that the dilemma between theory and practice—more specifically between theory-oriented and practice-oriented research—is a false dilemma. The practical-theological spiral is not just a pastoral method aimed at problem solving but also a strategy for developing theories in the scientific sense of the word—a grounded theory approach to theology. In this chapter I will expand on previous ideas about the pastoral circle, which I have renamed the practical-theological spiral, by reflecting on my discussions with third-world theology students and using methodological insights gained from the works of the French philosopher and sociologist Pierre Bourdieu (2000, 2002).

These reflections stem from a specific local context, that of a European university, more particularly the Catholic University Nijmegen (recently renamed Radboud University Nijmegen) and its Graduate School of Theology. But they seek to be global in their outlook and relevant to the grassroots. Our students come from all parts of the world—mainly Africa, Asia, and Eastern Europe—and their contexts differ greatly. Therefore, I restrict myself to the construction of African theologies and the debate between European and African theologians. I hope to show that both parties can benefit by using the practical-theological spiral. It can make European theologians less reluctant to engage in practice by showing that this approach helps to develop grounded theories in theology. African theologians, on the other hand, may become less hesitant to accept scientific methods if they are shown that academic theology can be very practical and relevant to the transformation of church and society.

My reflections are focused not only on ivory-tower debates at universities but also on everyday struggles for survival at the grassroots. Indeed, my aim is to show that the practical-theological spiral can help overcome this dichotomy, which is detrimental to both academics and activists. The "academic" versus "pastoral" dichotomy is overdrawn, say Holland and Henriot (1983, 7; Henriot 1998, 339–40). Nevertheless it appears in the debate between European and third-world theologians again and again. I prefer, therefore, to speak about the *practical-theological* spiral rather than the *pastoral* circle. I shall outline the four steps of the practical-theological spiral from the perspective of a grounded theory approach. But first, let me describe my journey with the pastoral circle and the methodological and epistemological questions that arise from that journey.

The Pastoral Circle

I studied philosophy, theology, and social sciences at Heerlen and Nijmegen in the late 1970s and early 1980s. At the time Edward Schillebeeckx dominated the debate in church and theology, not only at Nijmegen but throughout the Netherlands (Portier 1989). In those years Schillebeeckx embraced critical theory, and there was a critical climate in the whole of society. The mass protests against nuclear weapons, called Dutch disease or Hollanditis, are just one example. Political and liberation theologies were booming. After completing my studies, I was sent as a lay missionary to Sukumaland of northwest Tanzania in 1984. I had made quite a study of *ujamaa* socialism, and Julius Nyerere's thoughts on development as a condition for peace were widely admired in the Netherlands as manifestations of that same critical spirit, so I was eager to go. But I soon learned that the situation on the ground was very different from what I had read in books. In retrospect, I can say that this was where I became aware of the big difference between science and ideology (Mannheim 1960), between the official image of a society and what really goes on at the grassroots.

My further training as a missionary included a language course (Swahili) at the Danish Volunteer Training Centre at Arusha in northeast Tanzania and some seminars in cultural anthropology and pastoral theology at the (then) newly established Catholic Higher Institute (later renamed Catholic University) of East Africa in Nairobi, Kenya. Aylward Shorter (1972) introduced me to the work of Victor Turner and his ideas about root metaphors. Rodrigo Mejía (1993) introduced me to a new understanding of pastoral theology, using the pastoral circle. Later, when doing my doctoral research in Sukumaland, both introductions proved extremely useful. But in some ways I also found them unsatisfactory. Turner's multi-perspective and poly-method approach to studying the exegetical, positional, and operational meaning of symbols, combining phenomenology, structuralism, and action theory, helped me to understand Sukuma beliefs and practices. His analysis of what he called "the Ndembu inside view" (Turner 1969, 10–11) largely disregarded researchers' own contribution to the production of their research material. Consequently, I broadened my phenomenological analysis by including a hermeneutic slant, taking into account my pre-understanding and interest as a researcher and the influence of the production context on the research material; this was significant as I am a white, male, Western academic and my informants were black farmers.

When it came to the analysis of the positional meaning of symbols, Turner's "criss-crossing binary oppositions" (Turner 1969, 38) seemed rather arbitrary. Consequently, I looked for a more objective way of making a contrast analysis and found it in James Spradley's ethnographic semantics, as explained to me by Michael Kirwen at the Maryknoll Institute of African Studies in Nairobi. The analysis of the operational meaning of symbols also struck me as unsatisfactory. Although Turner presented rituals as anti-structure, he remained a functionalist in the sense that he saw rituals mainly as conducive to social harmony and cohesion. He did not take the conflict of interests and the division of power in Ndembu society sufficiently seriously. To overcome this omission I became interested in and used Bourdieu's theory of practice, which has influenced my further development as an academic to this day.

Mejía's introductions to pastoral theology in general and to the pastoral circle in particular greatly influenced my approach. I was inspired by his wide knowledge of both Latin American and African theology and his methodological thoroughness. The pastoral circle became the research design for my doctoral thesis, which—according to Janssen (1994, 226–28)—was unique at that time. In retrospect, what I had tried to do was to make the pastoral circle, which is basically a practice-oriented approach, more theory oriented. I wanted to make the pastoral circle a practical-theological research design. The debate about practical theology as empirical theology and the inauguration of the *Journal of Empirical Theology* at the University of Nijmegen, where I defended my doctoral thesis in 1994, provided the methodological and theoretical framework for my research (Van der Ven 1988).

After completing my doctorate I began using the pastoral circle in training missiology students in the Netherlands, preparing them for their overseas training programs, giving seminars on popular religion and evangelization for major seminarians and native priests in Tanzania and in a postgraduate practical theology program for Protestant ministers in Indonesia. My approach attracted the interest of other researchers, and my working papers were published in the *African Ecclesial Review* (Wijsen 1997a) and the *East Asian Pastoral Review* (Wijsen 1997b). They were then translated into German (Wijsen 1996) and Bahasa Indonesian (Wijsen 1999a).

My present context is the Nijmegen Graduate School of Theology, of which I am the director. The school offers master's and doctoral programs in intercultural theology. The slogan of the school reads: "Intercultural theology: A challenge for the 21st century." The presupposition is that constructing local theologies was a primary theological challenge for the twentieth century, in which the decolonization process took place, and it will undoubtedly continue on the various continents. Economically and politically the decolonization process may be complete (Mugambi 1995; Maluleke 2002), but from a cultural and religious point of view it continues (Magesa 2002). At the Nijmegen Graduate School of Theology we do not construct contextual theologies in the sense of local theologies (although, naturally, the Faculty of Theology at Nijmegen will continue to do so for the European context). On the assumption that our students have been thoroughly trained in the contextual theologies of their home countries, we seek to facilitate interaction between inculturated theologies.

It is this intercultural context that raises epistemological and methodological questions. Is a theology divorced from action necessarily irrelevant or uncommitted? Is commitment a condition for adequate knowledge, as the inaugural statement of the EATWOT seems to claim, or is the condition detachment? What is scientific knowledge? Do scholars in the West have a monopoly on methodology? Can they learn from scholars in the rest of the world? Or must scholars in the West stick to their own academic principles, and should non-Western students learn from them how to practice theology? Of course, it makes a big difference whether theology is studied at a university or a seminary, and differences between and within regions further complicate the picture. "The West" and "the Rest" are used as metaphors, with a sly wink at Chiweizu (1987), and show how wide the divide is. My experience is that many intercultural misunderstandings and even conflicts arise from different perceptions of what scientific knowledge actually is (Fox 1994).

A Grounded Theory Approach

Methodology handbooks in both Western and non-Western contexts make a distinction between theory-oriented and practice-oriented research (Verschuren and Doorewaard 1999, 33; Mugenda and Mugenda 2003, 4–5). According to this classification, theory-oriented research is undertaken at academic institutions, and practice-oriented research occurs at institutions for professional training. Put differently, academics primarily want *to know* (more) about things (knowledge development), not how *to do* things (knowledge implementation). Making scientific research practical or, even worse, problem-solving, is to lower its academic status. For a long time the ideal of science was to be "pure," producing knowledge for its own sake and not for its usefulness. One can distinguish among various forms of theory. There are everyday or pre-scientific theories, reflected or practice theories, and third-degree or meta-theories. Meta-theories offer reflections on reflected theories (Ziebertz 2002). Consequently, one can distinguish among popular, pastoral, and professional theologies (Boff and Boff 1987, 11–21). When I referred above to theory "in the scientific sense of the word," I had the third category of theory in mind.

Many third-world theology students find such distinctions artificial, even unethical. For them, scientific research must serve the needs of the people, not the other way round. They tend to inquire suspiciously who is going to profit from theological investigations. They adhere to the "primacy of practice" principle, or "doing before knowing" (Gutiérrez 1973; Boff and Boff 1987). These expressions, however, are often misunderstood. When early liberation theologians spoke about the primacy of practice and theology being (only) a second step, their main concern was to safeguard the social struggle of the people as a secular or autonomous reality (trade unions should not be confused with basic Christian communities), and social analysis of this reality should not to be dictated by a (hidden or overt) theological agenda. Their point was that practical involvement is a necessary step, but not necessarily the first one. This is one source of disagreement between European and third-world theologians. To what extent is commitment a necessary step in constructing authentic and relevant theology? Most European theologians would accept that commitment is important, but a scientific theologian cannot be overly committed, for it would entail a risk that the practice would no longer be critically questioned. Thus, whereas third-world theologians stress involvement in practice, European theologians stress distance from practice. The task facing theology is to strike a balance between the two (Fabella and Torres 1977, 269).

In third-world contexts many methods have been developed for pastoral purposes, such as the pedagogy of liberation (Freire 1971) in Latin America, training for transformation (Hope and Timmel 1984) or the Lumko method in Africa (Lobinger 1983), and the integrated pastoral approach based on that method in Asia. From a European perspective it is said that, while these pastoral methods may meet the needs of the people, they are not very helpful in generating scientific theories. But there are various examples to the contrary, such as the use of the Asian integrated pastoral approach for constructing an Asian Christology (De Mesa 2001), the use of the pastoral circle for constructing a social theology in Indonesia (Banawiratma and Müller 1999), and the use of the Lumko method of Bible sharing in small Christian communities for constructing an African biblical hermeneutics (Kalilombe 1999). The point at issue, however, is not so much whether or not theology should be theory oriented as *in what way* it should be theory oriented.

Methodology handbooks distinguish between theory-developing and theory-testing research (Verschuren and Doorewaard 1999, 33–36; Mugenda and Mugenda 2003, 198–201). Each research strategy has its own type of concepts (operational versus sensitizing) and design (linear versus cyclical). Whereas a theory-testing approach proceeds from defining a problem, formulating a hypothesis, and providing operational definitions to gathering and analyzing data and drawing conclusions, a theory-developing strategy is iterative (Spradley 1980, 26–28). In such an approach the researcher can start wherever he or she sees fit; in every stage the researcher can move backward or forward. This approach sets no starting point or end point, although the research must reach a conclusion somewhere. But the conclusion is open to fresh criticism. In my view the practical-theological spiral is best seen as a grounded theory approach to theology, based on a real dialectic relation between data sources (qualitative or quantitative empirical facts gathered through fieldwork) and knowledge sources (existing insights and theories developed previously by others that can be studied through secondary research) (Verschuren and Doorewaard 1999, 114–15).

I consider the Judeo-Christian tradition to be such a knowledge source, based on several thousands of years of human experience in the search for justice and liberation. In a book on theological method Edward Schillebeeckx (1974) claims that, just like any other science, theology starts from a hypothesis, namely, the truth of faith given in the Christian tradition, and that this hypothesis must be tested and possibly falsified by human experience. He later applied this methodological principle in his Christology (Schillebeeckx 1979, 617–19). From a social-science point of view, James Spradley writes that the researcher infers a hypothesis about cultural knowledge from what people say, the way they act, and the artifacts they use. This hypothesis must be tested over and over again until the researcher is relatively certain that this is indeed what people have in mind. Researchers can evaluate the adequacy of their knowledge by their ability to anticipate future behavior of the people they investigated (Spradley 1980, 10).

In previous studies I spoke about the research object in terms of a social situation that is experienced as problematic (Wijsen 1993, 12). A social situation is understood as people (actors) doing things (activities) in a physical setting or place (Wijsen 1993, 40; Spradley 1980, 39–42). In guiding students I discovered that the concept of social situation can easily lead to (excessively) broad research projects, so I narrowed down the research object to practice. I do not propose to elaborate on the concept of practice, as this has been done by others in some detail. Suffice it to say that I take practice to be "reflection based on experience and experience based on reflection," as Holland and Henriot defined it (1983, 8; Henriot 1998, 340), following Paulo Freire. Probably *praxis* would be a more appropriate term, as practice has the connotation of application of theory. Praxis, by contrast, is understood as co-constituting theory (Portier 1989, 30).

Definition of the research object helped me to clarify the research perspective. I am not primarily interested in ideas (beliefs) but in the dialectical relation between cognitive structures (such as cultural symbolism) and social structures (for example, power relations). This focus brings the actor back into the study of religion and theology. It makes the practical-theological spiral quite different from a systematic-theological approach, which is primarily interested in the contents of faith, more particularly in a coherent interpretation of those contents.

Participatory Objectification

The objective of the first stage of the practical-theological spiral is to acquire knowledge about the practice under investigation. The method (if it is a method) for this stage is called insertion (Holland and Henriot 1983, 8). Many approaches based on Joseph Cardijn's "see, judge, and act" scheme do not make a clear-cut distinction between observation and analysis. They give detailed directions for data analysis but not for gathering the data. In my earlier work I replaced the first stage of the practical-theological spiral, which Boff and Boff call "the preliminary stage" (1987, 22) or "step zero" (1987, 41), with participant observation. The reason for this is that the researcher's involvement in the praxis differs from that of the other participants in that it is more systematic and methodical and has preconceived intentions. The researcher cannot deny his or her past history and "second nature" (Wijsen 1993, 21; 1997a, 249). I shall return to this point when I discuss theological reflection.

Participant observation as a scientific method is known to be hotly contested in academia. It is considered subjective and biased. One criterion of scientific knowledge is its objectivity and neutrality. The classical ideal of science is to refrain from involvement and commitment as far as possible. Hence a questionnaire survey is seen as more objective than participant observation. There are, however, various degrees of participation, from nonparticipation through moderate and active participation to complete participation, with increasing degrees of commitment on the part of the researcher (Spradley 1980, 58–62). The point at issue is that of involvement (or its opposite, detachment) as a condition for the possibility of "true" knowledge. By true knowledge I mean that the reality "out there" corresponds to the mental representation of that reality.

A case in point that is fundamental to the construction of African theologies is the references to anthropological poverty in Africa. Most African students claim that missionaries and colonialists discarded African customs and traditions and replaced them with European and Christian values. Thus they speak about cultural schizophrenia in Africa, and even the cultural death of Africans. It seems to me that they use their own experience as

African intellectuals, having trained for twelve years or more in a European seminary or university system, as a lens to observe the reality in Africa, without seriously analyzing their own contribution to the production and reproduction of these statements. More detached research would stress the symbolic capital and even spiritual power that is alive as never before in African folk culture and popular religion, traditional medicine, and customary law (Huizer 1991; Wijsen 1999b).

According to Bourdieu, who started his academic career at the National Institute for Statistical and Economic Research of the University of Algiers, the idea of a neutral or disinterested science is one of the myths of our times (Bourdieu 2000; Habermas 1968). From his own experience he knows that statistical research is no more objective than participatory forms of research. One can manipulate—to a large extent—the product of statistical analysis, for instance, by combining two or more variables. Disinterested practice simply does not exist. A field (or market) is always a site of struggle, where people try to serve their own interests (or make a profit) using various resources (or forms of capital) in coalition (inclusion) or in competition (exclusion) with others. Universities are not exempt from this struggle. Academics fight over scarce resources, not only to accumulate symbolic capital (honor and prestige) but also for financial gain (research assistants, computers, funds).

Bourdieu (1990, 123) classifies himself as a constructivist structuralist or a structuralist constructivist. He tries to overcome the classical distinction between subjectivism and objectivism, phenomenology and structuralism, by stressing the dialectical relation between reality and the representation of that reality in the mind. By conducting research, scientists not only discover what is "out there," but to a large extent they construct what they try to discover. The "creation" of ethnic groups by cultural anthropologists serves as an example. Bourdieu tries to reduce subjectivism through participatory objectification. By this phrase he understands the objectification of the subject of the objectification, that is, the researcher himself or herself. The aim is not to analyze the researcher's experience but to analyze the societal conditions of that experience (Bourdieu 2002).

Analysis of Symbolic Power

The objective of the second stage of the practical-theological spiral is to gain insight into the observed practice. The method here is social analysis. Holland and Henriot stress the importance of symbolism. The language of technical social analysis is elitist, they say. Locked in the chains of technical language, it has little communicative power. "The alternative to this technical language is the symbolic dimension of popular culture. Thus we emphasize the need to explore the symbolism, myths, dreams, and visions of the ordinary people" (1983, 91). Fully in harmony with the dominant form of liberation theology—at least dominant in the reception of this theology in the Western world in the late 1970s—Holland and Henriot emphasize the socioeconomic aspects of their analysis. There was also another trend of liberation theology that has always been more interested in cultural symbolism and popular religiosity. This trend was developed mainly in the Argentinean school (Scannone 1998) and was shared by influential groups in Chile and Brazil. But it remained a minority position up to the 1980s.

The innovation in this second stage is the broadening and deepening of social analysis by combining it with cultural analysis (Wijsen 1997a, 241; Henriot 1998). But there are various ways of making a cultural analysis, and not all of them are helpful for the kind of theological research that I am advocating here. Surprisingly, among many African theology students it has become a fad to discover a people's world view as a starting point for constructing contextual theologies (Schreiter 1985). A people's world view is "their picture of the ways things in sheer actuality are, their concept of nature, of self, of society. It contains their most comprehensive ideas of order" (Geertz 1993, 127). By analyzing and reflecting on the proverbs or sayings of their people, these African students try to construct "ethno-theologies." Often they analyze the past more than the present situation, and the ideal more than the real. In many instances they romanticize the past based on "ideologies of home" (Robertson 1995). I recall sometimes painful debates with students from Tanzania and Kenya about a theology of African Renaissance, based on nationalist ideologies of *ujamaa* or *harambee*, which they may embrace in a rather naive way. My critical questions concerning *ujamaa* (Wijsen and Tanner 2002) met with suspicion that I was an "uncommitted" theologian. It takes these students quite some time to become more down-to-earth or empirical theologians. Perhaps this applies more to Catholic students, who are thoroughly trained in neo-Scholastic philosophy, than to mainline Protestant students, who have a solid background in biblical studies and are more inclined to protest.

Many theologians are trained in a form of cultural analysis derived from the Sapir and Whorf hypothesis. These American linguists maintain that language and culture are intrinsically connected. Thus they assume that one can study a culture just as one studies a language (Tanner 1997, 3–24). Based on a Saussurian or Chomskyan linguistics, making a distinction between language and speech, and competence and performance, they claim that one can understand a culture by studying the cultural grammar that underlies ritual and symbolism and thus discover, for example, the basic structure of African thought (Kirwen 2004). In theology, religiously oriented anthropologists such as Clifford Geertz and Victor Turner are quite influential. This is understandable, as they stress the autonomy of symbol systems independently of actors and social structures, a position held by theologians and phenomenologists of religion who say that religion exists *sui generis* (Schreiter 1985, 56–73; Küster 1999, 3–4). The anthropologist

Victor Turner (1975, 20) even said that he was looking for some evidence of ethno-philosophy or ethno-theology in Ndembu culture.

Bourdieu criticizes this type of cultural analysis that remains purely internal, overlooking the fact that symbolic classifications fulfill not only cognitive but also practical functions and that they are always oriented to the production of social effects. To interpret religious (political, scientific, or any other) speech acts requires not (only) the discovery of the cultural grammar underlying these acts, but (also) a thorough reconstruction of the field in which these speech acts are produced and reproduced, the interests that are served, and the (power) relations between the positions and agents in the field. He proposes that one should study the symbolism, myths, dreams, and visions of the ordinary people as cultural capital that is used by (groups of) actors to serve their own interests (Bourdieu 2000). In particular, he wants to know "how power creates religion" (Asad 1983).

Correlation or Confrontation?

The objective of the third stage of the practical-theological spiral is to evaluate the practice that has been observed and analyzed. The method for this stage is theological reflection. Holland and Henriot have already corrected the misconception that the first stage is pre-theological (Boff and Boff 1987, 22) and that theological reflection is merely a second step (Gutíerrez 1973). The idea that theological reflection is merely a second step is often misunderstood by Western theologians. Holland and Henriot write: "None of these parts can be totally isolated; theology is not restricted to that moment explicitly called 'theological reflection.' In a wider sense, all the moments of the circle are part of an expanded definition of theology. All are linked and overlap" (1983, 13). Thus what this model presents as an orderly sequence of stages in a process often happens simultaneously in reality.

That is why I spoke about preconceived intentions in the first step of the practical-theological spiral. The choice to be committed and engaged in action is a theological option and not a "step zero" or "pre-theological" stage. I have already explained why early liberation theologians spoke about theological reflection as a second step. But they had a further reason to distinguish clearly between social analysis and theological reflection: they wanted to avoid being branded Marxists by ecclesiastic authorities. Marxism was just a tool used by (them as) sociologists. But there is a pitfall. Early liberation theology inclines toward a two-stage model: first there is socio-analytical mediation, followed by hermeneutic mediation (Boff 1983). In the department of empirical theology at the Radboud University Nijmegen we do not speak about interdisciplinary study but about *intra*-disciplinary study to show straightaway that there is a dialectical relation between facts and norms (Van der Ven 1988). Intra-disciplinary study refers to theologians using the methods of empirical sciences, just as biblical scholars use literary methods, church historians use historical methods, and systematic theologians use philosophical methods. Of course, theologians' use of empirical methods must meet the standards of social scientists, which have to be confirmed and guaranteed by scholarly collaboration with them.

In keeping with the foregoing observations, my reflection on this stage of the practical-theological spiral concerns the theologian's "commitment" (Fabella and Torres 1977, 269). Some students at the Nijmegen Graduate School of Theology are attracted to Radboud University Nijmegen because they associate it with the hermeneutic method of Edward Schillebeeckx. In his later works Schillebeeckx (1984) defined theology as an "art of liberation." He developed this art in dialogue with third-world theologians, in particular with Gustavo Gutiérrez, with whom he shared an admiration for the new theology of French theologians such as Yves Congar and Marie-Dominique Chenu. But whereas Gutiérrez criticized Schillebeeckx for being too much of an academic theologian, too abstract, and too detached from the poor, Schillebeeckx in his turn held that Gutiérrez identified too much with the poor and that his theological reflection became too much part of their struggle (Borgman 2003).

Much the same debate goes on at the Nijmegen Graduate School of Theology. Whereas some of the third-world students say that the professors are too theoretical, the professors say that the students are too activist. By being too committed they are no longer capable of critical reflection on the practice. Theology becomes a justification of the practice. Some of my African students think in terms of Incarnation. They say that God was already present in Africa long before the missionaries came, working among Africans in mysterious ways. What the missionary does is to make explicit what had always been there. Incarnation theology undoubtedly fulfills a liberating function, recognizing the intrinsic value of African cultures, eliminating the pitfalls of the earlier adaptation theology that sought to jettison African culture and Christianize it from within. This theology served the interests of colonialists and missionaries who wanted African people to adapt to their point of view. In this sense it was an ideology (Mannheim 1960). But it is unwise to combat one ideology with another. Incarnation theology was a necessary step to overcome cultural and religious oppression, but when applied too radically it becomes naive.

Liberation theology never took root in Africa, except in South Africa (in the form of black theology) and in Cameroon, with outstanding scholars like Jean-Marc Ela and Fabien Eboussi Boulaga. In other countries liberation theologians remained basically prophets in the desert, such as Laurenti Magesa in Tanzania. But many of these scholars were either silenced (by the government or the church) or they turned secular. This is understandable in the context of growing church control and dependence on outside funding (Hastings 1989, 122–37). At present the debate is no longer between liberation and inculturation, but between reconstruction and renaissance (Magesa

2002; Kobia 2003, 103–50). In general, my African students are very en-
thusiastic about the potential of popular wisdom and the possibility of going back to the "path of the ancestors." They praise the African community
spirit (such as *ujamaa* in Tanzania or *ubuntu* in South Africa) and tend to
see it as a solution to (almost) all evils in society. But they tend to forget that
ujamaa was not a great success, and not only because of external influences
(Schweigman 2001). Much the same applies to Bénézet Bujo's *Ethical Dimension of Community* (1998) and Laurenti Magesa's *African Religion:
Moral Traditions of Abundant Life* (1997). However appealing these theologies may be, others feel they take the need to justify African traditions
too far (Maluleke 2002). A similar debate on ideology and science may be
found in African philosophy between ethno-philosophers and nationalistic
philosophers, on the one hand, and professional or scientific philosophers,
on the other (Hountondji 1983; Gyekye 1997; Appiah 1992; Wiredu 1996).

Theological reflection is not just an evaluation of experience "in the light
of living faith, scripture, church social teaching, and the resources of tradition," as Holland and Henriot seem to suggest (1983, 9; Henriot 1998,
340). The phrase "in the light of living faith" remains too much a one-sided
procedure. Schillebeeckx says that there is a correlation between human
experience and the Christian tradition, gospel and culture. And—as an adherent of social theory—he immediately adds that it is a critical correlation,
hence not only mutually clarifying but also mutually critical. Along with
African incarnation or inculturation theologians, he says that God and God's
kingdom are already present in Africa, but also yet to come. This is a condition for the possibility of negative contrast experiences, another basic category in Schillebeeckx's theological reflection. There is always a strong
eschatological and thus prophetic strain in his theology. Besides the primacy of practice, the hermeneutics of suspicion—another principle of liberation theology—should be applied to liberation and other emancipation
theologies as well. In some African students' research projects, commitment
and identification with the people and popular wisdom go too far. I challenge them to balance commitment and criticism. There is a continuity, but
also a discontinuity, between gospel and culture. Hermeneutic fusion of
horizons must be complemented by a hermeneutics of differentiation.

Empowerment of the People

The objective of the fourth stage of the practical-theological spiral is to
demonstrate conditions for the possibility of innovating the practice under
investigation. The method for this stage is pastoral planning. In discussing
the first stage of the spiral I referred to various types of participant observation (Spradley 1980, 58–62). In the last of these types (namely, complete
participation) there is no longer any distinction between the roles of observer and participant. The researcher has become an insider. This form is

more aptly called action research (Huizer 1979). Action research as a research strategy developed on the margins of academic studies; it became a hallmark of much third-world or liberation theology, where theologizing serves as a means of empowering the people—especially the most marginalized—through adult education and community development. Here the methodological principles of learning by doing and doing before knowing are applied in their purest form. The presupposition is that the best knowledge comes from below and from within.

An interesting example of an observer who became a participant is a Dutch anthropologist who studied spirit mediums in Botswana. He identified with his informants to such an extent that he became a spirit medium himself (Van Binsbergen 1991). He was prepared to trade his status as an anthropological fieldworker for that of a religious specialist. Becoming a *sangoma* offered him an inside view that is not accessible to participant observers who, however committed they may be, remain to a large extent outsiders. The author, a respected anthropologist with over twenty years of experience, was no longer able to write an ethnography but only to tell his story. In a later publication the same author, who moved from cultural anthropology to intercultural philosophy, dissociated himself from his earlier romanticizing of *sangoma* beliefs (Van Binsbergen 1998).

Action research emerged in social psychology just before World War II as a strategy in which the researcher learns about group dynamics and change processes by participating in or manipulating certain aspects of these processes. Kurt Lewin, who coined the term "action research" and was himself a Jewish refugee from Nazi Germany with a background in the *Frankfurter Schule*, once said: "If you want to know how things really are, just try to change them" (Lewin 1948). This type of research has been used in third-world contexts and elsewhere, in both urban industrial and rural agricultural settings, for the purpose of mobilizing the group power of workers and farmers through a pedagogy of the oppressed (Freire 1971) and training for transformation (Hope and Timmel 1984). It has given rise to a tradition of research-through-action, stressing indigenous knowledge and spiritual power (Huizer 1991). In general, the presupposition is that development or change must be people oriented or community based.

In line with my argument in the previous sections, such an approach can become naive and uncritical. One of my doctoral students, who was interested in developing a people-oriented biblical hermeneutics among the Pokot in West Kenya, discovered that community-based practice is not always good practice. To the Pokot, stealing from their neighbors is evil. But according to their popular wisdom there is nothing wrong with cattle raiding among the Turkana, as they do not consider the Turkana to be their neighbors. Clearly this practice, however people oriented or community based it may be, cannot be justified as good practice at a professional theological level. Maybe research-after-action could be an adequate alternative to research-through-action. While in research-through-action the action and research are undertaken simultaneously, research-after-action first commits available resources to action and only later to scientific recording and publication. "Research after action does not have that advantage of relevancy for the change process under review. It does, however, provide distance between the scientist and his activities allowing for more objective consideration" (Kronenburg 1986, 5–6).

Conclusion

The inaugural statement of the EATWOT cited at the outset confronts us with a dilemma between commitment and criticism, between grassroots theology and ivory-tower theology, theology in the West and theology in "the Rest" of the world. In this article I tried to bridge this divide by presenting the practical-theological spiral as a grounded theory approach to theology to promote understanding and collaboration between European academic or theory-oriented theologians and third-world applied or practice-oriented theologians. Of course, these labels are stereotypes and in reality these approaches and their advocates are more complex and differentiated. Moreover, the West and the Rest, European and Third World, are not primarily regional categories but refer to various ways of conducting research. The methodology handbook by Mugenda and Mugenda (2003) was developed at Kenyatta University in Nairobi, Kenya, but it reflects a largely Western approach; the methodology handbook by Verschuren and Doorewaard (1999) was developed at the Radboud University Nijmegen, Netherlands, but it is open to methods other than traditional ones.

The dichotomy between the two types of theology, academic and applied, is based on a false understanding of theory-oriented and practice-oriented research, as even a little reflection on the term *practice* reveals. I showed some strengths and weaknesses of both forms of theology. In reaction to a narrow-minded, scientific type of theology I tried to show that the commitment advocated by third-world theologians is not necessarily an inadequate principle for gathering "true" knowledge. This is a criticism of the dogma of scientific neutrality. On the other hand, I showed that the detachment advocated by European theologians can make pastoral projects more objective. The danger is that theologians who are overly engaged in practice may no longer be capable of critical reflection; they tend to identify with the people and offer justification for their practices.

Reflection on the four stages of the practical-theological spiral may make it more relevant to both European and third-world theology. In the reflection on the preliminary stage there is a shift from insertion to participant observation, and from participant observation to participatory objectification. Maybe this is the most important modification of the practical-theological spiral, as it is foundational for all the other steps. Researchers become far more aware of their own contribution to the material. Insertion always occurs in a specific social position. The accent is not on experience as a first step but on the social conditions of this experience. Concerning the second step, there is a shift from, or a combination of, social and cultural analysis—a form of cultural analysis that looks at cultural symbolism not only from the perspective of its underlying grammar but also from the perspective of power relations that shape cultures, of culture as symbolic capital. In the third stage there is not only an evaluation of culture in the light of the gospel but also the other way round. Theological reflection offers a critical correlation, but I have learned that it must be augmented by critical confrontation. In the fourth stage I moved from pastoral planning to action research, and from action research to research-after-action. In developing these steps I sought to strike a balance between commitment and criticism.

The real issue is not so much the use of methods as their underlying theory of science. In the 1970s and 1980s critical theory was accepted as scientific. Today this theory has largely disappeared from our universities, which equate science with positivism. Here I stand by Bourdieu's protest against the myths of our time, especially the myth of a disinterested science, and Schillebeeckx's view of theology as art of liberation. One question that still bothers me is whether or not academic standards are universal, irrespective of the context in which academic research is done. For the time being I maintain that in principle academic standards are universal, but in fact they are not. What our intercultural debate in theology can do is to make these standards more universal. This would mean that an academic standard created in a concrete context, by reason of historical significance and collegial cooperation, is embraced by other researchers in various contexts and finally achieves the status of universality, which is inclusive and accepted by all. But whether this will ever happen is questionable. It certainly has not happened in the recent past. So our struggle for symbolic capital in academia will also continue in the field of theology.

References

Amaladoss, Michael, ed. 1999. *Globalization and its victims*. Delhi: Indian Society for Promoting Christian Knowledge.

Appiah, Kwame. 1992. *In my father's house: Africa in the philosophy of culture*. Oxford: Oxford Univ. Press.

Asad, T. 1983. Anthropological conception of religion: Reflections on Geertz. *Man* 18: 237–59.

Banawiratma, J., and J. Müller. 1999. *Contextual social theology: An Indonesian model*. Manila: East Asian Pastoral Institute.

Becker, D. 1999. Der Westen gegen den Rest? In *Globaler Kampf der Kulturen*, edited by D. Becker. Stuttgart: W. Kohlhammer.

Boff, Clodovis. 1983. *Theologie und Praxis: Die erkenntnistheoretische Grundlagen der Theologie der Befreiung*. Munich: Chr. Kaiser Verlag.

Boff, Leonardo, and Clodovis Boff. 1987. *Introducing liberation theology*. Maryknoll, NY: Orbis Books.

Borgman, E. 2003. Theology as the art of liberation. *Exchange* 32, no. 2: 98–108.

Bourdieu, Pierre. 1990. *In other words*. Cambridge: Polity Press.

———. 2000. *Das religiöse Feld*. Konstanz: Universitätsverlag Konstanz.

———. 2002. *Ein soziologischer Selbstversuch*. Frankfurt am Main: Suhrkamp.

Bujo, Bénézet. 1998. *The ethical dimension of community: The African model and the dialogue between North and South*. Nairobi: Paulines Publications.

Chinweizu. 1987. *The West and the rest of us: White predators, black slavers and the African elite*. Lagos: Pero Press.

De Mesa, José. 2001. Making salvation concrete and Jesus real. *Exchange* 30, no. 1: 1–17.

Fabella, Virgina, and Sergio Torres. 1977. *The emergent gospel*. Maryknoll, NY: Orbis Books.

Fox, Helen. 1994. *Listening to the world: Cultural issues in academic writing*. Urbana, IL: National Council of Teachers of English.

Freire, Paulo. 1971. *Pedagogy of the oppressed*. New York: Herder and Herder.

Geertz, Clifford. 1993. *The interpretation of cultures*. London: Fontana Press.

Gutiérrez, Gustavo. 1973. *A theology of liberation*. Maryknoll, NY: Orbis Books.

Gyekye, K. 1997. *Tradition and modernity: Philosophical reflection on African experience*. New York: Oxford Univ. Press.

Habermas, J. 1968. *Erkentnis und Interesse*. Frankfurt am Main: Suhrkamp.

Hastings, Adrian. 1989. *African Catholicism*. London: SCM Press; Philadelphia: Trinity Press International.

Henriot, Peter. 1998. Grassroots analysis: The emphasis on culture. In *Liberation theologies on shifting grounds*, edited by G. De Schrijver, 333–50. Leuven: Peeters Press.

Holland, Joe, and Peter Henriot. 1983. *Social analysis: Linking faith and justice*. Maryknoll, NY: Orbis Books.

Hope, A., and S. Timmel. 1984. *Training for transformation*. Handbooks 1, 2, 3. Gweru: Mambo Press.

Hountondji, P. 1983. *African philosophy: Myth and reality*. London: Hutchinson.

Huizer, G. 1979. Research-through-action. In *The politics of anthropology*, edited by G. Huizer and B. Manheim, 395–420. The Hague: Mouton.

———. 1991. *Folk spirituality and liberation in Southern Africa*. Bourdeaux: Centre d'etude d'Afrique Noire, Universite de Bordeaux.

Janssen, H. 1994. Der pastorale Zirkel—eine Einführung. In *Inkulturation und Kontextualität*, edited by M. Pankoke-Schenk and G. Evers, 221–30. Frankfurt am Main: Verlag Jozef Knecht.

Kalilombe, P. 1999. *Doing theology at the grassroots*. Gweru: Mambo Press.

Kirwen, Michael C., ed. 2004. *African cultural themes*. Nairobi: Maryknoll Institute of African Studies; Minneapolis: Saint Mary's Univ. of Minnesota.

Kobia, S. 2003. *The courage to hope: A challenge to the churches in Africa*. Nairobi: Acton Publishers.

Kronenburg, J. 1986. *Empowerment of the poor*. Amsterdam: Royal Tropical Institute Amsterdam; Nijmegen: Third World Centre Nijmegen.

Küster, Volker. 1999. *The many faces of Jesus Christ*. London: SCM Press; Maryknoll, NY: Orbis Books.

Lewin, Kurt. 1948. *Resolving social conflicts*. New York: Harper.

Lobinger, F. 1983. *Towards non-dominating leadership. Aims and methods of the Lumko-series*. Delmenville: Lumko Institute.

Magesa, Laurenti. 1997. *African religion: Moral traditions of abundant life*. Maryknoll, NY: Orbis Books.

Magesa, L. 2002. African Renaissance. In *Marginalized Africa*, edited by P. Kanyandago, 13–27. Nairobi: Paulines Publications.

Maluleke, T. 2002. A rediscovery of the agency of Africans. In *Marginalized Africa*, edited by P. Kanyandago, 165–90. Nairobi: Paulines Publications.

Mannheim, Karl. 1960. *Ideology and utopia: An introduction to the sociology of knowledge*. London: Routledge and Kegan Paul.

Mejía, Rodrigo. 1993. The new understanding of pastoral theology. In *A light on our path*, edited by C. McGarry, R. Mejía, and V. Shirima, 27–37. Nairobi: St. Paul Publications.

Mugambi, J. 1995. *From liberation to reconstruction: African Christian theology after the Cold War*. Nairobi: Acton Publishers.

Mugenda, O., and A. Mugenda. 2003. *Research methods*. Nairobi: African Centre for Technology Studies.

Portier, William. 1989. Interpretation and method. In *The praxis of Christian experience: An introduction to the theology of Edward Schillebeeckx*, edited by R. Schreiter and M. Hilkert. San Francisco: Harper and Row.

Robertson, R. 1995. Glocalization: Time-space and homogeneity-heterogeneity. In *Global modernities*, edited by M. Featherstone, S. Scott Lash, and Roland Robertson, 25–44. London: Sage Publications.

Scannone, J. 1998. "Axial" shift instead of "paradigm shift." In *Liberation theologies on shifting grounds*, edited by G. De Schrijver, 98–103. Leuven: Peeters Press.

Schreiter, Robert J. 1985. *Constructing local theologies*. Maryknoll, NY: Orbis Books.

Schillebeeckx, Edward. 1974. *The understanding of faith: Interpretation and criticism*. London: Seabury Press.

———. 1979. *Jesus: An experiment in Christology*. New York: Seabury Press.

———. 1984. Theologie als bevrijdingskunde. In *Tijdschrift voor Theologie* 24, no. 4: 7–24.

Schweigman, C. 2001. Ujamaa: A phantom. In *Quest: International African Journal of Philosophy* 15, no. 1–2: 113–25.

Shorter, Aylward. 1972. Symbolism, ritual and history: An examination of the work of Victor Turner. In *The historical study of African religion*, edited by T. Ranger and J. Kimambo, 139–49. London: Heinemann.

Spradley, James. 1980. *Participant observation*. New York: Holt, Rinehart, and Winston.

Tanner, Kathryn. 1997. *Theories of culture: A new agenda for theology*. Minneapolis: Fortress Press.

Turner, Victor. 1969. *The ritual process: Structure and anti-structure*. London: Routledge and Kegan Paul.

———. 1975. *Revelation and divination in Ndembu ritual*. Ithaca, NY: Cornell Univ. Press.

Van Binsbergen, W. 1991. Becoming a sangoma: Religious anthropological field-work in Francistown, Botswana. *Journal of Religion in Africa* 21, no. 4: 309–44.

———. 1998. *Sangoma* in Nederland: Over integriteit en interculturele bemiddeling. In *Getuigen ondanks zichzelf*, edited by M. Ellias and R. Reis. Maastricht: Shaker Publishing.

Van der Ven, J. 1988. Practical theology: From applied to empirical theology. *Journal of Empirical Theology* 1, no. 1: 7–27.

Verschuren, P., and H. Doorewaard. 1999. *Designing a research project*. Utrecht: Lemma.

Wijsen, Frans. 1993. *There is only one God*. Kampen: J. H. Kok.

———. 1996. Der Pastorale Zirkel in der Ausbildung im kirchlichen Dienst. In *Zeichen der Zeit: Pastoraler Zirkel, Gesellschaftsanalyse, Bibel-Teilen*, edited by H. Janssen, 45–56. Aachen: Missio. Internationales Katholisches Missionswerk.

———. 1997a. The pastoral circle in the training of church ministers. *African Ecclesial Review* 39, no. 4: 238–50.

———. 1997b. The pastoral circle in the training of church ministers. *East Asian Pastoral Review* 34, no. 4: 325–36.

———. 1999a. *Lingkaran pastoral dalam pendidikan pelayanan*. Seri Pastoral 296. Yogyakarta: Pusat Pastoral Yogyakarta.

———. 1999b. Beyond the fatal impact theory. In *Globalization and its victims*, edited by Michael Amaladoss, 122–31. Delhi: Indian Society for Promoting Christian Knowledge.

Wijsen, Frans, and Ralph Tanner. 2002. *"I am just a Sukuma": Globalization and identity construction in Northwest Tanzania*. Amsterdam/New York: Editions Rodopi.

Wiredu, Kwasi. 1996. *Cultural universals and particulars: An African perspective*. Bloomington, IN: Indiana Univ. Press.

Ziebertz, H.-G. 2002. Normativity and empirical research in practical theology. *Journal for Empirical Theology* 15, no. 1: 5–18.

The Impact of the Pastoral Circle in Teaching Pastoral Theology

Rodrigo Mejía

It does not seem necessary to stress here the proper theological character of pastoral theology as a real theological discipline. The time in which pastoral theology was understood as a practical training for the administration of sacraments and other liturgical functions seems to belong to the past. Pastoral theology as a university discipline was officially recognized for the first time in Vienna in 1774. More recently, the Apostolic Exhortation of Pope John Paul II *Pastores dabo Vobis* (March 25, 1992) describes very well the scientific nature of pastoral theology: "It is a scientific reflection on the Church as she is built up daily, by the power of the Spirit; in history. . . . Pastoral Theology is not just an art. Nor is it a set of exhortations, experiences and methods. It is theological in its own right, because it receives from the faith the principles and criteria for the pastoral action of the Church in history" (no. 57).

This document of the church can serve us at the same time to introduce the role the pastoral circle can play in the teaching of pastoral theology. In effect, in the very same paragraph, commenting on the principles and criteria that should guide pastoral theology, the document says: "Among these principles and criteria, one that is specially important is that of evangelical discernment of the socio-cultural and ecclesial situations in which the particular pastoral action has to be carried out."

The pastoral circle proposes a process of analysis of social situations and structures as well as theological reflection on them; this corresponds very well to the short description of the "evangelical discernment" of the socio-cultural and ecclesial situations. We are allowed to think, therefore, that the methodological use of the pastoral circle in teaching pastoral theology is not only justified but also may be indispensable for pastoral theology. It is our purpose in this essay to share some reflections on the different aspects the impact this methodological use can have in the teaching not only of pastoral theology but of the whole of theology.

The Starting Point of Theology Revisited

The first consequence of the use of the pastoral circle in the teaching of pastoral theology is precisely at the very starting point. In order to appreciate this impact it is necessary to recall the traditional starting point inherited from Scholastic theology and more precisely from Saint Thomas Aquinas.

The starting point of the medieval theologians was the *lectio*, a reading from sacred scripture. It was from this reading that the *quaestio* was formulated and developed. The questions were born from the *lectio*, usually as a need to reconcile the apparently opposed views of two different authorities, namely, the Bible and the tradition of the church fathers, on the one hand, and the pagan philosophers, mainly Aristotle, on the other hand. This way of proceeding turned out to be a technique of teaching, as the French theologian M.-D. Chenu comments: "Even the points accepted by everyone and set forth in the most certain of terms were brought under scrutiny and subjected, by deliberate artifice, to the now usual processes of research. In brief, they were, literally speaking, 'called into question,' no longer because there was any real doubt about their truth, but because a deeper understanding of them was sought after" (Chenu 1964, 86–87).

In other words, the *quaestio* did not necessarily represent any real problem. Clarenbad von Arras, a theologian of that time, was quoted by Chenu: "It seems necessary to recall what the question is. . . . Hence, in the same treatise on the Topics, though in a different place [1, 3], [Aristotle] reminds us that a problem can be made up of every proposition. But these questions that are certain have nothing of a question but its form" (Chenu 1964, 67).

Introducing a question at the beginning of the teaching process is valuable, provided the question is a real one. The question can never be just a methodological pretext in order to read the biblical text.

The lack of realism and the lack of connection with human life of some of those theological *questions* were sometimes appalling. Discussions about the sex of the angels and whether the dove that appeared in the baptism of Jesus was a real dove or not are some examples. This led to the popular opinion that theologians are intellectuals who always have the right answers to the questions they invent themselves.

The first consequence of the use of the pastoral circle, therefore, is to qualify its starting point. The starting point is neither the *lectio* nor the question directly proposed by the biblical text, but rather real questions touching human life. Moreover, it is not enough that the theologian starts with a question, even if real, if it is a theoretical question with which the theologian has no direct experience. Real problems can also become abstract enunciations.

It is commonly accepted that the purpose of pastoral theology is to perform a critical theological reflection on the whole pastoral praxis of the church. This praxis is at the same time the material and the final object of its study. This is why H. Schuster called it "an existential ecclesiology" (1965, 4–9). However, this orientation to praxis can also remain at the level of a pure theoretical reflection if the starting point is not rooted in the real and historical situations of the church. If the pastoral theologian analyzes the praxis of the church in the same way a mortician performs a postmortem analysis of an anonymous corpse, the initial question, even if real, becomes an abstract formulation. By this, we want to underline the fact that it is possible for pastoral theologians to apply sound theological criteria and principles to situations with which they are not familiar at all and of which they have little or no personal experience, only secondhand information.

The pastoral circle is all about human experience, and it stresses the need for personal insertion as the adequate starting point for the whole process. Life comes first; theology comes second. Human experience is not only the raw material for analysis but the condition for the one who is going to perform the analysis. It is not that objective data, statistics, and published studies on the situation are to be neglected, but that nothing replaces the direct involvement of the theologian in the situation he or she wants to analyze. It is not the same to analyze the situation of war after having read several books on armed conflicts as it is to analyze it after having lived the real situation. The understanding of pastoral theology and of its purpose is very much conditioned by the human experience of the theologian, by his or her sex and cultural, social and financial condition, as Monika Hellwig demonstrated years ago (1982).

The term *insertion* does not imply that pastoral theologians have to live personally every single human situation as a protagonist or as a victim, but rather that they gain a personal and direct knowledge of them by presence and participation in them (see Chapter 7 herein). The more this participation is missing, the more the final product will be a pastoral theology taught "from hearsay" or a pastoral theology manual that is a *liber ex libris*.

The challenge posed here by the starting point of the pastoral circle was foretold and well formulated by Y.-M. Congar soon after the Second Vatican Council:

> If the Church wants to be close to the real problems of today's world and to endeavour itself to give answer to them, as it intended in the Constitution *Gaudium et Spes* and in the encyclical letter *Populorum Progressio*, it has to open a new chapter of pastoral and theological epistemology. Instead of starting only from the data of Revelation and Tradition, as classical theology has usually done, it will be necessary to start from the data and problems coming from the world and history. It is less easy. (Congar 1967, 72)

It is indeed less easy because it implies that the pastoral theologian cannot be satisfied with the peaceful atmosphere of the libraries but has to be inspired by the example of Yahweh, who said to Moses: "I have observed the misery of my people" (Ex 3:7). Theology has to be freed from its academic captivity by the university, and theologians have to be in closer contact with the daily life of the very people for whom their theology is destined, as all the theologians of liberation claim (Segundo 1976, 7–38). Even if difficult, the advantages of such insertion are obvious.

First of all, it follows the pattern of the formation of the Bible, which was the lived history of a community before it became a written document. We can never forget that even the *lectio* was human experience before being put into writing as a text.

Second, it also follows the model of Incarnation, because it allows the theologian a direct verification of the data by personally participating in the situation from within, even if his or her condition is not identical to the condition of those who are victims of the situation. The pastoral theologian becomes a witness, thus earning greater credibility. This is why the value of personal presence in the concrete social situation is today so much praised by the world of communications.

There is still a greater advantage, and it is the impact of the lived situation on the pastoral theologian. Without compromising the objectivity of his or her theological reflection, it is clear that the lived experience creates in the pastoral theologian a new motivation and a new commitment to doing theology.

Finally, the style of pastoral theology, either oral or written, may be also affected because it can become a narrative theology closer to the history style than to the conventional language of the manuals, a theology illustrated, confirmed, and seasoned by the historical memory of concrete events and circumstances. A good example of this narrative style is the well-known book of Fr. Jacques Dournes, SJ, *Dieu aime les païens*, in which his reflections about missiology are the visible fruit of a lifetime of experience among the peoples of Vietnam (1967). We can say the same thing of many of the theologians of liberation.

One Objection

Someone at this point could raise the objection that the insertion into a human situation from the very beginning can cause such an impact on the theologian that it can easily create a bias and diminish the objectivity of the subsequent theological reflection.

The background of this objection is the presumption that a method, in order to be valid, should be absolutely neutral and objective. It is the dream of a totally value-free methodology and a value-free science. Though objectivity and truth are indeed to be respected in all sciences, we cannot ignore the fact that the personal motivation and experiential background of the researcher is part and parcel of that "objectivity," as M. Heiddegger demonstrated with his theory of the hermeneutical circle, that is, the intimate relationship established between the reader and the text.

According to Heidegger, there is a certain pre-comprehension in the reader, caused by his or her own cultural and social background. This pre-comprehension affects his or her comprehension of the text. On the other hand, the text transforms the reader's own pre-comprehension. There is nothing revolutionary in this approach. Thomas Aquinas had established long before the Scholastic principle *Quidquid recipitur ad modum recipientis recipitur.* Theology is essentially a process of ongoing reinterpretation.

The practical consequence of acknowledging that the experience of the theologian may affect the theological content is a positive value, namely, the pluralism in theology. As a matter of fact, we have to admit that today we are far from considering theology as philosophy was once considered, as a sort of *theologia perennis.* The word of God remains forever because the words of the Lord "will not pass away" (Mt 24:35), but our theological interpretations and the living tradition of the church may change and improve. This pluralism today is a fact that no longer can be controlled, but it should not be envisaged as a threat to the unity of Christian faith or to the unity of the church itself (Rahner 1974, 3–23).

Practical Challenges

The first challenge here is for university professors, who, without losing their scientific rigor and method, need to liberate themselves from the ivory tower. To be credible, professors of pastoral theology need to be connected to the actual life of the local church. What the Second Vatican Council affirmed of theology in general has a particular application to pastoral theology: "Theological research while it deepens knowledge of revealed truth, should not lose contact with its own times" (*Gaudium et spes*, no. 62). A social theology is not just a theology dealing with social topics but rather a theology that is in permanent dialogue with society (Lane 1984).

The challenge is also present for students, who cannot do without a "pastoral fieldwork" as a necessary frame of reference for their own theological reflection. A final examination on pastoral theology has to reveal whether the students can analyze concrete situations and not just give back to the teacher the ready-made answers from the manuals (denounced by Paulo Freire as "banking education" [1971]).

Social Analysis

The second step of the pastoral circle is usually called social analysis. By this we mean analysis of the social situation—its structures and the root causes of problems—as completely as possible. This complex task calls for the use of human sciences, among which sociology plays a preponderant though not exclusive role. Anthropology, psychology, history, political science, and economics also play a crucial role in this analysis.

The legitimacy and necessity of the dialogue between theology and social sciences proposed by the Second Vatican Council is no longer a *quaestio disputata* but an acquired pedagogical principle (Gutiérrez 1990). It is good, however, to recall the words of the council when referring specifically to the planning of pastoral action: "In pastoral care sufficient use should be made not only of theological principles but also of secular sciences, especially psychology and sociology" (*Gaudium et spes*, no. 62). Here the contribution of the pastoral circle is obvious and does not need long elaboration. The challenge, however, is more in the practical field of teaching because the initiation to social analysis, as it was described above, implies an initiation to the disciplines involved in it. The pastoral theologian has to possess a fundamental knowledge of those sciences, without necessarily mastering all of them. What is practically impossible is that the pastoral theology professor alone may adequately initiate the students to all of them. Here interdisciplinary collaboration is necessary.

Of course, we must make a distinction between pastoral theology taught at a major seminary level and pastoral theology taught at a university level. Whereas for the major seminary a global and fundamental initiation to human sciences may suffice, at the university level the faculty of pastoral theology has to enter into interdisciplinary dialogue with those human sciences and organize its own curriculum accordingly. This is a serious academic challenge that perhaps may explain the fact that there are rather few faculties of pastoral theology at the university level in the world.

On the other hand, the initiation to those human sciences is not the responsibility of pastoral theology alone; they should constitute part and parcel of the philosophical preparation for theology. In order to introduce in theology a methodology that is more inductive than deductive, it is necessary to introduce at the same time a change of methodology and contents in the programs of philosophical studies preparing for it, as the Second Vatican Council recommended when referring to the philosophical formation of the candidates to priesthood in major seminaries: "They should be taught to use correctly the aids provided by pedagogy, psychology and sociology" (*Optatam totius*, no. 20). In the past the Scholastic tradition considered philosophy the "handmaid of theology." Today, in the interdisciplinary world of sciences, nobody is boss and nobody is handmaid, but human sciences are a necessary complement for theology, especially for pastoral theology.

Theological Reflection

The third step of the pastoral circle is known as theological reflection. Here, too, there is a contrast between the method of this reflection proposed by the pastoral circle and the traditional way of doing theological reflection. This tradition gave a priority to the deductive approach, or *dicta probantia* drawn from the scripture, as Karl Rahner underlines: "The theologians of the generation before our own went about their work in a theological territory which was already defined for them, one with which they were familiar. . . . They developed their scholastic theology along lines which were already determined by tradition. It was a sort of 'Denzinger Theology,' and they were convinced that they had at their disposal in the practice of this a sufficiency of clear, exegetically unassailable *dicta probantia*" (Rahner 1974, 70–71).

The simple and mechanical deduction of theological truths from selected texts of scripture is regarded very cautiously by theologians today because the text may become just a pretext to prove a particular idea. This way of proceeding may lead to a fundamentalist reading of the Bible. The same applies to the use of the texts of the magisterium, which, as with any other texts, have to be submitted to the same basic laws of hermeneutics.

The question here is not to choose between deduction and induction as if they were opposed and irreconcilable but to reach a balance in using them. The teaching of theology and all our catechetical methodology so far have followed the deductive approach. The Second Vatican Council, however, used the inductive approach in the pastoral constitution *Gaudium et spes* under the form of analysis. Since then this approach not only has been acknowledged but is recommended by the church itself even at the level of catechesis.

The inductive method had already been recommended by the Congregation for the Clergy in its document *General Directory for Catechesis* in 1971 (see no. 72). In the revised edition of 1997, when dealing with the inductive method, the *Directory* says:

> It is a method which has many advantages, because it conforms to the economy of Revelation. It corresponds to a profound urge of the human spirit to come to knowledge of unintelligible things by means of visible things. It also conforms to the characteristics of knowledge of the faith, which is knowledge by means of signs. The inductive method does not exclude the deductive method. Indeed it requires the deductive method which explains and describes facts by proceeding from their causes. The deductive synthesis, however, has full value, only when the inductive process is completed. (1997, no. 150)

The Special Theological Relevance of Catholic Social Teaching

At this stage of theological reflection it seems important to call attention to Catholic social teaching, one particular aspect of the magisterium of the church that has developed in a more systematic way since Leo XIII in 1891 with his encyclical letter *Rerum novarum*. It seems that despite all efforts made so far, Catholic social teaching still remains in major seminaries and even in faculties of theology "our best kept secret," as stated by Peter Henriot and his collaborators (DeBerri et al. 2003).

The positive reason for recommending the integration of Catholic social teaching at this point is not that it provides "ready-made theology" and universal solutions for all situations, but that Catholic social teaching is in itself a tool and a very sound guide for theological reflection on concrete situations. As Pope Paul VI explained:

> In the case of such different situations, it is difficult to say a single word or to propose a solution which will work everywhere. Such is neither our ambition, nor our mission. It is up to the Christian communities to analyze objectively the situation in their own country, to throw light on it using the immutable words of the Gospel, to draw ideas, norms for judgment and action plans for further action in the social teachings of the Church as it developed through the years. (*Octogesima adveniens,* no. 4)

Pope John XXIII, speaking in 1961 about the method of implementing Catholic social teaching, explicitly referred to the methodology of "see, judge, and act" long before the pastoral circle was proposed as a methodology:

> The teachings in regard to social matters for the most part are put into effect in the following three stages: first, the actual situation is examined; then, the situation is evaluated carefully in relation to these teachings; then only is it decided what can and should be done in order that the traditional norms may be adapted to circumstances of time and place. These three steps are at times expressed by these three words: observe, judge, act. (*Mater et magistra,* no. 236)

Planning for Action

The last stage and final purpose of the pastoral circle is to plan for a new pastoral praxis of the church. What can be the impact of this stage in the teaching of pastoral theology? It is clear that at the academic level of the major seminary or the faculty of theology in which there are students coming from diverse social and ecclesial contexts, the purpose of pastoral theology cannot be to offer them a pastoral plan applicable to their own local churches. Here the purpose of pastoral theology is rather to initiate the students in the principles and methodology of strategic planning applied to the pastoral field.

What is, however, more important is that pastoral action is not just an appendix to the whole process but the purpose of it. Pastoral theology is not motivated by an intellectual desire for theoretical knowledge alone but by the desire to evaluate and of improve the praxis of the church, "which, in a word, is called evangelization" (*Evangelii nuntiandi,* no. 14).

This makes pastoral theology a practical science, motivated by praxis and oriented toward praxis. It is not just a reflection on the praxis of the church, even on the intellectual praxis, as a subject matter but a critical reflection oriented to improve it in the future. Theology in general was oriented in the past only to gain a better understanding of faith. In modern times, thanks to the contribution of liberation theologians, theology is not only oriented toward a better understanding of faith but also toward a transformation of the world in the light of faith, that is, toward Christian praxis (Sobrino 1984, 7–38; Boff 1987, 221–31).

This fundamental orientation toward praxis is far from leading into an easy pragmatism. The reason is that the critical reflection on praxis is addressed by pastoral theology, first of all, to the praxis of the academy itself, that is, to the ways of doing and teaching theology today at the university. In this respect pastoral theology has to be faithful to its role among the theological disciplines, a role comparable to the role of a watchdog, which is supposed to alert the theological academy whenever there is danger of becoming isolated from the "joys and hopes, the grief and anguish of the people of our time, especially of those who are poor or afflicted" (*Gaudium et spes,* no. 1). A sound faculty or department of pastoral theology, which is faithful to its vocation, should keep the whole university body alive and alert.

Conclusion

Our purpose was to show the possible impact of using the pastoral circle in the teaching of pastoral theology. It is our hope that this impact has appeared clear and challenging not only in the field of pastoral theology but also, to some extent, in the teaching of other theological disciplines.

Some may think that whatever we have said here concerning the need for insertion in human situations and the need for a more inductive approach in introducing theological reflection may not be applicable to dogmatic and moral theology or to the teaching of scripture. It is true that the concern for the continuous renewal of the praxis of the church makes the pastoral circle more directly relevant for pastoral theology. However, the concern to start examining human situations first before going to look for solutions, the concern to be in an existential dialogue with the human society of our times, and the concern for the praxis of evangelization should be fundamental attitudes for all the fields of theology.

"Christ is the answer" is a popular slogan of the pentecostal church here in Africa. To that we could reply, "Of course, Christ is the answer, but what is the question?" In order to illustrate how the lack of concern for the human question may affect the whole world of theology and scripture, the history of the church, and even canon law, let me finish with a historical anecdote drawn from my personal experience of our staff meetings in one of the faculties of theology in which I have taught.

One of my colleagues, an eminent professor of Christology, was complaining about the students' lack of interest in his course. I asked him one question: "What are the major difficulties or problems your students have concerning the person of Christ?" He replied without hesitation: "I have no idea. I have to cover a vast and dense academic program in one semester. . . . I have no time to waste in asking this kind of personal question of the students."

Without asking further questions I immediately understood why the students were not interested in his course. I also understood something still more important: the greatest obstacle for the application of the methodology of the pastoral circle in the teaching of theology does not come from any serious objection from the academy or from the magisterium but from the lack of personal change of attitude on the part of the professor. Here, again, as in all aspects of Christian life, conversion is always required.

References

Boff, Clodovis. 1987. *Theology and praxis*. Maryknoll, NY: Orbis Books.

Chenu, Marie-Dominique. 1964. *Toward understanding St. Thomas*. Chicago: Regnery.

Congar, Yves-Marie. 1967. *Situation et tâches présentes de la théologie*. Paris: Les Editions du Cerf.

DeBerri, Edward, James Hug, Peter Henriot, and Michael Schultheis. 2003. *Catholic social teaching: Our best kept secret*. Maryknoll, NY: Orbis Books; Washington, DC: Center of Concern.

Dournes, Jacques. 1967. *Dieu aime les païens*. Paris: Aubier.

Freire, Paulo. 1971. *Pedagogy of the oppressed*. New York: Herder and Herder.

Gutiérrez, Gustavo. 1990. Theology and the social sciences (1984). In *The truth shall make you free: Confrontations*, 53–84. Maryknoll, NY: Orbis Books.

Hellwig, Monika K. 1982. *Whose experience counts in theological reflection?* Milwaukee, WI: Marquette Univ. Press.

Kasper, Walter. 1968. *The methods of dogmatic theology*. New York: Paulist Press.

Lane, Dermot. 1984. *Foundations for social theology*. New York: Paulist Press.

Rahner, Karl. 1971. Some critical thoughts on functional specialties in theology. In *Foundations of theology*, edited by Philip McShane, 194–96. Dublin: Gill and MacMillan.

———. 1974. Reflections on methodology in theology. *Theological investigations*, vol. 11. New York: Crossroad.

Segundo, Juan Luis. 1976. *The liberation of theology*. Maryknoll, NY: Orbis Books.

Sobrino, Jon. 1984. *The true church and the poor*. Maryknoll, NY: Orbis Books.

Schuster, Heinz. 1965. The nature and function of pastoral theology. In *(Pastoral theology) The pastoral mission of the church*, edited by Karl Rahner, 4–9. Concilium 3.

9

Teaching Missiology in Context

Adaptations of the Pastoral Circle

MADGE KARECKI

In the South African context the relationship between theology and life has been an uneasy one, but nevertheless, even in such a twisted and oppressive context, theology was an integral part of apartheid society. The Dutch Reformed Church played a major role in shaping the theological foundation for the political justification of apartheid. The use of a biblical theology to justify the systematic oppression of people of color under apartheid has caused and continues to cause people to be suspicious of the role theology might play in shaping life in post-apartheid South Africa.

Missiology as taught at the University of South Africa (UNISA) seeks to heal the rift between theology and life by using a praxis-based approach mission in its modules.[1] I use adapted versions of Holland's and Henriot's pastoral circle. Their innovative approach of rooting theology in a local context and of using social analysis to gain insight into the problems facing society has been and continues to be the inspiration at work within the three missiology modules discussed in these pages. The use of the pastoral circle was introduced as a means to enable students to *do* rather than simply to *study* missiology. Use of adapted forms of the pastoral circle engages students in ways in which they can make immediate connections between faith and life. What this has meant at Unisa is a change in the way missiology is taught. In this way we seek to be of assistance in the process of transformation that our students undergo in the learning process.

Why Transformation?

Transformation has become an integral part of the South African lexicon. Since the 1994 elections every aspect of South African life has been marked by psychological, political, social, and economic change. Higher education has not been exempted from this process but is an essential means of opening people to a deeper transformation as they take part in various educational experiences. In 1996 the National Commission on Higher Education issued a document that gives the reasons why the transformation of higher education is essential in our post-apartheid context: "The need for transformation stems from two sets of factors: firstly, the profound deficiencies of the present system which inhibit its ability to meet the moral, social and economic demands of the new South Africa; and, secondly, a context of unprecedented national and global opportunities and challenges" (NCHE 1996, 1).

Initial changes served to cultivate the fertile soil in which the process of transformation has taken root, but what we seek to facilitate is a deeper transformation of our students so that they can make a constructive contribution to the building up of South African society and find more credible ways to express their faith.

The pedagogical task of theology in any context is to affirm the deeper dimensions of the human person in relationship to ultimate reality, whether we name that reality God, Allah, YHWH, nirvana, satori, or the Supreme Being. But if personal transformation is true, it always extends outward to embrace the historical and social contexts of life. In this way theology does not give answers to questions about ultimate reality but only provides road maps for the journeys of exploration into the source of being and unity and ethical living in the world. It is what Groome calls "doing theology on our feet" (1987, 3). Such an approach provides people with the tools to understand what is happening in the depths of their being, to discern the events shaping the society in which they live and their response in differing contexts that have been shaped by historical events. They become the acting subjects of theology, not its passive objects (Freire 1970).

Higher theological education can do this when the educator facilitates this process through learning experiences that open possibilities for growth in knowledge and understanding. Learning becomes transformative as students grapple with their assumptions about faith and life and begin to understand their experience through a process of critical theological reflection on their own faith history as rooted in a particular context. When this happens, we have the makings of transformative and liberative education (Moore 1991, 164).

Holland and Henriot conceived the pastoral circle "to describe social analysis and its relevance to social justice action, to provide illustrations of analytical approaches to various problems and to explore suggestions and questions they raise for pastoral responses" (1980, 2), not as a teaching tool. It has nevertheless proved effective in enabling students to do missiology in context. By using the cycle, students begin to see that change is possible; with it they and their communities can do something to change their reality so that it reflects principles of justice and integrity.

In my teaching at Unisa I have tried to respond to these challenges by implementing the use of what I have called the cycle of mission praxis (Karecki 1999, 10). Though inspired by the pastoral circle, I decided to use the word *cycle* because it connotes a more dynamic movement within a process that is not only used once, but over and over as students do missiology in the context of their local situation.

Over a three-year period I adapted the cycle for use in three undergraduate modules that I designed. The cycle is presented as an interpretative tool for understanding and analyzing different aspects of mission. Each cycle is intended to help students develop a contextual approach to mission.

The aim of the three modules is to facilitate a reflexive mode of learning in which students are asked continually to relate missiological study material with the context in which their own mission praxis takes shape. This kind of reflection creates order out of experience. Students are able to create a system of meaning that contributes to the larger context of meaning within their specific social and cultural contexts (Jarvis 1993, 9). This is a movement "from the anecdotal to the analytical" (Holland and Henriot 1980, 4), as students learn to analyze different aspects of their lives and the contexts in which they live as well as the historical, social, and economic factors that shaped their contexts. When this happens, the students are able to work with others to make creative responses that address immediate as well as long-term issues.

Patterns of Mission Praxis

What I call the cycle of mission praxis is presented as an interpretative tool in the first-level compulsory missiology module *Patterns of Mission Praxis* (Karecki 1999, 10). All students who register for a bachelor of theology degree are required to take this module. Over the past several years we have found that this module has helped to change the perception that mission is done among other peoples and in other countries to one in which mission is done in every local context. Put quite simply, the aim of this module is not only to enable students to study missiology, but to facilitate a process in which they learn to do missiology in context, thus linking faith and life.

In this first-level missiology module students are led gently but systematically through a process of reflection on narratives that illustrate different ways that people engage in mission. This approach was chosen because it enables students to enter the world of other people in a way that is accessible to them. The majority of stories are of South Africans, so that students have a sense of familiarity with them. These are people they have read about in the newspaper, heard about on the radio or television, or learned about in history, like Albertina Sisulu, Francina Mofokeng, Trevor Huddleston, or Desmond Tutu. Other narratives introduce the students to people who have played a significant role in shaping the mission praxis, such as Robert de Nobili or Ntsikana. The cycle is then used as an analytical tool that students apply to the narratives. The learning experience is punctuated with activities in which they are asked to apply what they are learning to their own context through a project that is done in their local community with other members of that community. The metaphor that forms the framework for the module is that of journey. This in itself suggests change. The process respects the students' initial understanding of mission but seeks to broaden and deepen their ability to appreciate a variety of approaches to mission praxis.

The narrative approach works well because first-year missiology students are still suffering from the effects of an educational system that has not equipped them with the necessary skills to engage in learning that requires critical thinking and creativity. This approach initiates students into a method of doing missiology that starts in their immediate context and their own historical setting.

Figure 9–1. Cycle of Mission Praxis

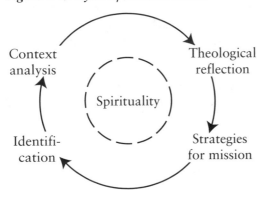

This cycle gives students a sense of agency as they begin a process of critically reflecting on the world around them. Their concept of mission is enlarged and deepened in the act of identification. Luzbetak defines identification as being in *communion* and in *communication* with the local community (1988, 215–16). Identification presupposes active participation in the community's life so that a sense of solidarity is built up among the members. It requires the building of "webs of relationships" (Geertz 1973) in which empathy and interdependence are nurtured and sustained. Relying on the feedback of students and my own experience, I maintain that this is more than insertion (Holland and Henriot 1983, 8–9). Students begin to see mission as a theological enterprise that is rooted in their own lives rather than something that happens in another place with other people. They are progressively led to develop the capacity to identify with the people who live and work in their community. It may be their community of faith, but it might also be the larger area of their neighborhood. Students are deliberately asked to begin this process of the construction of knowledge with an act of self-transcendence that is a deep shift in their frame of reference (Daloz 2000, 104). They are drawn out of themselves and into the life of the community, where their knowledge will be shared and where they will learn from those people with whom they interact.

The second stage in the cycle is that of context analysis. Through critical reflection on their context students begin to relate historical, social, economic, cultural, and political factors and see how they have shaped and continue to shape their immediate environment. The problems and needs of their contexts come in sharper focus by having students tap into "collective experience to arrive at a tentative best judgment" (Mezirow 2000, 11).

A word needs to be said about critical reflection. If analysis is going to be worthwhile and lead to creative action, it must be evaluative, hence critical. This is a "process of using a prior interpretation to construe a new or revised interpretation of the meaning of one's experience as a guide to future action" (Mezirow 2000, 5). The students use data previously compiled by others, critically reflect on it with the use of key questions so as to construct meaning that will result in an awareness of their own assumptions about their context (Mezirow 2000, 4). Mezirow contends that such critical reflection results in a change of perspective that facilitates action:

> Perspective transformation is the process of becoming critically aware of how and why our assumptions have come to constrain the way we perceive, understand, and feel about our world; changing these structures of habitual expectation to make possible a more inclusive, discriminating and integrating perspective; and finally, making choices or otherwise acting upon these new understandings. (Mezirow 1991, 167)

Such a process initiates a dialogue between the internal and external worlds of the students. They are led to see the interrelationship between analysis and theological reflection (Garrison 1992, 139).

Theological reflection is the third stage in the cycle of mission praxis. At this stage students bring into play the resources of their own faith tradition. Their critical reflection is done with the help of the lens of the sacred writings and teachings that shape their faith and theological understandings as individuals, but also as members of faith communities. They begin to develop what Farley calls a *habitus* for doing theology. He defines *habitus* as "a cognitive disposition and orientation of the soul, a knowledge of God and what God reveals." The context in which the student lives and works is the "geography," that is, the place that shapes analysis, but it is the faith experience of the student and the local community that creates the *habitus*, the capacity for theological reflection (Farley 1983, 35).

Habitus is more than subjective reframing and creative application of the resources of their faith. It is a deliberate and sustained dialogue in which the information gained in analysis is "brought to bear upon the situation, raises new questions, suggests new insights, and opens new responses" (Holland and Henriot 1980, 4) so that they can be brought to bear in the individual contexts of the students. It is often an emotional experience because students begin to reassess how they understand the relationship between faith and life and how theology supports a deeper form of reflection that either validates faith or challenges it. This kind of theological reflection clearly leads to action.

This kind of praxis-oriented learning is real and meaningful and engages students as whole persons. In this cycle, analysis and critical reflection lead to the development of strategies for mission. This stage of the cycle empowers students to take responsibility for mission in their own contexts. Once again the students are brought into a process of collaborative learning as missiological/theological responses are worked out that address real problems and situations of injustice in their contexts. Students interface their responses with the needs of their context and the viewpoints of members of their community. They are no longer receptacles being filled with the theological formulations but agents of change who participate in the *missio Dei* to bring justice, harmony, and the reign of God to bear upon the societies in which they live. In this process students become "socially responsible, clear-thinking decision makers" (Mezirow 2000, 8) who can act in ways that are integrated with the beliefs of their faith tradition.

Perhaps the most significant addition and adaptation to the pastoral circle lies at the center of the cycle of mission praxis. In an effort to enable students to develop the capacity for reflecting on their own motivation for mission, I have placed spirituality at the center of the cycle (see Figure 9–1). It is encircled with a broken line because it permeates every stage of the cycle. Spirituality informs the deeper motivation out of which people live and students are led through reflective activities to get in touch with their experience of ultimate reality.

In his book *To Know as We Are Known*, Parker Palmer makes a plea for what he calls "an education in transcendence" (1983, 13). He advocates a type of education that enables students to see beyond themselves and superficial appearance in order to grasp the deeper, hidden realities of life. Mechthild Hart and Deborah Holton (1993), two experienced adult educators, take a similar stance toward education and urge educators to help students to grow in their capacity for self-reflection.

Self-reflection is not an escape from the realities of life but a way to help students look at life at a deeper level. Interior spaces need to be created within a person so that the individual can engage in what Hart and Holton name "reflective withdrawal" (1993, 245). This is not to be confused with fleeing from reality or indifference to the needs in society. This kind of withdrawal is a necessity in emancipatory and transformative learning because it engages a person at the deepest level of identity. It has to do not with questions of function or skills but rather with meaning. It creates an inner awareness of true identity. The aim of such self-reflection is growth in the capacity to make meaning in a person's life. When an individual is able to reflect on his or her life and actions, there is growth in reflexive competency.

The person is then able to integrate real-life experiences in more meaningful ways. This is important because

> the shape of our knowledge becomes the shape of our living; the relation of the knower to the known becomes the relation of the living self to the larger world. And how could it be otherwise? We have no self apart from our knowledge of the self, no world apart from our knowledge of the world. The way we interact with the world in knowing becomes the way we interact with the world as we live in it. . . . The images of self and world that are found at the heart of our knowledge will also be found in the values by which we live our lives. (Palmer 1983, 21)

Spirituality is at the heart of our knowledge: of self, of the world, of others, of God. This is a type of knowledge that ushers us into a process which "decenters the ego where the self no longer obstructs us and where we can enter into other people's concerns with genuine interest" (Hart and Holton 1993, 248). This is the theological enterprise at its best. It engenders a shift from a concern for the self to what the self, inspired by faith, can do for the world. This is the kind of deeper transformation that theology can occasion if it is taught in a transformative way.

The addition of spirituality in no way diminishes the insights of Holland and Henriot, but rather, I think, enriches praxis because spirituality is "the inner heart of the whole enterprise" (Kritzinger 2002, 168). Putting spirituality at the center of the cycle of mission praxis simply acknowledges that all authentic mission needs to be informed and shaped by a spirituality that is infused with the grace of the Holy Spirit; then it is truly an expression of the *missio Dei.*

Still More Adaptations

Since that first cycle of mission praxis, I have created the cycles of cultural discernment, of Christian identity, and of interreligious encounter. In each one spirituality is at the center. This is a new dimension to missiology at Unisa and an addition to the original pastoral circle of Holland and Henriot. It is an attempt to present spirituality as multifaceted and motivational, not escapist and otherworldly; it invites students to look at life from a deeper perspective so that each learning experience becomes an invitation to deeper growth and development. Spirituality holds a central position in each of the cycles I have created because it is not a stage in each process but a motivational source that makes for a unique application in each context depending on who is using the cycle. To gain a better appreciation of how the cycles are used, it is necessary to say something about how the cycles are used in each of the modules.

Intercultural Christian Communication

The metaphor that shaped the module Intercultural Christian Communication as a theology of intercultural communication is "the person as mystery." In such a culturally diverse country as South Africa people often fear those who are different from themselves. I wanted to challenge students to take another perspective: seeing others as mysteries, not as problems or enemies. Like the cycle of mission praxis, the cycle of cultural discernment begins with the stage of identification. Since this is an advanced-level module,[2] the activities and assignments are more complex. In a developmental process students are taught principles of good intercultural communication, and they are made aware of barriers to it. To do this, each learner is asked to choose a learning partner of another cultural background so that both can learn firsthand about a culture other than their own.

At the second stage of the cycle, cultural analysis, students seek to understand "webs of significance" that form the culture fabric of the culture of their learning partner. They are guided by a series of questions that they ask of their learning partner. Through a serious and systematic look at a culture, students begin to learn the limitations of an etic (outer) view of the culture in comparison of the emic (inner) analysis provided by their learning partner. Some of the areas of cultural analysis that are considered are world view, foundational myths, symbols, gender differences, power distance, individualist versus collectivist stances, immediacy, privacy, work ethic, and the value of time. Stress is put on the need to make a tentative analysis of the culture that is brought into dialogue in sharing sessions with the learning partner.

Cultural analysis leads into the third stage of the cycle, missiological reflection. This stage is informed by four missiological issues raised at the 1996 meeting of the World Council of Churches:

- Christians should become "doers of the Word" (Jas 1:22) in every culture through culturally sensitive praxis-oriented evangelization.
- The church is called to be a community where all cultures can find a home. It cannot be part of power relationships that seek to enhance the power of a dominant group, while minorities are not given sufficient freedom of expression.
- Faith needs to be so incarnated/inculturated by people of a local culture that it can be lived within complex, modern societies in a credible way. Hence the church needs to help people to articulate an indigenous faith language that allows them to express their faith in a context of increasing secularization and globalization.
- Diversity is part of God's plan to reveal the risen Christ present in every culture. Only indigenous people can so incarnate the Gospel that it transforms culture from within. (Karecki 2000, 48)

Such reflection directs students's reflection on the relationship between mission and culture. It leads them to the next stage of the cycle, cultural discernment for mission.

Stories abound about how missionaries imposed their cultural perspectives and values on indigenous peoples. In order to avoid similar occurrences students need to develop the skill of cultural discernment. This kind of action is meant to lead to a deeper assessment of one's own culture or the culture in which one is living. In this way we take a sobering yet hopeful look at a specific culture. This is necessary because though the gospel needs to be incarnated in every culture, its incarnation takes different forms in every culture. It can support as well as challenge cultural values. It does this whenever people of faith have integrated their belief in Christ and manifest Christ's presence in their lives.

Using gospel accounts of Jesus crossing cultural boundaries (Lk 5:29–32; 7:36–50; and 14:12–14) as a backdrop, students seek to formulate answers to questions about the relationship between faith and culture. Some of the questions that are meant to inform their discernment are:

- Where are signs of God's presence at work in this culture?
- What cultural values can be enriched by the Gospel?
- What cultural values militate against the teachings of Jesus?
- Is there anything inhibiting questions of faith from entering public discourse about cultural values?
- Where do gospel values and cultural values lead to different actions?
- Is there an uncritical alliance between religious and cultural vested interests in political power?
- Who holds the power in this culture?
- Who remains voiceless in this culture?

Cultural discernment leads to deeper levels of identification and more authentic Christian witness that is founded on well-researched analysis, missiological reflection, and continued cultural discernment. The cycle continues.

One more aspect of this cycle needs to be highlighted because use of the cycle is dependent upon it and also is the fruit of its use. In this module I advocate a contemplative stance toward other people in which they learn the art of cultural discernment so that they can look critically at their own culture and that of their learning partner. The whole process is enhanced because students are asked to arrange to share a meal at the home of their learning partners. In a real-life context they apply analytical tools to "unpack" their experience so that they can learn from it.

Arranging to go to the home of the learning partner involves both humility and vulnerability. Though questions are provided to help students analyze their experience, they often express an overwhelming sense of humility before the graciousness of their learning partner and his or her family. In the context of a meal, new elements of intercultural communication are revealed through the obvious preparations that are made, the forms of greeting that are extended to the students, the food that is shared, and the conversation that ensues. Most students feel quite vulnerable as their relationship moves to a new level of familiarity and camaraderie. This step across boundaries adds new dimensions to their learning experience.

Intercultural communication in the setting of a meal leads them to a deeper appreciation of the mystery of the person before them. Differences are no longer barriers but expressions of the rich diversity that exists in the human family. Lines of communication across cultures are indeed possible, and the implications for building up intercultural communities become apparent in ways that could never have been imagined without a praxis-oriented approach to the study of missiology.

Dynamics of Interreligious Encounter

The third learning experience I have had an opportunity to design took shape in the module entitled Dynamics of Interreligious Encounter. The metaphor that brings unity and coherence to the module is pilgrimage. In this module students ask a pilgrim companion to share their learning pilgrimage with them. This time it is a person of another faith tradition. They are called pilgrim companions because they are in themselves "places" of pilgrimage where students can encounter faith in another, very tangible form. The idea behind this requirement is that many times generalizations are made about people of other faiths: *all* Buddhists do this; *all* Muslims behave like that; *all* adherents of African Traditional Religion believe this; *all* Jewish people are like that. I wanted to show that faith is embodied in and expressed by individuals. In this way it becomes more difficult to write people off because they have different beliefs.

In this study guide I have used two cycles: the first helps students reflect on their knowledge of and commitment to the Christian faith as they experience it within their own denomination. The second cycle prepares students for interreligious encounters with people of other faiths.

Through the use of the first, the cycle of Christian identity, I want them to feel secure in their identity as Christians so that they are not threatened when they enter into an interreligious relationship. The cycle again begins with identification, but this time it has to do with the sense of belonging students have to their Christian tradition. During the analysis stage students examine their level of commitment and involvement in their Christian denomination. At the stage of theological reflection students are asked to consider the impact that their faith commitment has in their life. Students are led to reflect critically on how the values inherent in Christianity are manifested in the choices they make. The action stage is called living with faith. Here students are asked to plan actions that will strengthen their Christian identity. They are asked to formulate strategies that will help them become more committed members of the church. Reflection questions are provided for each stage, but because this is also an advanced-level module, students are expected to take initiative in using the cycle as a way to prepare for encountering a person of another faith tradition.

A second cycle is used to aid students in the development of a level of competence that will serve them well in the process of developing a relationship with a pilgrim companion. This happens in two ways: through the use of the cycle of interreligious encounter and interaction with characters in a novel. Since interreligious dialogue is such a significant part of mission, I felt that a creative approach was needed to highlight its importance. Since the majority of Unisa's missiology students come from evangelical Christian denominations, I needed to come up with learning experiences that would respect their religious backgrounds while stretching their ability to be open to people of other faiths.

I wanted to find a way to invite students to analyze different approaches to mission that would help them grow in their competency to relate to people of other faiths. In order to do this I chose the novel *The Poisonwood Bible* by Barbara Kingsolver (1998). Through this story students would experience some dimensions of interreligious and intercultural relating. They could vicariously experience interreligious encounters and be able to analyze them by applying what they were learning from the study material. Kingsolver's novel is set in the Democratic Republic of the Congo during the years of struggle for self-governance. The main characters are Pastor Nathan Price, his wife, daughters, and various people of the village of Kilanga. They become the interlocutors of the students and reveal different ways to engage in mission and evangelization as well as bring out attitudes to African Traditional Religion and African culture. Activities provided in a study guide enable students to interact with the characters of the novel. They discuss different aspects of mission in an interreligious context, write letters to characters to share their feelings about intercultural encounters with them, and learn from them about how to be respectful participants in interreligious encounters.

The study materials include a collection of articles dealing with various aspects of interreligious encounter and information about other world religions. The aim of this module is to enable students to relate to people of other faith traditions with sensitivity and respect. It seeks to empower students by equipping them with the tools necessary to reflect in a missiological way about interreligious encounters in the South African and global contexts. The cycle of interreligious encounter seeks to ready the students for their encounters with their pilgrim companions and the people they will meet through them (Karecki 2001, 67).

Those familiar with the theology of Bernard Lonergan will recognize my application of his method of doing theology in the adaptation of this fourth cycle. The beginning stage of the cycle of interreligious encounter is being attentive. At this stage students are asked to become aware of themselves and their ability to listen not only to the words spoken by their pilgrim companions but also for the meaning they hold for the person. Max Warren's "A Theology of Attention" is required reading that forms the theological basis for this stage.

The second stage of this cycle is being open. Openness does not imply being wishy-washy about one's own faith. It simply means a willingness to learn from another and to let go of the need to have all the answers. Emphasis is placed on openness so that the students take the stance of someone who is a lifelong learner.

Being reflective is the focus of the third stage of this cycle. Reflection is the process of making meaning out of the experiences we have in life. Here again the inner and outer world converge. This stage represents a pause in our pilgrimage in order to construct meaning for ourselves about interreligious relationships and their effect on our mission praxis. Without such reflection we can have endless strings of experiences without learning from them in ways that enhance our faith and commitment to mission.

The movement through the cycle brings us to the stage of acting responsibly. In the context of interreligious encounters this means acting with integrity. It requires a high level of honesty about one's own faith commitment while at the same time being respectful of the person of another faith. It implies that partners work together to strengthen areas of common commitment that acknowledge our common humanity and common origin in God. Such responsible action encourages cooperation in action that will enhance the quality of human life and will restore justice in the face of oppression so that all people can experience the blessings of the reign of God (Karecki 2001, 69).

A Pattern Emerges

In the initial encounters that students have with their pilgrim companion there is an element of resistance to relating to a person who comes from another faith. One learner recorded this feeling: "I felt as if I was going against all I had learned about not mixing with people whom we called *heathens*." A young woman wrote that when she told her father that her learning partner was an adherent of African Traditional Religion, he said: "All of that is superstition. Be careful so that they do not put a curse on you." This filled her with a sense of anxiety that only went away after the third time she and her partner met together.

As the relationship develops through a series of encounters, one of which is working together on a social project that is sponsored by the pilgrim companion's faith community, students begin to become fascinated by what they are learning about the other person's faith. One student wrote: "I wanted to stay and listen to my pilgrim companion tell about the different rituals they perform in their homes. I could have stayed all day." After visiting a Buddhist temple, another student, whose pilgrim companion is a Buddhist monk, wrote: "What depth was revealed in our sharing. I am very attracted to their peaceful approach to life and their gentleness." Still another student observed: "My pilgrim companion's whole life is shaped by her faith. I sensed a wholeness about her and the way she lives." Many of the students feel a sense of attraction and are impressed by the commitment their pilgrim companions have to their faith.

The third phase that emerges through these encounters is marked by the students' reassessment of their own faith tradition. One student wrote: "I now feel free to relate to people of other faiths, and I feel more committed to my own. I want to keep learning about other faiths and my own." Still another student wrote: "We need to have more opportunities to meet people of other faiths. I no longer feel threatened by people who believe in another faith." An Anglican priest wrote: "Even in the small town in which I live we don't normally interact with the Imam. Meeting with my pilgrim companion helped to break down many stereotypes I had of Muslims." Another student wrote about the connection between peace and mutual understanding: "If we could see people of other faiths in a new light, we could work together for our communities. I don't have to give up my Christian faith to work together for peace with my Hindu sisters and brothers." It is obvious that such a learning process makes for exciting new areas of growth and development as students grapple with the challenges of living the Christian faith in a multicultural and multireligious world.

Conclusion

The pastoral circle designed by Holland and Henriot in 1980 has borne rich fruit in the missiological curriculum at Unisa. Our modules have become an exciting theological locus where students are introduced to ways of doing theology on their feet because Holland and Henriot shared the pastoral circle with us. Unisa's missiological cycles endeavor to equip students with praxis-oriented tools that continue to be sharpened, honed, and refined as the cycles are used in different ways in various contexts to construct local theologies that are both liberative and transformative.

Notes

[1] All teaching at Unisa is done through printed study materials and/or email. We only meet students in discussion classes or in the context of personal visits and through telephone calls.

[2] The bachelor of theology degree at Unisa comprises thirty modules. Students take ten compulsory modules and choose twenty from among advanced-level modules. These are selected in terms of the major discipline the student has chosen.

References

Daloz, Laurent. 2000. Transformative learning for the common good. In *Learning as transformation: Critical perspectives on a theory in progress*, edited by Jack Mezirow & Associates, 103–23. San Francisco: Jossey-Bass.

Farley, Edward. 1983. *Theologia: The fragmentation and unity of theological education*. Philadelphia: Fortress Press.

Freire, Paulo. 1970. *Pedagogy of the oppressed*. New York: Herder and Herder.

Garrison, D. R. 1992. Critical thinking and self-directed learning in adult education: An analysis of responsibility and control issues. *Adult Education Quarterly* 42, no. 3: 136–48.

Geertz, Clifford. 1973. *The interpretation of cultures: Selected essays*. New York: Basic Books.

Groome, Thomas. 1987. *Theology on our feet: A revisionist pedagogy for healing the gap between academia and ecclesia*. In *Formation and reflection: The promise of practical theology*, edited by L. S. Mudge and J. N. Poling. Philadelphia: Fortress Press.

Hart, Mechthild, and Deborah Holton. 1993. Beyond God the father and mother: Adult education and spirituality. In *Adult education and theological interpretation*, edited by Peter Jarvis and N. Walters, 237–58. Malabar, FL: L. Krieger Publishing.

Holland, Joe, and Peter Henriot. 1980. *Social analysis: Linking faith and justice*. Washington, DC: Center of Concern.

———. 1983. *Social analysis: Linking faith and justice*. Rev. ed. Maryknoll, NY: Orbis Books; Washington, DC: Center of Concern.

Jarvis, Peter. 1993. Learning as a religious phenomenon? In *Adult education and theological interpretation*, edited by Peter Jarvis and N. Walters, 3–16. Malabar, FL: L. Krieger Publishing.

Karecki, Madge. 1999. *Patterns of mission praxis*. Pretoria: Unisa Press.

———. 2000. *Intercultural Christian communication*. Pretoria: Unisa Press.

———. 2001. *Dynamics of interreligious encounter*. Pretoria: Unisa Press.

———. 2002. Teaching to change the world: Missiology at the University of South Africa. *Missionalia* 30, no. 1: 132–43.

Kingsolver, Barbara. 1998. *The poisonwood Bible*. London: Faber and Faber.

Kritzinger, J. N. J. 2002. A question of mission—a mission of questions. *Missionalia* 30, no. 1: 144–73.

Luzbetak, Louis. 1988. *The church and cultures*. Maryknoll, NY: Orbis Books.

Mezirow, Jack 1991. *Transformative dimensions of adult learning*. San Francisco: Jossey-Bass.

———. 2000. Learning to think like an adult: Core concepts of transformation theory. In *Learning as transformation: Critical perspectives on a theory in progress*, edited by Jack Mezirow and Associates, 3–33. San Francisco: Jossey-Bass.

Moore, M. E. M. 1991. *Teaching from the heart: Theology and educational method*. Minneapolis: Augsburg Fortress Press.

NCHE (National Commission on Higher Education). 1996. *An overview of a new policy framework for higher education transformation*. Available online.

Palmer, Parker J. 1983. *To know as we are known: A spirituality of education*. San Francisco: Harper and Row.

Warren, M. 1971. A theology of attention. In *Face to face: Essays on inter-faith dialogue*, edited by J. V. Taylor, 17–32. London: The Highway Press.

10

Punishment and Liberation

How the Pastoral Circle Transforms Our Theologies

GERRIT SINGGIH

After twenty-five years, thinking about the pastoral circle has changed considerably. But let me share with you how people at the theological faculty, Duta Wacana Christian (Protestant) University, Yogyakarta, Java, Indonesia, understand it. From 1986 to 1994 I taught an undergraduate course on social theology entitled "Church and Society." The main textbook was B. Herry Priyono's translation of *Social Analysis: Linking Faith and Justice* entitled *Analisis Sosial and Refleksi Teologis* (social analysis and theological reflection). In this translation J. B. Banawiratma wrote a foreword that emphasized the significance of culture. According to him, we have to distinguish between social analysis and cultural analysis. The first tries to see the power structures. Here questions are asked about who dominates the decision-making process, who profits from this process, and who loses. Cultural analysis, on the other hand, sees the values, which become the basis for action.

But, of course, you cannot separate these two kinds of analysis. In Indonesia, for instance, feudal culture is related to feudal structure. After insertion (which Banawiratma termed "situated common experience"), the next moment is analysis, in which you do personal analysis, social analysis, and cultural analysis. Social analysis and cultural analysis rely on the insights of the social sciences. Banawiratma does not explain personal analysis, but I think it serves as a bridge between insertion and analysis. If, for instance, you have a privileged position, then you can only follow the pastoral circle in a true sense if you "repent" *(bertobat)*.

Repentance is a religious term that is used mainly in evangelical-fundamentalist Protestant circles, but in Indonesia it is in this process. People who have been through this particular experience could have the same judgmental attitude toward others who are regarded as "unrepentant," meaning those who have not taken the side of the poor. Before, you have the fundamentalist way of dividing the world into two irreconcilable parts, the world of the "saved" and the world of the "unsaved." But if we are not careful, then what you will have is a *materializing* of this fundamentalist attitude in the domain of social theology, in which reality is divided into the world of the poor and the world of the rich. In Indonesia, very often it is not the liberals who become filled with social awareness but the fundamentalists. It is not difficult for them to move from the spiritual realm to the social realm. "Saved" becomes the poor, "unsaved" becomes the rich, and, as such, the rich are destined to be damned in hell.

In Holland and Henriot you find numerous warnings that our analyses and evaluations are not value free. They are all subjective, but it is important not to be stuck in the subjective factor where prejudice is not only acknowledged but given a very high appreciation (Gadamer 1975, 239–40), but to follow the circle or the spiral, in the sense that we must be always *open* to reality, or better, other concepts of reality. Insertion and personal analysis are not the easiest parts of the pastoral circle. Even in the first stage we have to take care not to let people fall into a fundamentalist mentality. Or maybe it is better to say, from the beginning, in our effort to live the preferential option for the poor, we have to prevent a fundamentalist understanding of this concept. We have to struggle to free people from fundamentalist traits, which could turn them into *social* fundamentalists (or if you like, leftist fundamentalists). But on the other hand, we ought to keep the fire, the spirit to fight evil and injustice, the desire to change the world so it will be a better place to live. Concerning the social fundamentalists, I think we have to persuade them to replace their judgmental attitude with a critical attitude. It can be done in a thorough fashion in the third moment.

The third moment, as we all know, is theological reflection, and according to Banawiratma, this is also analysis—*faith* analysis—based on *scriptural* exegesis, using the insights of *theological* science. I think I can understand why Banawiratma chose to combine reflection with analysis. In my experience with my students I discover that although they are theological students, they understand reflection in a narrow way, as a moment of reflection, and in their field reports the section on theological reflection takes only one or two short paragraphs with quotations from one or two biblical texts. Reflection means a short sermon. As modern-day theology students, they do not want to preach to the world, but in a true Marxist spirit, they want to change the world. They have to be persuaded to make a link between their study of theology and their social involvement. They have learned to practice exegesis in a rigorous way. In the same way, they must learn to relate certain texts with their situation.

Because most of them come from religious environments, which rarely see the relationship between spiritual concerns and social concerns, many of the students cannot immediately relate biblical texts with the social situation. The Bible is not related with society but with the church or with prayer fellowships. When they move to a more concrete awareness of the social situation, there is a break between their newly discovered analytical approach, which is based on the social sciences, and their theological beliefs, including their belief in the Bible as a spiritual guide. Most of them are not aware that there are many texts that can be used as points to ponder social injustice. They are used to reading the Bible with a certain spiritual filter, and now, in learning about the pastoral circle, they learn about a new filter, which we can call a social filter. But it takes a considerable effort to make them change filters, in order to be able to read the Bible with social awareness, and moreover, to read the Bible from the perspective of those who are the victims of injustice.

The picture gets more complicated if we take into consideration the tendency for people to become social fundamentalists. Members of Protestant congregations in Indonesia are more or less fundamentalist Christians. Most of the students at the theological faculty are also from these congregations. The gap between social awareness and theological belief concerning the Bible as a spiritual book could result in looking at some texts in a new way, but with dire consequences. Texts containing statements such as "woe to the rich" (Lk 6:24) are understood in a literal way as God's judgment against people who are in better positions than they are. I remember vividly one occasion when I participated in a workshop held in the university's conference center in Kaliurang, near Yogyakarta, in April 1996. As I took a morning stroll near the fish pond, I became aware of cries of excitement in the dining hall, where many participants were already watching television. The presenter had announced: "Our beloved *ibu* Tien Soeharto [the wife of President Soeharto] has suddenly passed away [because of sudden heart failure]." This announcement was followed by news clips of her past activities, and there were also many shots of people crying openly because of shock in hearing this sudden news. What strikes me is that the participants were not showing any sympathy toward the general and his family. They mocked him, threw insulting comments, made jokes about the deceased, and laughed derisively.

Now I am not an admirer of *ibu* (mother) Tien Soeharto. Together with her husband and her children she contributed in no small measure to the suffering of the people. I can also understand why the participants behaved in such a way. Before, she was an all-powerful person; you could not do anything against her. But now she is dead; she cannot do anything against you. Still, I think that what the participants were doing was not right. I think they were unaware of this, because they think that Tien Soeharto could be judged by applying the "woe to the rich" texts to her. God punished her! See here the workings of a "punishment theology." Later on I will elaborate on this theology, but let me end this part by stating that the participants ought to show respect for the dead and for people who mourn their dead. In many cultures of the world the way people handle their dead shows how they appreciate life, and life belongs to human beings. When you cease to regard others as human, even if they are your enemy, then everything is lost.

In this course students are required to do a "live in" for about two weeks in villages within a certain area, which has acute social problems. Usually we chose the western part of Yogyakarta, the Kulon Progo area, or the southern part, the Gunung Kidul area. Under the rule of Soeharto's New Order this enterprise can be risky. Every visit to a different area involves requests for official permits. The local government is usually very suspicious of students who come to live with the people in the villages. With a class of about fifty to seventy-five students (male and female), it takes time and energy to organize the visits. Our partner in this project is the Social Institute of the University, called in Indonesian the LPM. It handles the technical problems of the "live in," and, because it has contacts among the people in the area, the people agree that students can come and live with them. Students are divided into small groups, and they disguise themselves as Bible-study teams that are going to parishes in the country. The congregations in that area are asked to help in harboring the students.

As long as the students are seen as people doing "spiritual activities" among their own and are not involved in proselytizing, then they are usually tolerated and given official permission to stay in the area. The problem comes after they have been through this course. Some of them maintain close contact with the staff of the LPM, whom they admire very much. They start to involve themselves in social work, and not infrequently they return to the place where they did their "live in" in order to participate in the people's struggle to have a better life. Practically, this means helping people to stage protest meetings and marches. In the course of time, the LPM and the university are accused of inciting people to oppose government policy and have to face threats and intimidations. I was once involved in this difficult situation, living for a whole week in fear of being picked up at night by the soldiers.

This shows that living the pastoral circle is not just an academic exercise but also a practice of vocation. After they completed the course entitled "Church and Society," some of my students of their own initiative went to live in the slums of Yogyakarta to express their solidarity with the people. As a result of this, many of them became very ill from contagious diseases. I remember that I literally had to carry one of them out of the slums, before it became too late for him. Seen from the present perspective of a post–New Order period, which in Indonesia is called the Reformation period, I feel proud of my students. They have taken part in the struggle to transform society. Now they are in a different situation. Many have become parish ministers in large cities. But I hope they keep their love for the people and make the effort to relate the "people" and the "people of God" (the congregation). It is the problem of defining this relationship that I want to discuss in the second part of this essay.

The People of God and the People

At that time the course was called "Church and Society" *(Gereja dan Masyarakat,* abbreviated *Germas).* But in the period of the New Order regime the term *masyarakat* was used by social workers as a cover term for "people," which in Indonesian is *rakyat.* The term *rakyat* is discouraged by the officials because in the past it was a popular term in the vocabulary of the Indonesian Communist Party and its sympathizers. Above, I referred to the students disguising themselves as Bible-study leaders, and so we see the use of a term to cover another term. It was a common practice in Indonesia during the totalitarian rule of Soeharto. Because the term "liberation" *(pembebasan)* is anathema, people use the term "independent" *(merdeka,* which during the period of Soeharto's predecessor, Soekarno, was the official term of greeting). But the term "preferential option for the poor" seems to be tolerated and is translated almost literally. The struggle to transform society involves strategies of the poor and weak to survive, and one element that has to be seen in a positive way is fear. There are two kinds of fear: the first is paralyzing fear, and the second is fear indicating the will to live. It is the second kind of fear that ought to be brought into planning of action.

Let us go back to the reference to people above. The course "Church and Society" actually should be named "Church and the People" *(Gereja dan Rakyat).* In this course we want to treat people as subjects and not as objects of research. But the question is, of course, are students, especially *the ology* students, part of the people? In Indonesia students regard themselves (and are regarded) as being apart from the people. During the student riots after 1965 to topple Soekarno, the army and the students were seen as two classes within society that collaborated to defeat the government. Even now, in the Reformation era, many students live in the margins of society and are working (unsuccessfully I think) to create a student revolution to overthrow the present government as "traitors" of the Reformation; they persuade people not to participate in the general election. Most of the theology students are sent by their churches, which also provide their scholarships. Different from the *minjung* theology of South Korea, which regards *all* the oppressed and suffering people as people of God, it is common for Indonesian Protestants to see the congregation *(Jemaah)* as the people of God, which is categorically different from the people.

So it is not easy to place the students in the insertion. Together with the students I discover that in this first moment of the pastoral circle we are not going to learn in an abstract way about people but that we have to translate abstract terms into concrete terms of individual or collective experience.

We are not talking about hunger, unemployment, and injustice generally but are seriously asking ourselves whether we are now hungry, unemployed, or experiencing injustice. After this, in the second moment, we are encouraged to ask why all of these things happen to us. The question why is becoming very important. In the New Order educational policy students were discouraged from asking questions, and as the result of this policy, even now in the post-Soeharto era, it still takes a lot of effort for students to ask analytical questions during class meetings. After the questioning, it is our task to link all the factors that are related to our hunger, our unemployed situation, and our experience of injustice. Later, in the moment of theological reflection, the question why will inevitably be directed to God, and contrary to many assumptions that Indonesians (presumably because of having an Islamic world view) have no theodicy or cannot ask questions that are related to theodicy, we discover that people in the villages are not strangers to the theological problem of relating a powerful God to a good God.

But back to the above question: Are the students hungry, unemployed, or experiencing injustice? Although most of them receive meager scholarships, we can say that they are not hungry, unemployment is not (or is not yet) a problem for them, and as far as I know none of them experiences injustice. From 1998 to 2001, as the result of the economic crisis that started in 1996 and which deeply hurt the people, many become hungry. As a response to this situation, many churches in the urban areas organized "lunch from God" programs. Some of our students, who hitherto were helped financially by their parents, stopped receiving money, because their parents became bankrupt or lost their jobs. The theological faculty issued food coupons for them. But this policy lasted only for about one year. After that the students themselves refused to accept these food coupons and looked for scholarships to continue their life as students.

In general, the situation of the students is better than the people's. One-third of the students at the theological faculty are of Chinese descent. Traditionally, Chinese and Javanese people live apart. It is common in Java to hear stereotypical comments about the Chinese as rich and the Javanese as poor. As many Chinese are also Christians, you often hear a double stereotype: on one hand, there are the Chinese Christians, who are rich; on the other hand, there are the Javanese Muslims, who are poor. Here we see ethnicity as an important social factor, which is not mentioned in *Social Analysis*. In the beginning it is especially hard for the Chinese students to do a "live in" in the villages. But I discovered that their so-called fundamentalist faith enables them to overcome their reluctance and see this venture as a vocational experience. If they are now learning about a social situation by following the pastoral circle, then what is needed is empathy and commitment. The students are not hungry, unemployed, and experiencing injustice, but they want to understand the struggle of the people to overcome their problems and they want to help the people. They are in the villages for only a short time (two weeks). Some maintain contact with the villages (and cause problems for the institution), but most continue with their "normal" activities. So it is important to emphasize to the students that they are in the field as observers, but observers with empathy (participant-observers). They are there to help, but it is important to insist that they not impose their views or their plans on the people. It is their *togetherness* with the people that counts. And as they are theological students who later will become parish ministers, then one of the aims of involvement in the course "Church and Society" is to develop a vision of how a better way of practicing diaconal work could be achieved, based on social analysis and theological reflection.

If they are there as helpers and assistants, how should they do their social analyses and theological reflections? We have seen above how Banawiratma insists on theological reflection including biblical exegesis as an academic discipline. At the same time they must make social analysis of practical experiences. This is a dilemma for the teachers of social theology. On one hand, it is a course run within a higher education institution, and as such, it has to maintain academic standards; on the other hand, the "live in" is done together with the people as subject and for the interests of the people. For the moment, I think that both kinds of work should be done: students should not lose the academic dimension of their work (we can say that this is the theoretical part), but they should also do analysis of their problems from their life experiences, and reflect their faith (in their non-academic Bible studies) starting also from their life experiences. The people's insights become material for the students (the practical part).

In 1991 the theological faculty started its master's program in theology. In this program students are encouraged to do contextual theology. Practical theology becomes very important, and at first there was informal cooperation with several experts in practical theology in the Netherlands to enhance it. Later Duta Wacana undertook formal cooperation with the theological faculty of Nijmegen University, and since then we learned about a version of the pastoral circle (the practical-theological spiral) from Frans Wijsen. Numerous students in practical theology have followed this circle as their way of doing field research. But different from the course "Church and Society" in the undergraduate program, graduate students are not doing a "live in." They do their one-semester field research in an individual way, before, during, or after they follow a course on research methods and one of the subjects of practical theology. Although Wijsen emphasizes that in this circle both theory and practice are important, and that they are in a dialectical relationship, the result is often one sided; students are either too theoretical or too practical. The problem is that students do their field research at a long distance from the university, and so far, there is no way to monitor them in their work. (I am also involved in practical-theology courses in the graduate program, but I must confess that somehow the excitement I felt in the undergraduate "Church and Society" course is not much evident in the graduate research programs.)

The Pastoral Circle and Religious Pluralism

The faculty is still looking for ways to improve the "Church and Society" course. Recently the name was changed to "Social Theology," following the custom of our Catholic Jesuit friends at the neighboring seminary. The content is clear: social involvement and social theory. Besides Joe Holland and Peter Henriot's book, the other main textbook is J. B. Banawiratma and J. Mueller, *Berteologi Sosial Lintas Ilmu* (a cross-disciplinary social theology), which has been translated into several languages. In the analysis part, participant-observation is stressed; in the reflection part, there are points on economy and ecology, development and the kingdom of God, and the culture of poverty. As far as I know, there is still no reference to religious plurality and ethnicity (which is now acknowledged as one of the most acute social problems in Indonesia). We propose to the twelve churches as the owners of the theological faculty (the stakeholders) to lengthen the time of "live in" to become three months, the same length of time that is used for the students to do their practical work in the congregations. Out of theological and/or financial considerations, the churches have refused to accept this proposal. They understand the need to finance students who want to do ecclesiastical practical work, but they cannot comprehend why they have to finance students who want to do social work, which, according to them, is not the concern of the churches.

But one of the reasons for this proposal to lengthen the time of the "live in" has come out of the reflections concerning the context. I have referred above to students who go to the villages disguised as Bible-study leaders. They enter the society through the congregations, which is part of the community. But the aim of the "live in" is to reach out to the people, who are not Christians but Muslims. Many lead a kind of contextualized Muslim life, but they should be identified as followers of Islam, not followers of the Javanese religion, as has often been done in the past by some Christian missiologists. Sometimes students forget their disguise and start to evangelize. They are immediately discouraged by our monitoring team from the LPM, but I can understand that they are doing this because it is their concept of reaching out to non-Christians; mission to others is evangelization aimed at converting people. But even if they are not evangelizing, there is still a gap between their identity as students of a Christian theological institute and the people, who are Muslims and (this is very important, I think) have had several bad experiences with Christian groups who initially came to their areas as social workers or activists but ended up as missionaries. For them, social ministry was a means for mission.

We are lucky not to have participated in the Muslim-Christian conflicts and tensions that have been going on for years in Indonesia, precisely by trying not to mix social theology and missiology. (This, of course, can lead to problems of definition: What is social theology? What is missiology? They are difficult questions. But to give you a picture, although missiology at Duta Wacana, both in the undergraduate and in the graduate programs, is not identical with evangelization, missiology and social theology are taught as different disciplines.)

In Korean *minjung* theology and in some Latin American liberation theology, the people are the poor, and because they are poor, they are regarded as the people of God. This idea is derived from the biblical notion of the kingdom of God, which is not identical with the church. This understanding is different from that of many Christians in Indonesia, who regard themselves as the people of God, and not the others, not even the poor. (In many charismatic congregations that follow a "success theology," the rich are considered the people of God. In the middle of the economic crisis that started in 1997, there are Christians who do not seem to be aware of the crisis or, maybe precisely because of the crisis, tend to show that they are not affected by it. They "witness" to their mainly Muslim neighbors that they are thriving because of their faith as Christians. They put slogans such as "We are a happy family" on their front porches.)

From these liberation theologies we can learn to change our understanding of the people of God, not just by limiting them to the congregations but by including those who are poor, "the least of my brothers." But for the context of Indonesia, even that is not enough. Following Aloysius Pieris, we have to consider seriously two contexts of Asia: poverty and religious plurality (Pieris 1988). Social theology in Indonesia has paid sufficient attention to the context of poverty, but it is only beginning to learn about the context of religious plurality. The "other" is not only the poor, but the Muslim. We have learned to serve the *poor* Muslim, but we still have to learn to serve the *Muslim* poor! From the perspective of religious plurality as the context of Indonesia, I think it is important that we learn to see our congregations not as the people of God but as the disciples of Jesus Christ *(Isa Almasih)*, and *all* the peoples as the people of God.

I have referred to the practice of *diakonia* in the congregations. This practice is almost always the least done, compared with the practices of *koinonia, leitourgia,* and *marturia.* In large urban congregations, in which membership could reach five thousand, members who receive diaconal help may be only around fifty. It is as if the churches are reluctant to acknowledge that the poor are among them. Indonesian churches have to tackle the problem of poverty among Christians. But this problem should not make them neglect the other problem; that is, that non-Christians never become subjects of diaconal service or ministry. They only become recipients when they are seen as showing signs of becoming Christians. One of the aims of the social-theology course is to enable the churches to practice *diakonia* in a wider sense, to become church-community building. But not only that. At the same time, *diakonia* should be transformed to become community building that involves non-Christians. Both church-community building *(Pem-bangunan Jemaat)* and community building *(Pembangunan Masyarakat)* are important parts in the life of the churches.

To give one example of how this could be done, let me share with you the cooperation between the theological faculty and the LPM from 1986 to 1991. In this period the LPM was working with the people in the Gunung Kidul area. This area consists mostly of arid soil and, compared with other areas in the province of Yogyakarta, is very poor. Its inhabitants are usually reluctant to admit where they come from when they are in the city of Yogyakarta. During the dry season, people and cattle suffer from lack of drinking water. In that area small congregations that belong to the Javanese Christian Church live together with their Muslim neighbors. When people from these congregations came to the institute to ask for help to overcome their problem, we convinced them that they cannot do this alone but have to involve the whole community, including the non-Christians who form the majority. This was agreed. Christians and non-Christians then worked together with the LPM as their consultant to install pralon (hard plastic) pipes, which could channel the flow of water from springs high in the hills down to the villages. Committees were organized to regulate the use of this precious drinking water, and members of these committees were both Christians and non-Christians. When it became clear that all in the community benefited from this project, and that Christians did not harbor hidden agendas (doing communal service as "tools" for evangelization and targeting the villagers as would-be converts), relationships improved. Students who were involved in this cooperative project already have a picture of how they are going to do diaconal work when they become congregational leaders. They no longer have to build clinics and design projects *for* the people but *together with* the people; because of this, they have to bring awareness to the members of their congregations that working together with non-Christians is a precondition to restoring a normal relationship with the Muslims, which up to the present time is still in a very bad condition.

Within the perspective of religious pluralism it is, of course, questionable if the Bible can function in the same way as it has functioned in Latin America (De Wit 1991). If non-Christians are involved, then the Bible cannot become the sole source for theological reflection. The students (and the teachers) are at first at a loss in this situation. Their background of fundamentalism with exclusive claims makes it very difficult for them to undertake this form of interreligious theological reflection. But slowly they come up with reflections on parallel themes, which are referred to by Stanley Samartha as "inter-scriptural hermeneutics" (Samartha 1987). In the Bible and the theological traditions of Christianity as well as in the Qur'an and Hadith, there are parallel themes on how to cope with suffering, injustice, hope, and liberation. But it is also clear that in all scriptures there are texts that are negative toward people outside the flock and condemnations of their tenets. My idea of parallel themes is taken from studies of two Muslim theologians,

Ali Ashgar Engineer from India (Engineer 1993), and Farid Esack from South Africa (Esack 1997). Both stress the liberation element in the Qur'an. Based on these parallel themes in their scriptures and religious traditions, both Christians and Muslims could reflect on their problematic situation. In turn, this interreligious reflection could inspire them to act together.

Are We All under Divine Punishment?

We have seen above how people reflect on the Bible from their situation. It is not easy to theorize about the function of the Bible in the pastoral circle. Just as the pastoral circle has undergone many changes, so biblical hermeneutics has also undergone many changes. As a reaction to dogmatic use of the Bible, where biblical texts are used or manipulated to conform or legitimize the confessional teachings of the Western Protestant denominations, in many Indonesian Protestant theological institutions that belong to member churches of the Protestant Communion of Churches (PGI), students are encouraged to learn about the historical-critical method in a moderate way. The result is ambiguous: on one hand, the effort to acquire the so-called original meaning neutralizes Western traditional assumptions; on the other hand, there is a wide gap between the past and the present, between "what it meant" and "what it means." I think mainly under the influence of liberation theology and feminist theology, the gap is being filled. It is important to have perspective in reading the Bible. In Indonesia the historical-critical method is combined with commitment.

But a lot of people are also interested in modern (or postmodern) ways of reading the Bible. In contrast to the historical-critical method, which emphasizes the world behind the text (and sometimes assumes that it is the only "objective" method), many are now involved in the narrative or literary-critical method, which emphasizes the world within the text. In this method people are suspicious of theological assumptions wrapping the texts, and they try hard to liberate the Bible from theology (or ideology). But precisely because of this, the Bible again becomes far from the struggle of the people. As in some feminist circles the Bible is identified with patriarchy, in this circle the Bible is identified with oppression.

The most recent approach is the reader-oriented interpretation of the Bible, which emphasizes the world in front of the text (meaning in the mind of the reader). Actually in literature concerning biblical hermeneutics, a historical-critical interpretation of the texts using perspectives such as feminist or liberation perspective is close to this approach. The problem is that this approach can also be used to maintain the status quo. A lot of recent publication in Asia (including from mainland China) concerning the newer approaches actually resists the struggle to break the status quo. So we see that in biblical interpretation there is a number of approaches, and each approach can be used for or against the interests of the people. In other words, in biblical studies subjectivity is now being acknowledged. But precisely because of that—as I mentioned in the introduction—we should always take care to be open and broad enough to take into consideration the insights of other approaches, to relate in a dialectical way the text and context, or text and reader.

My task as a teacher of "Church and Society" was done in the heyday of Soeharto's New Order regime. In 1994 a younger colleague took over the course. Soon afterward the situation changed. General Soeharto's grip on the nation weakened, and Indonesia became "a nation in waiting" (Adam Schwarz). On Ascension Day, May 21, 1998, Soeharto stepped down after weeks of student demonstrations and days of riots in the capital of Jakarta and other urban centers. But all agree that the beginning of the end was in 1996, when together with her Southeast Asian neighbors, Indonesia plunged into the worst economic crisis in its history. This crisis gave birth to other kinds of crises. In the furthest western point Aceh separatist guerrillas escalated their attack on government installations and on the Javanese settlers, and in the furthest eastern point the Papuas demanded more autonomy and even independence. In Kalimantan, the Dayak people started communal warfare against the Madurese settlers, and in the northern coastal areas of Java hundreds of churches were burned or ransacked by mobs. Factories closed, and many people lost their jobs. In almost every region people resorted to violence to address their problems. Petty thieves were doused with gasoline and burned alive. A few days before Soeharto's fall there were riots in the streets of Jakarta. Department stores were burned or looted from day to night, while vehicles burned on the streets. Hundreds of people were trapped in department stores and died because of the fires. A number of Chinese people were also killed. Many Chinese women were raped and afterward thrown alive into the fires. The whole country was in shock.

But when Soeharto was replaced by Habibie, the crisis did not end. During the referendum in East Timor, military-backed militias organized massacres. In 1999 the already tense relationship between Christians and Muslims in the Mollucas erupted into communal warfare that lasted until 2002. This was soon followed by Christian-Muslim conflicts in Halmahera and Poso. The religious conflicts in Eastern Indonesia, the ethnic communal conflicts in Kalimantan, and the problem of Aceh and Papua persisted during the presidencies of Abdurrahman Wahid and Megawati. The many violent and chaotic situations caused people to wonder whether Indonesia was being punished by God.

It is interesting to see that the above situation was not brought into analysis but was immediately brought into theological reflection. There has been, of course, much analysis in the mass media, but the conclusions are so different from each other that none is wholly convincing. Perhaps the enormity of the situation makes it difficult to analyze, and because of that no clear plan of action can be envisaged. At the recent presidential election campaigns the five candidates explained their programs, but according to social observers, none of them really has concrete plans to deal with the difficulties. What is clear is the reality of violence and suffering, and because Indonesians are a religious people, they have begun to reflect in theological terms. On Good Friday and Easter 1997 the director general of the Protestant Department (Dirjen Bimas Kristen) of the Ministry of Religions asked Christians to fast as a form of Christian response to the situation. In this situation, where church buildings were burned by the hundreds and where people lost their feelings of security, Christians feel that God is angry with the people, that God is punishing them, and that one way to assuage God's anger is to fast as a sign of repentance. This request to fast is unusual, as most of the Protestant churches in Indonesia are from Calvinist and Lutheran traditions, which regard fasting negatively, as a human effort to achieve salvation. Only the pentecostal charismatic churches and fellowships are preserving this tradition, beside the Catholics (in a more lenient form). It indicates that pentecostal-charismatic influence is being felt among the Christian authorities. Within the Chinese churches this request was largely ignored, but within the Javanese churches many responded positively. They still maintain cultural affinities with their Muslim neighbors, who keep fasting as one of their main tenets.

In February 13, 2000, Djohan Effendi, one of the department heads at the Ministry of Religion (he served as minister of state secretariat during Abdurrahman Wahid's presidency) and a Muslim scholar, stated in a newspaper interview that the nation was under God's punishment. All of the people, including the religious groups, have fallen under the sin of materialism, he said. They compete in building expensive worship buildings and in performing spectacular religious events, but they ignore the pleas for justice by the poor. In March 2000 the PGI held its general assembly at Palangkaraya, with the theme "Seek Ye the Lord" (Amos 5:6a). The context is about injustice, divine punishment on religious people, and (a small possibility of) repentance. Although many Christians reject fasting, even they can agree with their Muslim compatriots on one theological point: Indonesia is under divine punishment.

How are we going to evaluate this theological point? The tendency to relate suffering with divine punishment is common in Indonesian religious thinking. But it has to be noted that there are also many, both in Christian and Muslim circles, who no longer believe in divine punishment. The reason is that this theology of divine punishment has been used to explain suffering away, and because of that nothing has been done to remove the suffering. There was a great outcry when a conference of Muslim religious leaders issued a statement concerning people with HIV/AIDS. The statement said that because people with HIV/AIDS are under punishment of God, they should not be given governmental help but should receive lethal injections instead. The statement was hastily withdrawn, with the explanation that it was one of the drafts to be studied, but it was leaked to the press.

I was invited to the PGI general assembly to give the main Bible study on Amos 5:6a. I did not choose the theme. It was close to theme of the World Council of Churches general assembly at Harare, "Turn to God." But I can understand why the organizers wanted to reflect on Amos. They were angry at the decision of the PGI leaders to send gold to Soeharto's residence in 1997, when the government, in imitation of the Thai government, asked the people for help in getting out of the crisis. Nothing was heard of the gold after it was in Soeharto's hands. For many, the visit of the PGI leaders to the president, which the leaders termed "a pastoral visit," was compared with the offering of the golden calf by Aaron in Exodus 32. It symbolized for them the cooptation of the Protestant churches under the New Order regime, the ignorance of church leaders of the changing political situation, and their fatal mistake in identifying the people with the state/government. The general assembly was intended to become a meeting where Christians (especially the PGI leaders) would be expected to confess their sins, to acknowledge divine punishment, and to repent.

In my Bible study I started from the present rejection of a theology of divine punishment. To some extent I agreed that this dominant traditional theology gives a picture of God as cruel and violent, and that it should be asked whether this is consistent with the picture of God as a God of love in Jesus Christ. I am also a follower of Taizé spirituality, and repeatedly I read in their reflections that in God there is no punishment but only love. In modern pastoral care we should take care not to explain suffering as divine punishment, even if there are biblical texts that could be used to support this idea. My colleague Robert Setio rejects this theology; later my reflections at the assembly were published together with his long response. He represents the younger Indonesian biblical scholars, who tend to liberate the Bible from theological constraints and, as such, are not interested at all in theological notions, especially traditional themes such as divine punishment. There is a lot of truth in their rejection.

I am always unhappy with biblical texts that refer to punishment on a cosmic scale, such as the flood. Humankind is regarded as evil, but there is no description of what kind of evil human beings have done. They all died (except Noah and his family), and all the animals (except those in the ark) died too. In divine cosmic punishment, the innocent suffer and die. There is (from our present point of view) a certain arbitrariness in God's punishment. How about the people who suffer under the present multiple crises? How about the Chinese women who were raped and burned to death in May 1998? Are they punished by God? How about the perpetrators? Why are they left free? Whether they are Christians or Muslims, people who suffer ask a lot of questions to God. Of course, religious leaders comfort them with terms such as *providence (kehendak Allah, takdir)*, but that does not prevent them from asking these questions. I have also stated above that I disagree with the attitude of those who derided the death of Tien Soeharto.

But, after all these considerations, I think I can be open to a limited application of the concept of divine punishment. After years of following the process of the pastoral circle with my students, I cannot always hold onto my liberal views, which I inherited from modern study of theology in the West. The suffering people, the Chinese women, are victims of violence. Their suffering and their deaths should not be interpreted as divine punishment. When I was teaching the course "Church and Society," I detected the hope of the people that God as a just God would punish the powerful ones who make the people suffer. So the crisis was interpreted as punishment from above toward the corrupt political-military leaders and the avaricious business leaders of the country. And when Soeharto and his cronies did fall, this unpredicted event was seen as fulfillment of the people's hope. Soeharto was punished in order to liberate the people, in the same way Pharaoh *(Fir'aun)* was punished to let Israel free.

I object to a theological concept of divine punishment used to maintain the status quo, but if there is a theological concept of divine punishment that inspires people to break the status quo, what is wrong with that? Of course, I think we should return to the Bible and see that not only enemies are under punishment but also Israel as the people of God. My studies on punishment as a theological theme in the prophetic tradition made me aware that historically the idea of punishment of Israel as the people of God came late into the people's understanding. The individual in Israel could be punished by God, but not Israel as the elect of God. The prophetic tradition did a turn in this understanding, and it was Amos who first referred to this turn. Precisely because they were known to God, they could be punished by God. The Indonesian people themselves are not free from the wrongdoings they see in the New Order regime. After more than thirty years under Soeharto, even they are under some influence of the New Order's ideology. Seen from the present stagnant process of the Reformation, when people start talking about the resurrection of the New Order, it seems that the judgmental attitude toward the "other" as wrong and the "self" as right is detrimental to the welfare of the nation.

Was the expectation of the assembly organizers above fulfilled? No, not at all. The PGI leaders defended their decision, and no apology was offered. A new leadership was chosen at the Palangkaraya assembly, but the leaders have to work in the shadow of the failure of the last leadership to maintain integrity within the structures of injustice and oppression. The PGI lost credibility in the eyes of many people, and while waiting for the next general assembly, the new leadership had to work very hard to rebuild relationships. In a way, we can say that even the PGI is under God's punishment. But, as we all know from the Bible, punishment is related to hope and liberation. Although in some prophetic texts the notion of hope is seemingly absent, later additional work by redactors (readers) that refers to hope indicates in general that liberation is the other side of the coin. As stated by Zimmerli, "Yahweh's No is also (dialectically) Yahweh's Yes" (Zimmerli

1977). This can be applied to the member churches of the PGI but also to the whole nation.

Conclusion

Let me conclude with a last reflection. In beginning the pastoral circle process we start with our own theological assumptions. My students are fundamentalists, while I am liberal. But when we relate our theological assumptions to the reality of our context, these terms are called into question. In the course of following the moments of the pastoral circle, I struggled to free my students from their fundamentalist traits, but, in turn, I discovered that the people caused me to relativize my own liberal convictions. At first I thought that only my students would have to change, but later I also had to change my views. I believe that I have been experiencing what Holland and Henriot refer to, in citing Juan Luis Segundo's use of the "hermeneutical circle," as the necessity of constantly evaluating my own pre-understanding and my own conclusions (Holland and Henriot 1983, 8).

At the most basic level of either social action or theological reflection, what is essential is the welfare and the interests of the people. If our interpretations are not helping them in their struggle to have a better life, then we should change our assumptions. Going around the pastoral circle transforms not only social situations but also theologies and, indeed, individuals. Whether we are undertaking social analysis or theological reflection, we should be critical, even of ourselves, and be open to new horizons.

References

Banawiratma, Johannes, and Johannes Mueller. 1993. *Berteologi Sosial Lintas Ilmu.* Yogyakarta: Kanisius.

Engineer, Ali Ashgar. 1993. *Islam dan Pembebasan.* Yogyakarta: LKiS. This is a translation of Ali Ashgar Engineer, *Islam and its relevance to our age* (Bombay: Institute of Islamic Studies, 1987).

Esack, Farid. 1997. *Qur'an, liberation and pluralism.* Oxford: Oneworld.

De Wit, J. H. 1991. *Leerlingen Van De Armen.* Amsterdam: VU Uitgeverij.

Gadamer, Hans-Georg. 1975. *Truth and method.* New York: Seabury Press.

Holland, Joe, and Peter Henriot. 1986. *Analisis Sosial and Refleksi Teologis.* Translated by B. Herry Priyon. Yogyakarta: Kanisius. This is a translation of Joe Holland and Peter Henriot, *Social analysis: Linking faith and justice* (Maryknoll, NY: Orbis Books, 1983).

Pieris, Aloysius. 1988. *An Asian theology of liberation.* Maryknoll, NY: Orbis Books.

Samartha, Stanley. 1987. *The Search for new hermeneutics in Asian Christian theology.* Madras: Christian Literature Society.

Zimmerli, Walther. 1977. Prophetic proclamation and reinterpretation. In *Tradition and theology in the Old Testament,* edited by Douglas A. Knight, 69–100. Philadelphia: Fortress Press.

Part III

Challenges for a Future Use

T he pastoral circle was proposed twenty-five years ago. It was not meant to be an untouchable "magic formula" for pastoral analysis or theological teaching. If it is to maintain its relevance, it has to face the evolving challenges of human life. Such is the purpose of this third part, in which the contributors describe some of these challenges for the present and the future.

The first challenge is pluralism, and it is addressed by Michael Amaladoss, a Indian Jesuit theologian who is particularly well placed to talk about it. Reacting against a Catholic theology presented in the past as universal and uniform, Amaladoss stresses the undeniable fact of cultural pluralism, which obliges the theologian to contextualize the notions and to express the essence of the gospel message in concepts that are locally understood. The use of the pastoral circle is not an attempt to endorse all the cultural structures and values of a given particular culture, but it should help theology to be in permanent dialogue with cultures and not be "monolithic."

Maria Riley makes us aware of the growing emergence of the role of women in society and of the gender issue as a permanent component of all theological reflection. Catholic social teaching as well as the use of the pastoral circle should integrate this gender concern as a dimension present in all its stages and become a more inclusive methodology.

James Hug warns against a possible dichotomy in the understanding and application of the different stages of the pastoral circle, particularly between social analysis and theological reflection. Though sociology is an autonomous science, the use of social analysis cannot be considered deprived of any religious or theological value. Those doing social analysis are inevitably under the influence of their own religious and spiritual values, whether orthodox or liberative. In other words, social analysis in the pastoral circle cannot be considered as just a profane and secular stage, whereas the theological reflection would be the only religious one.

This parts ends with the contribution of Dean Brackley, who raises the question of how to do theology and apply the pastoral circle in a relevant way in a postmodern society. He proposes that by taking seriously the three main dimensions of experience—the world outside us, the world inside us, and the cultural word about the world—theology could respond to the challenges of a postmodern society increasingly tending toward globalization.

11

A Cycle Opening to Pluralism

MICHAEL AMALADOSS

The pastoral cycle proposed by Joe Holland and Peter Henriot twenty-five years ago systematized and clarified the underlying method of the theologies of liberation that had emerged in Latin America a decade earlier. It showed how theological reflection emerged from an experience-insertion in the reality of life and an analysis of that experience leading to a correlation with the scriptures and the tradition of faith. Theological reflection led to discernment and action. The cycle continued. The context was the poor and the need for creating a society of justice and equality. An awareness of the method helped theologizing and theological education at all levels in many parts of the world, especially in the Third World. Focusing on methodology, the book mentions culture and religion in passing. The need for the church to become prophetic and the role of the basic Christian communities are noted. In the project of "faith doing justice," the focus was on the process, experience calling for analysis and correlation with faith tradition, which in turn lead to discernment and praxis.

In the second edition of the book (Holland and Henriot 1983) Joe Holland added a preface about the need to be open to the creative transformation of civilization and to the spiritual roots of creative energies. We have to move from a mechanistic to an artistic root metaphor in looking at society and its future. "The social and spiritual creativity of rooted communities in solidarity" has to be discovered and engaged. In this project the laity had a special role.

Nearly a decade earlier Aloysius Pieris, speaking at the third general assembly of the Ecumenical Association of Third World Theologians (EATWOT), had suggested that the theology of liberation has to take the religiosity of the people seriously, at least in Asia (Pieris 1988, 69–86). Moving from Latin America to Africa, EATWOT discovered the role of culture in liberation. Going then to Asia it realized the importance of religion. Latin America, of course, had an overarching Hispano-Portuguese culture and the religion of Catholicism in its various elite and popular forms. But the contexts of Africa and Asia presented a situation of cultural and religious pluralism. This pluralism affects the pastoral cycle at all levels. At the level of experience the situation is complicated by intercultural and interreligious conflicts, when cultures and religions are used to legitimize economic, political, and social domination. Social analysis cannot ignore cultural and religious pluralism as an important element of society. Reflection then has to be dialogical, taking the many cultures and religions into account. Praxis, too, has to provide for the factor of cultural and religious pluralism. On the one hand, we cannot ignore cultural and religious factors in talking about justice. On the other, culture and religion can also be causes of injustice. In this context the faith that links to justice has to become multicultural and multireligious.

The Indian Story

Before I explore and explain how pluralism is an integral dimension of the pastoral cycle today, I would like to share the story of the use of the pastoral cycle in India, which provides the experiential basis for my reflections. The practice of social analysis came to the serious attention of social activists and theologians in India through a seminar given by François Houtart in Bangalore in 1974. The analytical scheme presented by Houtart was based on Marxist theory, as was the analysis of the first generation of liberation theologians. It was heavily economic and political, with little place for culture and religion. Religion was seen mainly as alienating. The social activists took to it enthusiastically. Theologians, however, felt keenly the absence of a positive role for religion in social transformation. This led to tension between the two groups. A mixed group of theologians and social activists met twice in the Indian Social Institute at Delhi. The meetings did not bring mutual understanding, but the theologians took up the challenge of integrating social analysis in their theologizing.

This was facilitated by the emergence of theological centers in Indian languages (Arokiadoss 2002). A program of inculturating formation led the Jesuits to stress the need to root formation in contextual experience and to use local languages. At the level of theological formation this meant starting regional theological centers in the different linguistic areas of the country. The program started in 1978. These centers made an effort to contextualize both theological reflection and education. Social analysis was used to link experience and reflection. This pioneering effort was further helped by Holland's and Henriot's *Social Analysis*, which had an Indian edition in 1984. Continuing use of the method, with a search to give a more positive role to culture and religion both in reflection and praxis, led the theologians to develop a framework of an integral analysis taking into account the various elements that constitute society: economics-politics, person-society, and culture-religion. I shall explain this scheme below.

Ten years after launching the program of inculturation in formation, a review commission insisted on the importance of contextualization by launching the slogan "Formation, not only for mission, but in mission." At the level of theology it recommended an effort to integrate the social sciences and philosophy with theology. Accordingly, a program for integrated religious studies was developed and is waiting for one or other regional theological centers to implement it as an experimental project. The concept of integration insists on an interdisciplinary approach while respecting the identity of the various disciplines like the social sciences, philosophy, scriptural studies, and theology.

The program for contextual regional theology, started by the Jesuits, has now been taken up by a few other religious congregations. Independent of this program, the pastoral cycle also is active in the emergence of liberation theologies focused on oppressed groups like the Dalits (the untouchables of the Indian caste system), the Tribals, or indigenous people and women. The pastoral cycle has also animated the annual efforts at theologizing on various themes by the Indian Theology Association during the last twenty-five years (Parappally 2002). It is in this context that we feel that the pastoral cycle must not only give a positive role to culture and religion in an integral framework of social analysis but also take seriously cultural and religious pluralism.

Why Pluralism?

There are at least four reasons why pluralism becomes an essential dimension at all levels of the pastoral cycle. When a scheme for social analysis was presented to us in 1974, it was proposed as *scientific,* though it was based on Marxist ideology. The term *scientific* carried with it overtones of something objective, authoritative, and universal. In a postmodern world, with the devaluation of totalizing theoretical narratives, science itself has become pluralistic (Kuhn 1970). It does not evoke the same awe. The collapse of socialistic societies and the multiplication of experiments of mixed economies also have contributed to the deflation of the aura that surrounded scientific social analysis. Today we could speak of a pluralism of ideologies at this level.

Second, today we are living in a globalized world. We may not like the particular form it is taking. We may resent that the globe is becoming unipolar and demand a multi-polar world. But the globalization of communications and its impact on social, economic, commercial, and political relations has come to stay. We may still defend the importance of respecting pluralism of all kinds: ethnic, economic, social, political, cultural, and religious. But all these are part of a global world. We can choose to live in a ghetto, but then we have to build walls around ourselves. We cannot wish globalization away. We can only insist that it respect justice, diversity, and equality (Amaladoss 1999).

In its beginnings, Latin American liberation theology focused on the United States of America as the source of all evil, as the dominating and exploiting power. Attention was also directed toward local dictators, who were often supported by the United States. When dictators disappeared and democracies were established, then people were forced to turn their attention to local and internal dominations, exploitations, inequalities, and injustices. Even today the condemnation of American hegemony, its war in Iraq, and its support of Israel cannot solve local socioeconomic and political problems, the caste system in India, the ethnic divisions in many places, religious conflicts, the oppression of women, the destruction of nature, and so on. Fighting for justice today has to take both local and universal forms, and at both levels it has to take into account various sorts of pluralisms and the challenges of collaboration.

Finally, traditional analysis sees the world in a dualistic mode, divided between the oppressors and the oppressed, and often uses the language of revolution. Some local dictators may even be overthrown by a revolutionary movement. But revolution does not automatically bring about the desired transformations. The Philippines has democratically thrown out two presidents, Marcos and Estrada. But have the poor really been empowered and liberated? At some stage we have to realize that we are not going to overthrow and destroy once and for all the oppressors and establish a classless paradise. Our struggles have to take the form not only of protests, but also of constructive negotiation and creative action. The South African experience offers an example. Apartheid as a sociopolitical system was overthrown, and democracy was established. But this did not automatically change attitudes or restore community. A community cannot be built up through ongoing conflict, but only through reconciliation (Schreiter 1989). So the government established a Truth and Reconciliation Commission. Its chairman, Bishop Desmond Tutu, speaks of restorative, rather than retributive, justice (Tutu 1999). Reconciliation, dialogue, and collaboration are insisted upon. The focus and the results of the Truth and Reconciliation Commission may be limited, but I think that it provides a model. At some stage we will have to promote dialogue, negotiation, and collaboration to build up a new community of equality and justice. Protest should be part of the dialogue. The revolution will have to be constructive and nonviolent and, therefore, inclusive. This is true at local, national, and global levels. It is good to affirm that an alternative world is possible, but at some stage we have to become part of the local and global processes and challenge them from within to move toward alternatives. Protests from the outside can create awareness and conscientize. Creative transformation, however, can come only from within. At that stage we cannot escape a pluralism of perspectives and ideologies and, therefore, dialogue, negotiation, and collaboration.

An Integral Analysis

In order to place these various pluralisms in context, we have to have an integral analysis of society (Amaladoss 1994, 30–42). I think that this can be done by taking into account the different elements that constitute society. I would spell these out as economics-politics, person-society, and culture-religion—six elements grouped into three pairs. Every element influences all the others. While economics-politics concerns the material conditions of life, person-society deals with the agents or the people who live this life, and culture-religion evokes the symbol systems that make their lives meaningful. Let us take a brief look at them, considering both their positive and negative dimensions.

Economics deals with the production and distribution of goods. Production is helped by science, which discovers the laws of nature, and technology, which devises machines that can be used to control nature and use it for production. An exclusive dependence on science may lead to a materialistic outlook. Technology may give rise to a sense of power. The way that science and technology are used may lead to the exploitation of nature, of women, and of the poor.

Mass production of goods is related to the ability to market them. Marketing is made possible by the promotion of consumerism, which, in turn, is encouraged by advertisements. Production and marketing are driven by the profit motive, so it is the quest for profit that drives the whole process. Money is the medium that facilitates these processes. Today money itself is bought and sold in the market. Money by itself can make more money. On the other hand, given the capacities of production and distribution today, it is possible to meet the needs of everyone on the planet.

Politics is a game of power. It determines who controls the means of production and the market. In former times the rich people also held political power. Today the rich prefer to control power through professional politicians who do their bidding. Even democracies are controlled by groups of oligarchs who use money to buy political influence. People in power seek to promote personal and class interests rather than the common good. There is, however, an increasing desire on the part of the people for participation in decision making and for democracy. There are movements to empower the poor, but it is an uphill battle.

The *people* today grow through various personal and social conditionings. One wonders how free and creative they really are. The quest for pleasure (consumerism) and for power alienates them in various ways from the body, from society, and from God. A spirit of egoism is further strengthened by individualism and competition. In some situations this may lead to isolation and anomie. Positively, today, people seek identity, autonomy, and personal development. There is also an increasing interest in the defense and promotion of human rights.

Social groups are organized in various ways. Even in democracies some dominate others in the name of wealth, power, ethnic identity, caste or social status, or even religion (ritual status). Often these factors are interlinked. Some groups, like the Dalits in India or women everywhere, suffer multiple domination and exploitation. Migrants are the victims of new kinds of social discrimination and exclusion. On the other hand, voluntary associational groups seem one way of overcoming divisive and exploitative social forces. Contemporary democracy that is rule by the majority may have to move toward more consensual models to promote real equality and the participation of everyone.

Culture consists of world views, attitudes, and systems of values with the symbols and rituals that help to express, celebrate, and transmit them. It is conditioned by economic, political, and social factors. In turn, it integrates them into a meaning system provided by the world view and the value system. Culture is also the source of identity of social groups. Multiculturalism can lead to mutual attempts at domination and conflict. All through history military conquests and migrations have led to intercultural interaction. Such interaction is today multiplied by communications, both as the exchange of information and as travel. Cultures can be manipulated and dominated by small groups of people. Today all cultures have to handle the impact of science and technology. Contemporary globalization may lead to newer kinds of domination. But it also leads to groups of people defending their cultural identity. The native peoples everywhere have carried on such a struggle for identity for centuries.

Religion is also a quest for meaning, but it focuses on ultimate questions like origins and ends and the problem of evil or unmerited suffering. Cosmic religions are aspects of culture that concern the cycles of nature and of life. Meta-cosmic religions appeal to the special experiences of founders and leaders or to revelation by the Transcendent, expressed in scriptures. They also make space for gurus and mediators. Religions are rooted in and tend to legitimate existing social structures. But in the name of the Transcendent they also prophetically challenge structures to change. Under the impact of science merely cosmic religiosity may disappear, resulting in secularization. Meta-cosmic religiosity, on the contrary, may give rise to fundamentalism or to a move from institutional to personal religion.

An interesting exercise at this stage would be to take a particular issue, like poverty, the oppression of women, the Dalits, or ecology, and try to analyze it according to the scheme proposed above (Amaladoss 1994, 37–42).

Ideologies

One element that seems to cut across the meaning system provided by culture and religion is ideology. Aloysius Pieris describes it as follows:

A world-view, which is essentially programmatic about a this-worldly Future to be realized, not without struggle, in the socio-political order, with the aid of certain tools of analysis or a method of discernment based on its own (i.e. ideological) premises, and requiring by its own intrinsic nature to be transcended by the Truth it seeks to articulate. (Pieris 1988, 24)

Pieris compares it with religion:

Religion, primarily and normatively (therefore not exclusively) points to an Absolute Future, a Totally Other, so that the horizon of final liberation is given a metacosmic ultimacy. . . . But, contrary to a widespread misconception, religion does emphatically teach that the Absolute Future has to be anticipated here in this life not only through the spiritual achievements of individual persons but also through visible structures in human society. . . . It is usually the case that a religion, in incarnating the Absolute Future here on earth, makes use of visible social structures, strategies and institutions that (this-worldly) ideologies provide. (Pieris 1988, 25)

Though ideology directly concerns the sociopolitical order, I think that it is a dimension of culture. It should not be identified with culture, which includes other elements of identity and meaning at linguistic and symbolic levels. Just as ideologies mediate the impact of religion on society, ideology can also mediate the impact of culture on society. Ideologies can, however, come from any source: economical (capitalism-socialism), political (democracy-dictatorship), person (patriarchy), social (caste or race), culture (nationalism), or religion (fundamentalism-communalism). Some ideologies may not be merely a-religious. They can also be antireligious. Other ideologies may seek legitimation from religion (Amaladoss 2004).

Some Preliminaries

People belonging to different cultures and religions may come together around the same ideology. People belonging to different ideologies may belong to the same religion or culture. But in the coexistence of ideologies, cultures, and religions, a certain friction of meanings cannot be excluded or, probably, avoided. In this essay, however, I am not going to analyze the interactions among ideologies, cultures, and religions. I want to take as my starting point the pluralism of ideologies, cultures, and religions both locally and globally and ask how we can carry on our analysis-reflection-action project in such a situation of pluralism. Should pluralism necessarily end up in conflict, or can we think of collaboration (Amaladoss 2003)?

I am also not going to focus on the Christian theology of the pluralism of religions (Amaladoss 1992; Kuttianimattathil 1998; Dupuis 1997). Whatever may be the attitude of the church to the other religions the church has accepted at the Second Vatican Council the principle of religious freedom at the civil level. People are free to follow any religion according to their conscience. John Paul II has also called for collaboration among religions at the civil and social level (*On social concerns,* no. 32). I shall keep the discussion at that level, though toward the end I would like to reflect on the impact of such a praxis on theological reflection.

Talking about interreligious collaboration at the civil and social levels does not mean any attempt to privatize religion. Although ultimately it is the believers who collaborate, not the religions, the believers need not bracket their religious convictions in collaborating. They bring them into the dialogue. This involves three stages of theological reflection. First, they have to reflect within the Christian group to find inspiration and legitimation for the concrete action that they wish to propose to the other believers. Second, they may talk about their faith convictions as part of the dialogue with others. Such dialogue may lead to mutual challenge. At a third stage they reflect on their faith convictions in the light of the dialogue and praxis.

I am also limiting my discussion to interaction at the level of civil society, leaving aside the exploration about how the conclusions can be turned into political programs. Let us now look at the various requirements of a dialogical reflection. This reflection includes the last three steps in the pastoral cycle, namely, analysis, reflection, and discernment of plans for action.

Dialogical Reflection

The first requirement for dialogical reflection is the establishment of a framework to guide the discussion on which all can agree. This will consist of a vision of society that we wish to create. It is from this point of view that we are going to evaluate what is wanting in the present and make suggestions for future action. Every religion, culture, and ideology has its own utopia. But is it possible to agree upon a common utopia? Moving beyond broad themes like peace, justice, and democracy, there is the Universal Declaration of Human Rights and other conventions on social and economic rights that the United Nations has evolved over the years. Though there may still be discussion on issues like whether the East and the West have the same approach to human rights and though the people in power may not have accepted all these declarations, they do embody a large agreement on basic values. The liberation of women and the protection of nature have also been objects of UN efforts at building an international consensus. At the time of the Second World Parliament of Religions the participants agreed upon a global ethic that all could promote (Küng and Kuschel 1993). The leaders of various religions who met in Rome in January 2002 also proclaimed a Decalogue of Assisi for Peace. It is not necessary to analyze all these statements here and evolve a unified document. It may be that a "final" statement will not be helpful, because it might stop ongoing discussion and possible changes in one or other area, such as the place of women in Islam or the problem of female circumcision in Africa.

In postmodern societies people seem to be so sensitive to their personal liberties and freedom of opinion that they wonder whether a dialogue is possible. All I can say is that, in so far as people do not retire into a hermitage and choose instead to live in a community and share an economic, political, and social system and expect that system both to support and to respect their personal project, they have to agree with the others who also belong to that system in order to keep it functioning. They cannot avoid some form of a dialogue that will help them to arrive at an overlapping consensus. A community that may be denied at an ideological level will have to be accepted at a practical level. One cannot insist on one's rights without recognizing and respecting the rights of others.

Dialogical reflection therefore supposes that there is an attitude of openness to and acceptance of the other groups, big or small (as is noted also in Chapters 5 and 10 herein). The usual tendency is for the majority to ride roughshod over minority groups. Sometimes a powerful minority that thinks of itself as enlightened or specially favored is likely to marginalize the majority. People who have reflected on the problem of multiculturalism have come up with three basic principles of tolerance: recognition, respect, and acceptance (Gutmann 1994; Taylor 1993). First of all, we must recognize that there are others who are different from us. Appreciation of difference is not always easy. Our own convictions seem so obvious and inevitable to us that we wonder how anyone can think differently. Recognition of difference already shows a certain openness. Those who are different from us are humans with freedom and a capacity to experience and reflect. They have a cultural, religious, or ideological tradition that guides them. We must therefore respect them and their difference. Recognition and respect should lead to acceptance. This does not mean that we have to accept their perspectives and options. We accept their right to be different and to think differently from us. This will lead us to listen to them and dialogue with them toward achieving an overlapping consensus.

As preparation for dialogue, each religious, cultural, and ideological group, correlating its experience with its theoretical perspectives and moral convictions, should be able to develop concrete policy options and action programs to transform society and build community within the agreed framework and bring it to the community for discussion (Amaladoss 1997). The aim of the discussion is not to arrive at an agreement on theoretical perspectives or even a plan of action but at an overlapping consensus on the goals that they can pursue and on the action projects they can initiate together (Rawls 1993). This will involve some give and take. A consensus at this level will lead them to collaboration in political action. Political action will be easier if the civil society has been prepared through ongoing dialogue and discussion and consensus formation. The dialogue can take place in groups, in the media, in seminars, in universities, in publications, and so on. These constitute the public space. Action can take the form of a movement focused on a particular theme that seems important at a given moment.

The Process of Dialogue

How can such dialogue take place effectively? The pastoral cycle is essentially dialogical, because it puts sociocultural analysis in dialogue with the word of God, and it puts people in dialogue among themselves. Perhaps this cycle can be enriched by the methods spelled out by Jürgen Habermas and Hans-Georg Gadamer. Distinguishing communicative action from instrumental and strategic action as promoting communication and consensus, Habermas talks about the "ideal speech situation" (Habermas 1984, 1987). The conditions for creating an ideal speech situation are these: everyone is honest and does not aim to deceive the others; everyone is free and expected to speak his or her mind, participate in the discussion, ask questions, propose objections, and discuss; and there are no underlying power relations in the group so that no one is manipulated by another. Where there is an atmosphere of common commitment, mutual trust, and freedom, it is possible to create such an ideal speech situation. One would expect every authentic discussion group to operate in such a manner. Otherwise there is no dialogue, only one or more monologues.

When such dialogue is taking place between people who belong to different religions, cultures, and ideologies, there may be a common goal but no common intellectual ground. Each one looks at the others from his or her own context and perspective. That is why we would need the "fusion of horizons" of which Gadamer speaks (Gadamer 1975). Those who speak are not merely presenting conclusions but are able to spell out the perspectives and convictions that led to such conclusions. By doing so, they lay themselves open to questions and challenges directed at their perspectives and convictions, which must then be explained or even defended. Challenge may lead to rethinking and modification. Those who listen are also able to spell out how they understand the others' proposals from their own perspectives. Such an interaction leads to a dialogue between perspectives and convictions. We could call this phenomenon a fusion of horizons. The fusion may not lead to a consensus but to a convergence that supports a consensus at the more practical level of projects for action.

Latin American liberation theologians usually speak of basic Christian communities as the agents of liberative action. Asian theologians have often spoken of the need in Asia for basic *human* communities that would be interreligious. We can widen the concept to include multireligious, multicultural, and multi-ideological groups at local and broader levels. Living in the same area or focused on a common project, they share a commitment to common action that brings them together.

An Example

Mahatma Gandhi is an example of a person who was capable of animating and leading such basic human communities. He had a goal of social and political liberation with which people from different religions could identify. He had interreligious ashrams where he trained committed workers for social and political revolution. He designed interreligious prayer services to inspire them. Given his strong personality and qualities of leadership, there may not have been much dialogue and discussion in the manner I described above. But the structure was open to such dialogue. In the process of opening up to other religions, Gandhi developed his own brand of Hinduism. His name for God was Truth, and he called his project *Satyagraha* or "clinging to truth." Nonviolence was an essential dimension of his method. It involved protest and struggle, but it respected the basic humanity of the other and was therefore open to negotiation and compromise, so that individuals could advance one more step together (Gandhi 1945).

Challenges to Theologizing

The aim of the pastoral cycle is action. I would like to focus here on the consequences for theologizing that emerge out of the kind of dialogue that I have been proposing. In the past theology normally functioned as "faith seeking understanding." It started and ended with faith. The scriptures and the tradition of faith provided the starting point and context for reflection. Such theology used to be systematic, whether dogmatic or moral. Today theology starts and ends with life. Its aim is not faith seeking understanding, but faith transforming life. Correlation between experience and the tradition of the faith is a process of mutual hermeneutics, in which faith enlightens and guides life while life grasps and expresses the faith in new and creative ways. Theological reflection is systematic, but it does not create an abstract, objective system.

When theology reaches out to the "other" who is not a believer, it becomes apologetic, seeking to explain theological perspectives and convictions in a way that the "other" can understand and perhaps even accept. Apologetic theology focuses not on the authority of revelation and tradition but on reasonableness (Lakeland 1997, 87–113). Traditional apologetics used to be on the "defensive" with rationalists and "offensive" with regard to others who were open to conviction. But in a situation where a Christian is engaged in a dialogue with other believers, theology has necessarily to become apologetic in a new manner. It cannot base itself on authority but has to show itself reasonable and relevant to life experience. Therefore, both the preparation for dialogue and the dialogue itself require apologetic theology. We may be inspired by our faith tradition. But we must be able to give reasons for our convictions to make them intelligible to others who do not share our faith. As Peter reminds us: "Be ready at all times to answer anyone who asks you to explain the hope that is in you" (1 Pt 3:15, Good News Bible). The correlation of our faith with our experience may also lead to a reinterpretation of our faith expression. Our faith expression is not fixed once for all. The object of our faith commitment is God, and God does not change. But our understanding of God and of God's plan as expressed in our faith statements can be subject to reinterpretation. Even the so-called systematic theology is actually contextual, conditioned by the context and the tools of reflection that are accessible to us at a given time and place. There is little universal in it. That is why there are different schools of theology and why theology keeps changing over the centuries.

In the course of dialogue when there is a "fusion of horizons" our faith convictions are challenged by those of other believers. These challenges may lead us to rethink our own presuppositions and perspectives. Such rethinking may lead to reinterpretation and reformulation. Theology here is becoming dialogical. Its reflection is taking place in dialogue with other religions, cultures, and ideologies. So we move from apologetic to dialogical theology. Such dialogical theology would normally be mutually prophetic, especially when religions tend to justify existing unjust structures. But it is for each religious group to interiorize the challenge of the other and transform itself. Challenges can come from outside, but transformation cannot be imposed from outside. It has to come from within.

Dialogical theology will eventually affect our systematic theology. I have already indicated that every systematic theology is contextual. When the context is pluralistic and this pluralism is taken seriously and is allowed to affect our reflection, then our theology will necessarily change. Such change is welcome because it is bound to strengthen our involvement and commitment to social transformation. This is what makes contextual theology also transformative.

The theology that emerges out of the pastoral cycle therefore will be apologetic, contextual, dialogical, and transformative. It will also be systematic in the sense that its different areas will be consistent with one another and not contradictory. But it will not be systematic in the sense that it will follow a particular philosophical framework. Neither will it be an abstract rational deductive system derived from doctrinal first principles. On the contrary, it will be responsive to contextual experience. Theology will be at the service of life, and not life artificially adapted to theology.

Conclusion

Religion often tends to legitimate particular cultural structures. Hinduism justifies the caste system. Islam does not always seem to be just to women. When theology becomes dialogical, then it is inevitable that the tight fit between religion and culture changes and cultural change leads to the reinterpretation of religion itself. While this will not affect the core beliefs of a religion, it can transform much of its embodiment and self-expression in particular cultures. Religions tend to be partial to the cultures they encountered first. Many people in authority in the church even now think that the Greco-Roman culture in which the Christian faith had its first serious self-expression is not only exemplary but normative to all other cultures. Dialogical theology will challenge such pretensions and release religion from its unnecessary cultural moorings. The way that the church treats its women is an example of such cultural moorings.

The pastoral cycle, therefore, can lead not only to social transformation but also to religious purification. Such purified religions will be, in turn, much readier for dialogue and for collaboration for ongoing social transformation.

The pastoral cycle starting with an experience of cultural and religious pluralism gives rise finally to theological pluralism. The catholicity or universality of the church does not consist in its having a universal, monolithic theology. The many contextual theologies have indeed a common source in scripture and tradition. But scripture and tradition are themselves contextual and pluralistic and in need of interpretation. Unity will have to be found at the level of a common commitment to a self-revealing God. The unity is therefore experiential, not textual, living that is not based on formulas. At the level of life and experience, even cultural and religious pluralism can be transcended, while recognizing and accepting it. Life experience, then, is not simply pluralism but convergence in community.

References

Amaladoss, Michael. 1992. *Walking together: The practice of interreligious dialogue.* Anand: Gujarat Sahitya Prakash.

———. 1994. *Towards fullness: Searching for an integral spirituality.* Bangalore: NBCLC.

———. 1997. *Life in freedom: Liberation theologies from Asia.* Maryknoll, NY: Orbis Books.

———. 2003. *Making harmony: Living in a pluralist world.* Delhi: ISPCK.

———. 2004. Changing dialogue: From religions to ideologies. In *Encounters with the word*, edited by Robert Crusz et al. Colombo: The Ecumenical Institute for Study and Dialogue.

Amaladoss, Michael, ed. 1999. *Globalization and its victims as seen by the victims.* Delhi: ISPCK.

Arokiadoss, P. 2002. Inculturating priestly formation. In *Renewed efforts at inculturation for an Indian church,* edited by Erasto Fernandes and Joji Kunduru. Bangalore: Dharmaram Publications.

Dupuis, Jacques. 1997. *Towards a Christian theology of religious pluralism.* Maryknoll, NY: Orbis Books.

Gadamer, Hans-Georg. 1975. *Truth and method.* London: Sheed and Ward.

Gandhi, M. K. 1945. *The story of my experiments with truth: An autobiography.* Ahmedabad: Navajivan.

Gutmann, Amy, ed. 1994. *Multiculturalism.* Princeton, NJ: Princeton Univ. Press.

Habermas, Jürgen. 1984, 1987. *The theory of communicative action.* Vols. 1 and 2. Boston: Beacon Press.

Holland, Joe, and Peter Henriot. 1983. *Social analysis: Linking faith and justice.* 2nd ed. Maryknoll, NY: Orbis Books.

Kuhn, Thomas. 1970. *The structure of scientific revolutions.* Chicago: University of Chicago Press.

Küng, Hans, and Karl-Josef Kuschel. 1993. *A global ethic.* London: SCM Press.

Kuttianimattathil, Jose. 1998. *Practice and theology of interreligous dialogue.* Bangalore: Kristu Jyoti Publications.

Lakeland, Paul. 1997. *Postmodernity: Christian identity in a fragmented age.* Minneapolis: Fortress Press.

Parappally, Jacob., ed. 2002. *Theologizing in context: Statements of the Indian Theological Association.* Bangalore: Dharmaram Publications.

Pieris, Aloysius. 1988. *An Asian theology of liberation.* Maryknoll, NY: Orbis Books.

Rawls, John. 1993. *Political liberalism.* New York: Columbia Univ. Press.

Schreiter, Robert J. 1989. *The ministry of reconciliation: Spirituality and strategies.* Maryknoll, NY: Orbis Books.

Taylor, Charles. 1993. *Reconciling the solitudes.* Montreal: McGill Univ. Press.

Tutu, Desmond Mpilo. 1999. *No future without forgiveness.* New York: Doubleday.

12

Engendering the Pastoral Cycle

MARIA RILEY

Revisiting Peter Henriot and Joe Holland's popular book *Social Analysis* some thirty years later provides a perspective on the strengths and weaknesses of the pastoral circle. The book combines explanations of analytical process, examples of the authors' then current social analysis, and some future projections. Although dated in its analysis, the project of the book remains important for those engaged in social justice work because it provides a process for people involved in the social mission of the church to continue to analyze the historical context of their work whether it is local, national, regional, or global. It is also a reminder that the task of the pastoral circle is ongoing and must become a habit of mind if social analysis is to be an effective tool in planning pastoral responses to issues of injustice. The pastoral circle might better be defined and used as a pastoral cycle that deepens and expands with each revolution.

Whereas the social analysis presented in the book is shaped by the particular historical context of the late 1970s, it also suggests some of the developments that would evolve during the 1980s, 1990s, and into the new millennium. Some of the projections are more optimistic than the reality that has unfolded, but the analyses also identify some emerging trends that have become dominant or significant in the context of the twenty-first century. Among them I would list the current model of global economic integration, which has followed the third stage of industrialization, national security industrial capitalism, described in the book. The New Right, which emerged in the 1970s, has hardened in some cases into a form of radical fundamentalism that is driving not only some religious groups but also the economic fundamentalism shaping economic globalization. But as is true of all future projections, unforeseen events happen that have a profound effect on human history. In this period it was the collapse of Soviet Russia and the end of the East-West conflict that opened the way to the rapid global economic integration of this era. More recently, 9/11 ushered in national security regimes in many parts of the world, especially in the United States.

Social movements, foreseen as a strategic response to national security industrial capitalism, have become an increasingly important political voice in recent years. And the women's movement and feminist analysis, briefly alluded to in the text, have developed both politically and theoretically. The rapid development of information technology, which has enabled not only global economic integration but also the rise of the social movements both from the right and from the left, was not foreseen at the end of the 1970s when the book was written.

Because social location is a critical element in the social-analysis process, I begin by introducing myself. I am an Adrian Dominican Sister and have worked at the Center of Concern in Washington, D.C., for twenty-five years. Peter Henriot and Joe Holland were my colleagues during some of that time. My responsibility has been the Global Women's Project, which has brought me in contact with women in many parts of the world, enabling me to develop both working relationships and friendships with many. My perspectives have been honed through active participation in the UN World Conferences on Women, on Human Rights, and on Social Development, and the ongoing work of my colleagues at the Center of Concern. Of particular importance was the series of regional conferences the center sponsored on Catholic social thought in celebration of the centennial of *Rerum novarum.*

My approach to social analysis is shaped by a feminist gender lens. While I realize the word *feminist* can be problematic for some, it defines a particular perspective concerning gender relations that is important to recognize. I might also add that feminism is not a rigid category, as some believe. At the UN World Conference on Women in Nairobi in 1985, the understanding of feminism was situated in global context with the clear assertion that feminism can only be defined within its local context. There is no single expression of feminism, but many feminisms based on the context in which women find themselves:

> Over the past twenty years the women's movement has debated the links between the eradication of gender subordination and of other forms of social and economic oppression based on nation, class, or ethnicity. We strongly support the position in this debate that feminism cannot be monolithic in its issues, goals and strategies, since it constitutes the political expression of the concerns and interest of women from different regions, classes, nationalities, and ethnic backgrounds. While gender subordination has universal elements, feminism cannot be based on a rigid concept of universality that negates the wide variation in women's experience. There is and must be a diversity of feminisms, responsive to the different needs and concerns of different women, and *defined by them for themselves* (Sen and Grown 1987, 18).

The significance of this agenda becomes readily apparent in examining the multidimensional agendas of women's groups in a given country or region. For example, due to the high number of Filipina women who migrate outward because they cannot support themselves and their families, cross-border labor rights and protection for women workers are critical concerns of Filipina feminists. This issue is of less importance for women's groups in India, for whom outward migration is a lesser problem. Their struggles focus more on the rise of religious fundamentalism with its revival of cultural traditions such as the dowry and its impact on women, including bride burnings. In the rural areas there is also a return of *sati* (cremating a woman alive upon the death of her husband). Some agendas remain a constant concern of women globally, but the particularities of a country or region set the agenda. Sex trafficking is such an agenda. Filipina women have worked against sex tourism and trafficking since the 1970s, but the issue has taken on more importance in Africa and India due to the HIV/AIDS pandemic. What is vital is that the women of the country and/or region define the critical issues and the appropriate political and cultural approach to addressing those issues. This understanding of feminism shapes my gender analysis.

Finally, my current work is within the context of the International Gender and Trade Network, which was founded at a Strategic Planning Seminar on Gender and Trade sponsored by the Center of Concern and DAWN Caribbean in 1999. The network is organized in eight regions: Africa, Asia, Caribbean, Central Asia, Europe, Latin America, North America, and the Pacific. It acts as a technical resource and political catalyst to bring gender, social development, and equity concerns into trade policy and agreements. Equity includes not only gender equity but also equity among peoples and nation states.

Given this perspective, what is striking but not particularly surprising is the critical absence of gender analysis in the social-analysis process developed by the authors. When the book was written, the global women's movement had begun, but gender-aware knowledge was at a very early stage. The same cannot be said today. In this essay I chart the evolution of feminist gender analysis in relevant areas of social and economic policy with the intent and hope that gender analysis will become an integral part of future social analysis and pastoral planning processes. In particular, I explore the changing analytical lens, changing approaches to gender issues, and the necessity of a transformed social and economic agenda if development is to progress. Finally I raise some issues for theological reflection and pastoral response.

Changing the Analytical Lens

The last thirty years have witnessed the increasing mobilization of women worldwide and their growing political presence and power, not only at women's conferences, but also throughout the UN system, in national politics, in economic participation, and in social movements. These decades also have witnessed a changing and deepening of the focus and critique women bring to economic and social issues. The lens of feminist analysis has expanded to include an integrated approach that links the household to local, national, and global systemic macro-economic policy and has moved from a WID (women in development) approach to GAD (gender and development) and beyond.

Shift to Macro-economics

By the mid-1980s the effects on women of the economic crisis of that decade and the solutions of the World Bank and the International Monetary Fund (IMF) were becoming evident. A Commonwealth report stated that "the economic crisis of the 1980s, and the types of stabilization and adjustment measures taken in response to it, have halted and even reversed the progress in health, nutrition, education and incomes which women had enjoyed in the developing countries during the previous three decades" (Commonwealth Secretariat 1989, 3). It was becoming clear that the WID solutions of the 1970s to address women's poverty, such as credit availability, land reform, and training and education, were inadequate in the face of the new macro policies that were negating progress at the local and national levels. It also was becoming clear that women and men did not experience the economic crisis in the same way. Feminist economists began the task of unmasking the so-called gender-neutral macro-economic policies in the stabilization and structural adjustment packages.

Women's multiple roles were identified as the core distinction between women and men. Whereas men, for the most part, can confine themselves to economically productive roles—the cash economy—often women are not only involved in economic production, but they also carry primary responsibility for the work of social reproduction that is the care of the household and the well-being of community–the care economy (Commonwealth Secretariat 1989). Social reproduction, the care economy, is unpaid, economically invisible, and undervalued in all cultures. According to the 1995 UN Development Programme's *Human Development Report,* the estimated value of women's care work equals about US$11 trillion. This gender division of labor is deeply embedded in cultural and social expectations, in the social roles assigned, and in various forms of discrimination in women's and men's lives.

At the household level the gender division of labor traditionally defines women's role primarily as family maintenance. This work is unpaid, taken for granted, and invisible in economic terms, but it has significant impact on the quality of women's lives, opportunities, and well-being. It is also the foundation of all other work in the society. When women assume paid work, they also assume a double workday, paid and unpaid. It should be noted that in some cases the traditional gendered division of labor is breaking down, notably among young adults in some industrialized nations; however, these examples remain more the exception than the norm.

With the economic crisis of the 1980s more and more women entered the cash economy in order to sustain the household. In addition, when women entered the productive economy they continued to be located in low-wage, often hazardous working conditions with little potential for advancement and high vulnerability to sexual harassment and other forms of discrimination. The exploitation of young women workers in export processing zones has been well documented. In times of economic downturns women are often the first fired. The growing trend of the flexibilization and casualization of employment through outsourcing, contract and part-time labor, and homework has only increased women's vulnerability in the work force (United Nations 1999).

The invisibility of women's unpaid work and the undervaluing of their paid work remains a critical issue in national and international macro-economic policy. For example, the application of IMF and World Bank stabilization and structural adjustment policies (SAPs) caused many countries to cut back on government sponsored or subsidized social services. Women bear the burden when public-sector services switch to the household, thereby increasing the burden of unpaid work on their already stretched energy and resources. This reality explains why women are in the forefront demanding that essential services, such a water, health care, education, and energy sources, be removed from trade negotiations, such as the World Trade Organization's General Agreement on Trade in Services. The privatization of essential services shifts the costs to the consumers and often leads to inferior and inadequate services to vulnerable households and areas.

The inequities resulting from the asymmetry between women's and men's work account for the differential impact of stabilization and structural adjustment. As the recession and SAPs cut into family incomes, social services, and subsidies, more and more burden fell upon the household, and therefore upon women and girls, to provide the basics for the well-being of the family. These realities shaped the emerging feminist economic analysis of macro-economic policies and challenged mainstream economic theories and the financial institutions that promulgate them to attend not only to economic efficiency, but also to the social and gender impact of their policies from the household to the global. The conceptual framework for the new gender-aware approaches to macro-economic analysis is neatly summarized in the *World Survey on the Role of Women in Development*:

> Although social institutions may not be intrinsically gendered themselves, they bear and transmit gender biases. Being socially constructed institutions, "free markets" also reflect and reinforce gender inequalities.

The cost of reproducing and maintaining the labor force in a given society remains invisible, so long as the scope of economic activity does not include unpaid "reproductive" labor. Thus, unpaid work needs to be made visible and the economic meaning of work redefined to include unpaid reproductive labor.

Gender relations play an important role in the division of labor, the distribution of work, income, wealth and productive inputs with important macro-economic implications. By extension, economic behavior is also gendered. (United Nations 1999, 60)

Although some progress has been made in bringing these issues into economic discourse at the macro level, actual policy changes are slow in coming. It has become conventional wisdom among development "experts" that there can be no authentic development without integrating women's agendas and perspectives into the development process. However, this position continues to be mostly rhetorical.

From Women in Development to Gender and Development and Beyond

In addition to changing the analytic lens to macro-economic policy, women have also changed their approach to achieving more equitable social structures. The shift from WID to GAD was particularly important because it transformed the approach to gender issues. The WID agenda focused on two main goals: to generate discussions and research on the role of women in development; and to institutionalize a women's focus within development agencies and governments with the mandate to integrate women into development (Razavi and Miller 1995).

The WID solution, integrating women into the development process, did not question the kind of development that was being fostered by the donor nations or the financial institutions. Furthermore, WID focused on women and generally ignored the consequences of different social realities, such as the gendered worlds of women and men, race and ethnic differences and economic status. It focused on women's productive capacity, arguing that women were more efficient in the use of resources than men and therefore supporting women was a more efficient way to achieve development. But in so doing the WID focus continued to render women's reproductive work invisible. The argument joined equity to efficiency to legitimize the promotion of women, but in effect it instrumentalized women in the service of economic development, not development in the service of the advancement of women (Razavi and Miller 1995).

The critique of the WID approach led to a reexamination of it assumptions, particularly that it "tended to isolate women as a separate and often homogeneous category, [and] it was 'predominantly descriptive,' as well as being 'equivocal in its identification and analysis of women's subordination'" (Razavi and Miller 1995, 13). The GAD approach uses gender, rather than women, as an analytic category to understand how economic, political, social, and cultural systems affect women and men differently. Gender is understood as the social roles, expectations, and responsibilities assigned to women and men because of their biological differences. Gender is a cultural and often ideological construct that shapes women's and men's realities. Because the GAD analysis focuses on social relations, it also opens the way to identify other social and ideological constructs such as race, ethnicity, and class.

The movement toward GAD signals three important departures from WID: (1) it identifies the unequal power relations between women and men; (2) it reexamines all social, political, and economic structures and development policies from the perspective of the gender differentials; and (3) it recognizes that achieving gender equality and equity will demand "transformative change." The GAD approach demands transformative change in gender relations from household to global politics and policy and within all the mediating institutions, such as governments, the World Bank, the IMF, and the World Trade Organization (WTO).

But the question continues to be: How does transformative change take place? Two processes are currently advocated: gender mainstreaming and empowerment. They approach the question of transformation from two different perspectives: "top down" or "bottom up" development. Gender mainstreaming was officially recommended at the UN Fourth World Conference for Women in Beijing in 1995. Its advocates call for mainstreaming gender analysis into all, not just women-focused, policy and programming both in design and in impact assessment. It is primarily concerned with the reform of decision-making processes within development institutions, such as the World Bank or the US Agency for International Development. Empowerment is the work to create space for women to exercise their power and voice in decision making on the issues affecting their lives.

Both approaches have their critics. It is evident that in the ten years following Beijing gender mainstreaming has not worked. In its original concept, gender mainstreaming was understood as a process "for ensuring equity, equality and gender justice in all the critical areas in the lives of girls and boys, women and men. As such, it is a moral and ethical imperative as well as fundamental to human rights in all its forms" (Williams 2004, 1). But in its present form gender mainstreaming has been instrumentalized as a programmatic goal or a mechanical tool. Institutions, agencies, and governments have not lacked the vision, the political will, and the resources that would make gender mainstreaming a reality. Also gender mainstreaming, as its name implies, does not carry a critique of the current neo-liberal framework in which development decisions are made, whether at the World Bank, the IMF, the WTO, or national development agencies. It does not focus on the macro-economic environments that shape local economic realities but instead seeks compensating mechanisms to address the failures of the macro-economic policies. As such, it falls back into the WID stream of seeking to integrate women into current development models, rather than the transformative GAD stream, which seeks to transform the economic structures (Williams 2004).

The empowerment approach also has limitations. Its focus on local participatory development can blind it to the macro-economic issues in play. The limitations in participatory development's ability to change economic and social structures remain a question. The state must play a role in regulating macro-economic forces and directing development policies toward more gender-equitable outcomes. Both of these strategies are essential, but they both need to be transformed by the GAD approach and its focus on the relationship between the micro-economic and macro-economic structures. However, more important is the agenda that the different groups and approaches bring to their advocacy. If that agenda is in support of current directions in neo-liberal economic policies as illustrated by the international financial institutions and the World Trade Organization, there will be no significant transformation of economic policy. For that we must look to the social movements and in particular the feminist voice within those social movements.

Beyond empowerment and gender mainstreaming, women today are demanding the full exercise of their human rights and are developing a rights-based approach to economic policy. In the June 2000 special edition of *World Development*, Caren Grown, Diane Elson, and Nilufer Cagatay advocate "a rights-based approach to economic policy which aims directly at strengthening the realization of human rights, which include social, economic and cultural rights, as well as civil and political rights. Such an approach goes beyond viewing gender concerns as instrumental to growth to recognize women's agency and their rights and obligations as citizens" (Grown, Elson, and Cagatay 2000a, 1154). This approach clearly illustrates a profound political shift that became evident at the Fourth World Conference on Women, where women no longer focused on a narrow range of so-called women's economic issues but demanded voice in all arenas of economic policy making.

Women bring a particular perspective to the human rights agenda. Over the decades of the growth of the global women's movement, women realized the most progress in the areas of social, economic, and cultural rights. However, these rights were considered the second generation of human rights after civil and political. In preparation for the UN World Conference on Human Rights, the Global Campaign for Women's Human Rights organized women from the local to the global levels to ensure that social, economic, and cultural rights were fully recognized. The *Vienna Declaration and Programme of Action* (1993) clearly states the "the human rights of women and of the girl-child are an inalienable, integral and indivisible part of universal human rights." It also affirms that all human rights are "indivisible, universal, interdependent and interrelated" (World Conference on Human Rights 1993, no. 5), thus insisting that economic, social, and cultural rights are as important as civil and political rights. Success in including women's human rights in a UN Document does not automatically guarantee success in eliminating all violations of those rights. It does, however, provide an effective tool for activists to use in the work of advancing women's human rights, particularly their social and economic rights.

New Agenda—Gender and Trade

The WTO was inaugurated in 1995, the same year as the UN Fourth World Conference for Women in Beijing. SAPs were the predominant macro-economic issue at the conference, but beyond that little attention was given to the process of growing economic integration, which is at the center of globalization. Nor was there much awareness of the relationship between SAPs and global economic integration. However, in reexamining SAPs from the point of view of trade liberalization and intensification, it is clear that one of the goals of SAPs reforms was to prepare countries' economies for the increasing liberalization of trade and investment fostered by the WTO and its most powerful players—Canada, the European Union, Japan, and the United States.

As liberalization has progressed, the gap between the rich and the poor both within and among nations has widened. Privatization, the partner of liberalization, has become the norm for many public-sponsored programs that address social needs. Women have witnessed the erosion of services that address basic needs such as health care, education, water, and sanitation, which has increased the burden in the household—witness the Asian financial crisis with its contagion effect that virtually wiped out years of progress for people in Thailand, Korea, and Indonesia. South Korean studies showed that women suffered the greatest setbacks during this crisis, as they were the first to lose jobs and security due to traditional discriminations and social role expectations. Furthermore, the prescriptions to relieve the Asian crisis were built on the traditional SAPs model that continues to shift the burden of social responsibilities onto the household and women. Clearly the economic model is not working.

Liberalized trade and investment are relatively new to the women's economic agenda. Feminist economists and the NGO community have only begun to address the issues since 1995 when the WTO came into existence as the successor to the GATT (Generalized Agreement on Tariffs and Trade). Since the First Ministerial Meeting of the WTO in Singapore in 1996, women have been actively engaged in bringing a gender perspective into trade policy at the WTO and at regional and country levels. The task is formidable, because trade economists and negotiators consider trade and investment gender neutral, and because the major NGO groups addressing trade and investment issues, such as organized labor, environmental groups, and many southern NGOs, generally do not have a gender analysis. The resistance is deep and often unconsciousness.

Transformed Policies

Women activists and feminist women's organizations are pressing for a new approach to economic policy because they know the failures of the current models from their own experiences. They are critical of macro-economic policies that focus on market-based criteria with an overriding emphasis on stabilization and a diminished role for the state. This macro approach includes social-policy concerns primarily as a "safety net" when and where market-driven policies fail. Women are seeking to put social policies at the center of economic policies.

Putting social policies at the center of economic policies would change the criteria for judging effectiveness. The soundness of economic policies would not be based on market criteria, per se, but in terms of whether they ultimately succeed in bringing societies to greater social justice. "Thus desired social outcome such as distributive justice, equity, provisioning of needs for all, freedom from poverty and discrimination, social inclusion, development of human capabilities become the ultimate goals of policy-making, including macro-economic policy making" (Grown, Elson, and Cagatay 2000b, 1348). It should be noted that the feminist economic agenda addresses the well-being of all members of society, not just women.

Back to the Pastoral Circle

What does all this say to social ministers in their work for social justice? The first obvious answer is to include gender analysis and women's perspective in all phases of the pastoral circle—insertion; social analysis of the political, economic, social, and cultural structures; theological reflection; and pastoral response. In the social-analysis moment it is critically important to look at the interrelatedness of the various levels of society, beginning with the household, and to analyze how local, national, and global economic policies influence all people's ability to attain a sustainable way of life. There is much to learn from analyzing the structures that shape women's and men's political, social, economic, and cultural experiences at this time, as we chart our work to shape a more just society for all.

Theological reflection offers some specific challenges. In 1963, in *Pacem in terris,* Pope John XXIII identified women's growing participation in public life as one of the "signs of the times" (no. 41). Since then, women's growing consciousness of their human dignity and human rights has been one of the most far-reaching social evolutions. It has been God's revelation breaking history, challenging the time-honored human theory that men, by virtue of being male, deserve the right to govern and control all dimensions of society and that women should be subordinate to them (Riley and Sylvester 1991). How should social ministers be reading this "sign of our times"?

Gender analysis also challenges the traditional approaches of Catholic social teaching to the human person, woman and man; to the understanding of family roles; and to the definition of work. Consistently, the social-teaching documents, while affirming women's full humanity, define women in terms of their "appropriate role," and their "proper nature." Such language is never used when referring to men. It raises the question of whether the church implicitly holds a dual anthropology of human nature; there is human nature for which man's experience is normative and then there is woman's "proper nature."

Catholic social teaching explicitly defines the care of the family as women's primary role. The father's role in the family is seen only in economic terms. To so emphasize that women are primarily responsible for the quality of family life diminishes the social role and value of fatherhood. It disenfranchises men from the full potential of their fatherhood while it disenfranchises women from the full potential of their personhood (Riley and Sylvester 1991). Finally while Catholic social teaching recognizes women's responsibility for the family, it lacks a political-economic analysis of social reproductive work—the care economy and the role it plays in social structures as well as in women and men's lives.

A Recent Example

A publication from the Vatican Office for the Doctrine of the Faith in May 2004 presents an interesting case of the Vatican struggling to answer the feminist critique of its anthropology of the human person, female and male. Written by Joseph Cardinal Ratzinger and approved by Pope John Paul II, the title is "A Letter to the Bishops of the Catholic Church on the Collaboration of Men and Women in the Church and the World." It attempts to address the changing social realities of women and men while maintaining an essentialist approach to women's primary role.

In its theological reflection, the document draws heavily on Pope John Paul II's document *Mulieris dignitatem* (1988), reiterating the traditional Catholic teaching of the common human nature of women and men made in the image and likeness of the Creator, their essential equality, the importance of their sexual differences, their spousal relationship, and their complementarity.

The third section of the document, "The Importance of Feminine Values in the Life of Society," seeks to apply this theology to women's lives today. It is here that the document tries to maintain an essentialist understanding of women, her role of motherhood, and her values, while at the same time recognizing and encouraging the many roles women play in society today.

However, the document continues to make women's capacity for bearing children the defining factor of their lives. In naming "feminine values" it universalizes and idealizes women for their "sense of the concrete" and opposition to abstractions. It invites women to bring their special values to humanize society, but what does this implicitly say of men? In an interesting aside, the document observes that women's virtues are values to which both women and men are called by the Christian imperative. This observation begs the question of why the Vatican has never written a comparable document on men.

The document continues the tradition of the importance of women's role in the family but insists that women should also bring their values to the wider society through work outside the home. It says that work should be organized to accommodate both worlds of women's work, the family and the workplace—a position that women's advocates have held for a long time. But the document does not sufficiently recognize man's essential role as a nurturer of the family as well.

The fundamental problem in this document is that, while seeking to address the question of collaboration between women and men, it speaks only to women's identity and roles in the family and society. It does not speak to men's identity and roles. It has an exalted sense of the "genius of women," and in doing so diminishes men. It bases its arguments of complementarity on sexual difference and union but fails to speak to the wholeness and integrity of each human person and the mutuality that wholeness should call forth in all relationships. It decries what it calls certain approaches that create opposition between women and men, but its approach sets up polarities between women and men. It fails to treat women's and men's realities and experience equally.

Conclusion

The changing realities of women's and men's lives today call for a rethinking of these issues in Catholic social teaching and in the pastoral circle. This statement raises another important issue regarding the development of Catholic social teaching. It challenges the traditional model of constructing social encyclicals and calls upon the church to develop its social teaching in more open, participatory, and accountable ways. To keep this living tradition alive and authentic, "its methodologies must become more inclusive, building upon the full range of social, cultural, economic and political experience and social judgment of the human community" (DeBerri, Hug, Henriot, and Schultheis 2003, 39).

Finally, social ministers must seek to include the usually silent and marginal voices in planning the pastoral response to the unjust context they are addressing. In this case we are focusing on women, but effective pastoral planning will embrace all those on the margins created by injustice. Part of the process is empowerment of those who are most affected by the injustice. Empowerment is not something we give to people, it is opening the space for them to use their own power and, as such, is essential as part of pastoral planning.

Women and those dependent upon women persistently remain the largest social group mired in poverty worldwide. This reality is not an accident; it is the direct outcome of the effect of social roles and social expectations placed upon women and of discrimination. Catholic social teaching's expressed "option for the poor" is an option for women. I think a serious challenge that confronts social ministers is to first understand the resistance to addressing the women's agenda and second to find explicit ways to overcome that resistance. This challenge goes well beyond the process of the pastoral circle and addresses the ministers' attitudes, often unconscious, as they have been shaped by the historic and time-honored structures of patriarchy that are evident, active, and legitimated by all our social structures, including the church.

References

DeBerri, Edward, James Hug, Peter Henriot, and Michael Schultheis. 2003. *Catholic social teaching: Our best kept secret.* Maryknoll, NY; Orbis Books; Washington, DC: Center of Concern.

Commonwealth Secretariat. 1989. *Engendering adjustment for the 1990s: Report of a Commonwealth expert group on women and structural adjustment.* London.

Grown, Caren, Diane Elson, and Nilufer Cagatay. 2000a. Introduction. *World Development* 28, no. 7 (July): 1145–56.

———. 2000b. The social content of macroeconomic policies. *World Development* 28, no. 7 (July): 1347–64.

Razavi, Shahra, and Carol Miller. 1995. *From WID to GAD: Conceptual shifts in the women and development discourse.* Geneva: UNRISD.

Riley, M., and N. Sylvester. 1991. *Trouble and beauty: Women encounter Catholic social teaching.* Washington, DC: Center of Concern, Leadership Conference of Women Religious and NETWORK.

Sen, G., and Caren Grown. 1987. *Development, crises, and alternative visions: Third world women's perspectives.* 2nd ed. New York: New Feminist Library, Monthly Review Press.

United Nations. 1999. *World survey on the role of women in development: Globalization, gender and work.* New York: United Nations Publications.

UNDP. 1995. *Human development report.* New York: Oxford Press.

Williams, Mariama. 2004. Statement of Mariama Williams: Roundtable discussion on mainstreaming gender perspectives into all policies and programs in the UN system. Available online.

World Conference on Human Rights. 1993. *Vienna Declaration and programme of action.* New York: United Nations Publications.

13

Redeeming Social Analysis

*Recovering the Hidden Religious Dimensions
of Social Change*

JAMES HUG

Joe Holland and Peter Henriot and all who have translated, adapted, taught, developed, and implemented the pastoral circle methodology through the years deserve warm appreciation and gratitude. They have promoted the spread of a simple planning process that teaches structural awareness, draws attention to the systemic causes of suffering and injustice, and results in consciously faith-filled planning appropriate to the complexities of the situation. That is no small contribution.

The critique of the pastoral circle and the recommendations I offer here for modifying it are intended to make it more adequate and to strengthen it for addressing the important challenges facing those who use it to effect social change for greater justice in today's world. My colleagues and I prefer to call it a pastoral spiral. Since the process of experience or insertion, social analysis, theological reflection, and pastoral planning is aimed at change, the end point is, ideally, not the same as the beginning point. The "circle" does not close; it gives rise to a new experience that then must be analyzed, reflected on theologically, and then gives rise to further action. Hence, spiral seems a more apt symbol.

My Social Location

The context within which the pastoral spiral has become a regular tool in my work is no longer the academic world (from which I have come) or the world of pastoral ministries as they are usually understood in faith communities today. The daily arena of my work is the world of policy advocacy and negotiation dealing with the pervasive realities of contemporary globalization.

What is new and of extraordinary importance in the contemporary wave of globalization is that the technologies of this age have extended the global interconnections farther than ever before, making global communications nearly instantaneous. This has allowed an unprecedented emergence of powerful transnational corporations. For their profitable functioning, they require an orderly and predictable set of global markets.

In recent decades, then, these corporations have been pressing national governments for stable institutions and laws of global governance to serve their trading needs. They want a systematization of critical economic concepts (such as ownership, property rights, and so on) and local/national systems of regulatory legislation that will protect their business interests and efforts.

Those business interests and activities have proven in many cases to be destructive of local communities' needs, rights, and even their very sustainability. As this has become more and more apparent to the poorer nations and peoples of the world, the drive to produce a business-friendly global governance system has met more resistance—both on the streets and in official intergovernmental venues.

The context in which I make use of the pastoral spiral method embraces the international processes where the struggles over the shape and control of this new stage of global political life are being waged. This is the world of UN conferences, meetings of the World Bank and International Monetary Fund, negotiations at the World Trade Organization and in regional arenas, as well as the meetings of global civil society that often accompany the official meetings or are called to address the issues they are dealing with. More specifically, my day-to-day work on these issues is carried out in Washington, D.C., in the United States, the sole superpower, which is now attempting to dominate the global scene. This highly conflictual context has highlighted certain characteristics, strengths, and weaknesses of the pastoral spiral process that are worth reflecting on for other contexts as well.

Attending to Subjectivity in Conflict

The first of these is that any process designed to promote social change will be implemented in a conflictual situation. There are almost always people who benefit from the status quo and will resist change. Those who approach their reality with a goal of significant change are choosing to enter or to provoke a conflict. They need to understand the perspectives and values of the others involved in the conflict as well as their own.

Second, most if not all major conflicts involve differences in fundamental values. That fact makes it important to recognize and acknowledge the impact on each person's perceptions and responses of those values and all that shapes them: their social location, formation, and experience. This demands self-knowledge, willingness to dialogue, and community involvement in the processes of the pastoral spiral.

The advances in psychological, philosophical, and scientific understanding of human processes of knowing and valuing have made us aware of the focusing and limiting influence that gender, culture, social and economic status, personal and group expectations, ideologies, beliefs, values, and so many other factors exert on perceptions and consciousness of experience. Each person's experiencing has unique focusing elements, both positive and negative. Those elements give rise to particular insights and to personal blind spots. The only authentic way to move beyond this fundamental subjectivity is to make the elements of the personal experience explicitly conscious and bring them into dialogue with other people involved in the same context. The limits and distortions of personal subjectivity can only be overcome by discerning communities.

In other words, we need to be aware that entering upon the process of the pastoral spiral is never a simple or clean start. We never start from zero. We enter a richly diverse, dynamic historical flow bringing the dynamics of our own history and identity. Those dynamics shape our perceptions of the reality we experience, sensitizing us to some dimensions of it and blinding us to others. It is quite clear from the differences in the chapters of this book that the sensitivities and concerns of people immersed in the academic world are quite different from those of fully engaged pastoral ministers, and both are quite different from those of policy advocates. And when the context is one of high-stakes conflict, understanding and dealing explicitly with what is shaping our experience and that of our competitors are essential.

This context of subjectivity in conflict suggests that in preparing to use the pastoral spiral method, it is important to begin on a confessional note within an adequately diverse community context. By "confessional note" I mean the explicit expression of the major types of experience each person brings to the process and the sensitivities and concerns the person has.

As a white, North American, male member of a Catholic Christian religious community committed to a faith that does justice, for example, I come to the issues of globalization intent on finding ways to bring about a situation of greater justice for all people on the planet. My spontaneous vision of that justice shares many elements with the middle-class American lifestyle and security I enjoy. I do not bring a firsthand experience of the injustices that contemporary globalization dynamics create for women, for people trapped in poverty, for racial/ethnic minorities in societies, for Africans, Asians, or Latin Americans, for people of other faiths. Nor do any of us imagine justice or identify the paths toward justice in quite the same way.

For that reason the implementation of the pastoral spiral methodology will be more adequate to the reality being addressed when all of the major types of people involved in and affected by that reality participate together in the analysis, discernment, and planning. In gathering this community, special attention must be given to including those whose experience, perspectives, and values are most often overlooked or ignored—those in poverty and marginalized or oppressed in the situation.

An Illustration

An instructive example of the difference that the degree of diverse participation and the preferential concerns of those involved in moral judgments make occurred in the US Catholic church when it set out to evaluate the US economy in the 1980s.

The rapid proliferation of official documents on Catholic social teaching since 1961 called attention to the religious and moral values involved in the policy decisions of public life at all levels. While that social teaching developed its critiques of capitalism and communism through the decades since, Catholics in business in the United States and in other wealthy Western countries moved into positions of leadership and acquired significant wealth and public status.

In the early 1980s, while the US Catholic bishops were preparing a document on the US economy, a number of these business leaders came together to publish a document of their own: *Toward the Future: Catholic Social Thought and the US Economy: A Lay Letter* (Lay Commission 1984). It offered a preemptive theological defense of the US system of neo-liberal or democratic capitalism then (and still today) dominant in the West, grounding its positions on three basic principles of Catholic social thought: the unique dignity of each person, the social nature of human life, and the principle of subsidiarity. Published just a week before the first draft of the bishops' pastoral letter appeared, it attracted an immense amount of media attention and set up the conflict situation in which the moral discernment would be carried out.

Economic Justice for All: Pastoral Letter on Catholic Social Teaching and the US Economy (NCCB 1986) was much more critical of the structures and operations of the economy, drawing upon a much broader array of principles from the scriptures and Catholic social thought.

The reason for the difference between the two documents becomes very clear when we look at the processes by which they were created. *Toward the Future* was developed by a panel of twenty-nine prominent Catholic lay men and lay women engaged in business, public service, education, labor, law, journalism, and the not-for-profit sector. They held six private hearings over a roughly two-month period, receiving testimony from other prominent people in business, government, and academia, principally people with a pro-business perspective (Lay Commission 1984, 81–88). The focus of the document is set in the two questions with which the text begins:

- What have I produced with the goods and talents God has given me?
- Can I tell God I am giving a fair amount of my personal time and treasure to help those in need and to help them to achieve economic self-reliance? (Lay Commission 1984, ix)

The experience, the point of view, the perspective, and the values are clearly those of entrepreneurs.

Economic Justice for All, in contrast, was the fruit of more than three years of open consultations across the United States and around the world. Drafts were published widely and critiques invited. Tens of thousands of pages of comment were reviewed and weighed. Open hearings drew testimony from all sectors of society, taking special care to include the experiences of people trapped in poverty. The process was the most participatory and inclusive of any used for the creation of a church teaching document, a serious effort to discern the Spirit active in the community. This document also opens with questions that reveal its approach and values:

Every perspective on economic life that is human, moral, and Christian must be shaped by three questions: What does the economy do *for* people? What does it do *to* people? And how do people *participate* in it? (NCCB 1986, no. 1)

The letter is very consistent in looking at the issues and problems from the perspective of their impact on all people, especially those in poverty. Its analysis and recommendations were much more nuanced and appropriate to all dimensions of the economic reality and much more adequate to the full range of Catholic social vision than *Toward the Future*.

After these economic controversies quieted down, *Toward the Future* slipped unheralded into the past. The same cannot be said, however, for the theological vision it articulated and promoted. US President George W. Bush, a self-proclaimed born-again Christian with a mission to make the world more free, has worked more than any other president in memory to bring religious language, values, and institutions into public life. The vision of religion that he promotes and that he claims legitimates the policies of his administration is fundamentally the same theology put forth in *Toward the Future*. That makes it a good example in the rest of this chapter, as I explain the principal modification to the pastoral spiral process that I recommend: the conscious integration of theological or faith elements in each step of the process.

Attending to the Religious Dimensions of Reality

In addition to being confessional and communal, I believe our approach to the pastoral spiral process needs to be explicitly religious from the beginning.

I confess that I come to this work as a trained theologian. I am convinced that God is active in history, in the events and dynamics of our daily lives. I believe that all reality is sinful and graced. The secular and the sacred are not different worlds; they are simply different ways of conceptualizing the same reality or different languages for describing and discussing it.

Why is it important, then, to be explicit about the religious dimensions of our experiences at the beginning of the pastoral spiral process? Because those religious dimensions have become part of us and are shaping our perceptions either consciously or unconsciously. They are an important element in the subjectivity of each person that has just been discussed. When we make them explicit, we make them available to ourselves and to the discerning community so that we can determine together whether they are deepening our grasp of the reality or blinding us to its real meaning.

Holland and Henriot acknowledge the presence of faith and religious reflection in all dimensions of the pastoral spiral process. They write: "We can say that social analysis contains within itself, implicitly or explicitly, a theology of life. The theological process has already begun in what appears to be a secular analysis of society" (Holland and Henriot 1983, 13). They proceed in the very next paragraph, however, to declare that "in this study, we will concentrate on social analysis, the second moment of the pastoral circle. Yet, we do so in a theological context—that is, one inspired by a faith commitment. For the present, however, we postpone more extended reflections on the third and fourth moments of the circle, namely theological reflection and pastoral planning" (Holland and Henriot 1983, 13–14).

But what about the influence of faith and religious experience in focusing our attention on details of our experience in the *first* moment? What about the theological process that is actively part of the *second* moment? What happens when those doing social analysis have different faith commitments from the ones that guide Henriot and Holland? Religious values and institutions play a structural role in shaping our perceptions and analyses of reality, as well as the reality itself to be perceived and analyzed. Restricting attention to the function of faith in the life processes to the *third* moment of the pastoral spiral process overlooks critical elements of experience and of analysis and leads to inadequate and distorted results. The religious element of each moment in the pastoral spiral needs to be explicit to do justice to reality and to direct social change in fruitful directions.

Experience: The First Moment

Faith experiences and beliefs often have discernible effects on people's dispositions and shape their awareness of future experiences and responses. Paul's experience of his own weakness evoked for him the image of Christ crucified and the realization that God often reveals the greatest power in our weakness. That predisposed him to see the wisdom and power of God working in the poor and weak in Corinth and inviting the conversion of the powerful. The Johannine community's experience of the hostility of the Jewish community heightened its consciousness of the threats around it and predisposed it to find God in the experience of acceptance and belonging. In the midst of hostility, longing for belonging, community members recalled the words of Jesus that confirmed that their special relationship with God and that the strength of their communion in love were the fullest revelation of God's presence in the world:

> In other words, then, the intuitive responses to specific social contexts embody affective dispositions which are linked with experiences and images of God deep in the pre-conscious of the human spirit. By consciously entering into the affective disposition, we can draw upon a type of spontaneous "logic of the affections" to call into consciousness the sense of God from which and to which we are responding. (Hug 1983, 291–92)

The foundational senses of God that guide our intuitive responses to specific contexts depend upon our needs or longings and how they have been met and have evolved in our personal histories. People with strong security needs will be subconsciously alert to dangers and searching for security; they are predisposed to recognize God as their rock, their fortress, the all-powerful One who grounds their sense of security. Those yearning for justice are especially attentive to what is wrong in society and have often found God in prophetic voices, judgment, and the triumph of justice. The restless, lonely heart seeking love and intimacy has often found in God the loving parent or intimate friend.

Systematic theologies reflect different efforts to identify and articulate the variety of patterns in the most important foundational religious experiences, the resulting variety of names for God, and the perceptual and moral predispositions that have, as a result, shaped specific religious traditions. Many of these theologies combine in some order:

- *a sense of dependence* or radical contingency that calls forth a sense of God as Creator or Source and predisposes us to awe and appreciative gratitude of creation;
- *a sense of grateful love* that evokes more intimate images of God filling our lives with care and gifts and calling forth dispositions of gentleness and caring for all around us;
- *a sense of repentance*, which provides a sense of God as judge and focuses our attention on human weaknesses, calling us to more critical self-awareness;
- *a sense of obligation*, which brings with it images of God as One who has established order in creation and predisposes us to seek and follow God's laws;

- *a sense of possibilities* through which God is experienced as Redeemer, as the source of new possibilities and hope, inspiring human creativity and countering despair; and
- *a sense of direction* that sees God as the final goal, the driving force and fulfillment of history, evoking a desire to participate in and cooperate with God's purposes for creation. (Hug 1983, 293–98; Gustafson 1975, 82–116)

These six "senses of God" and patterns of perceptual and moral predisposition have been acknowledged through history as authentic types of religious experience. God has been experienced as One who creates and supports, loves, judges and forgives, orders, liberates, and guides (Hug 1983, 298).

The theologies of *Toward the Future* and of the current faith-related justifications of neo-liberal capitalism focus upon the freedom of the individual in the context of the order established by God the Creator and the accountability of that individual to God as the final judge. God creates each individual as a free person, expects all persons to use their freedom creatively to liberate the wealth hidden in creation, and will judge them on the decisions they make and how well they respect the freedom of others. These are the two concerns that are reflected in its legitimation of the capitalist market system as "the only system built upon the liberty of its participants" (Lay Commission 1984, 26) and its heavy emphasis upon the decisions of the entrepreneur, the responsibility of the agent for his or her choices.

That singular—indeed, practically absolute—focus on freedom, personal creativity, and responsibility concentrates one's attention on individual choices and not upon the social realization of God's reign that a sense of direction would keep in front of us, or upon the social trends of God's redeeming work in the possibilities for a better future that are emerging. It is not surprising, then, that this theology sees personal failure at the root of almost all evils or injustices and fails to notice other dimensions of the experience.

Social Analysis: Filling Out the Picture

Social analysis, the second moment of the pastoral spiral, is defined "as the effort to obtain a more complete picture of a social situation by exploring its *historical and structural relationships*" (Holland and Henriot 1983, 14). The broad structures identified are economic, political, cultural, and sociological. The process is diagnostic: an identification and explication of the structures and historical dynamics shaping the experience, generally an experience of injustice, that we are addressing. Social analysis asks: What are the structures and dynamics at work creating the situation we are experiencing as it currently exists?

Theological reflection or faith analysis, the third moment, grows "out of the analysis" (Holland and Henriot 1983, 93). It is an evaluative moment that assesses the analyzed situation "in the light of living faith, scripture, church social teaching, and the resources of tradition. The Word of God brought to bear upon the situation raises new questions, suggests new insights, and opens new responses" (Holland and Henriot 1983, 9).

This is the pivotal point in the pastoral spiral process. Our analysis of the structural and historical dynamics creating our current reality is judged against the touchstone of our personal and communal faith experience. This is a discernment process by which we identify our own deepest values, determine the directions we must go to improve the situation as we have analyzed it so that it will accord more closely with those values, and then move to creating specific plans for bringing about a more just alternative social situation.

In other words, in the pastoral spiral process, the theological-reflection stage does not differ from the social-analysis stage by being explicitly religious while social analysis is purely secular, drawing upon the social sciences. Theological reflection differs from social analysis as evaluation and judgment differ from explanation and interpretation.

If then, in answering the social-analysis question—What are the structures and dynamics at work creating the situation we are experiencing as it currently exists?—we discover that religious beliefs, values, institutions, and structures shape, motivate, legitimate, and/or sustain the current situation, we must include them in the analysis. Only then will we be able to understand the situation accurately, evaluate it appropriately, and develop adequate plans for effective social change.

The neoliberal social analysis of the US economy in documents such as *Toward the Future* offers some illustrative examples. In its analysis, the cause of poverty in society is the failure to create adequate wealth. That failure is traced to personal or structural faults. The personal faults are failures of the initiative and entrepreneurial values that provide the "*moral élan* of the US economy" (Lay Commission 1984, x). The structural faults are traced to ignorance of the processes and dynamics of wealth creation in a community or the political suppression of the personal dynamics and virtues that lead to the creation of wealth. It is the genius of the US system, according to this analysis, that it overcomes poverty by balancing democratic politics with market economy and strong cultural support of entrepreneurial values, especially creativity and enlightened self-interest:

> From before the time of Jesus multitudes have lived in poverty and under tyranny. To further their liberation, our forefathers designed an order of political economy in which the poor and needy might routinely raise themselves out of poverty by methods economically wise and conducive to unparalleled economic creativity. (Lay Commission 1984, xi)

In prior ages, one part of society could gain only at the expense of others; capital investment and creativity changed the rules. "For the first time in human history," [Walter] Lippmann wrote, human beings had constructed "a way of producing wealth in which the good fortune of others multiplied their own" and "the golden rule was economically sound." The production of wealth and the abolition of poverty moved in tandem. Poverty could no longer be regarded as the natural state of a majority but as an ever shrinking problem which could be overcome. (Lay Commission 1984, 23)

In other words, they are arguing that the political economy conceived by the "Founding Fathers" of the United States harnessed self-interest to the service of the common good. Only by meeting the needs of people can the entrepreneur succeed.

There are a number of fairly obvious problems with this analysis. Entrepreneurs respond to the needs of those with the resources to buy their goods and services, not to the needs of those in poverty. The production of wealth without adequate social mechanisms for redistribution does little to abolish poverty. Marketing has long since transformed luxuries into "needs" in affluent societies, while the survival needs of those in poverty are overlooked or ignored. Ecological limits preclude growing the world out of poverty. Concentration of wealth allows those who dominate the economy to disrupt the balance of democracy, markets, and virtue-supportive culture, and to corrupt the whole process to their advantage.

The point I want to call attention to here is that supporters of the neoliberal vision cannot see and deal with these problems *because of their foundational religious beliefs*. First, they consider personal freedom and choice as the core human religious act. They identify God as the Creator who judges those choices, rewarding or punishing the individual. Social structures and systems have their purpose and meaning in serving individual freedom. If that freedom is present and poverty remains or grows worse, it must be fault of personal choices by those "few bad eggs" whose greed for wealth or power is creating the problem:

We wish to observe that many critics, in our experience, criticize the *system* for faults that are more properly attributed to the *persons*—to ourselves—who fail to use the liberties afforded by this system wisely or well. That a free system cannot, of its very nature, coerce human beings into moral behavior is the flaw in all schemes by coercive utopians. After invoking some sanctions and some incentives, after education and encouragement, a free system can do little more than offer human beings the liberty to act morally. This means, of course, that some will act immorally; in fact, that every one of us will sometimes fail. But it is no more just to blame the system for the failings of free persons than to blame our blessed Creator for making us free, or for allowing tares to grow up with the wheat (Mt 13:24–30). (Lay Commission 1984, 34–35)

Proponents of the neoliberal economic theologies see market capitalism as the only system built upon the liberty of its citizens, encouraging the good use of that liberty through private property, market incentives, and the discipline of profit (Lay Commission 1984, 26, 46). It provides the context for what is considered the important religious moments: the personal free choices each person makes before God and God's judgment of that person:

> As Catholics, we do not value the market either as an idol or as an automatic "Invisible Hand" instantly making all things right. The market is an opportunity, an open place. It allows us our liberty of conscience. What we make of it defines our character and prepares us to meet our Judge. (Lay Commission 1984, 26, 44)

As a result, these proponents are prone to refer to America with such Puritan biblical images as "the shining city on the hill" meant to be "a light to the nations." *Toward the Future* quotes the US Catholic bishops at the Third Plenary Council of Baltimore in 1884 at some length:

> We think we can claim to be acquainted both with the laws, institutions and spirit of the Catholic Church, and with the laws, institutions and spirit of our country; and we emphatically declare that there is no antagonism between them. . . . We believe that our country's heroes were the instruments of the God of Nations in establishing this home of freedom; to both the Almighty and His instruments in the work, we look with grateful reverence. [We urge Catholics] to take a special interest in the history of our country, [and we] consider the establishment of our country's independence, the shaping of its liberties and laws as a work of special Providence, its framers "building wiser than they knew," the Almighty's hand guiding them. (Lay Commission 1984, 7–8)

Echoes of that sense of divine guidance and of a religious mission can be heard in the writings and speeches of President George W. Bush to this day, for example, in the State of the Union Address 2004. And while less explicitly religious in tone than *Toward the Future*, for example, *The National Security Strategy of the United States*, released by President Bush in September 2002, just a year after the tragic events of 9/11, is built upon the same principles. In the covering memo presenting the strategy paper, Bush stated:

> Freedom is the non-negotiable demand of human dignity; the birthright of every person—in every civilization. Throughout history, freedom has

been threatened by war and terror; it has been challenged by the clash-ing wills of powerful states and the evil designs of tyrants; and it has been tested by widespread poverty and disease. Today, humanity holds in its hands the opportunity to further freedom's triumph over all these foes. The United States welcomes our responsibility to lead in this great mission. (*The National Security Strategy of the United States of America* 2002, 2)

That mission, *The National Security Strategy of the United States* notes in its very first paragraph, is the result of the unprecedented and unequaled power of the United States, which bestows on it the mission of promoting "a balance of power that favors freedom." It is a moral and religious mis-sion: the goal is not just to make the world safer; it is to make it better by promoting the universal values of economic and political freedom, peace, and respect for human dignity. The document goes on to catalogue how this sacred vocation legitimates everything from unilateralism in international relations to preemptive war and market liberalization.

These religious beliefs give rise to a social-analysis that is remarkably uncritical of the workings of democratic capitalist systems, hypercritical of systems that impinge on any freedoms, and dedicated to creating a world order committed to freedom.

In this social analysis moment of the pastoral spiral, it is also instructive to step back and take a broader perspective. The neoliberal social analysis of the economy offered in *Toward the Future* was developed and published to play a particular role in its historical context. That role itself needs to be the object of critical-analytic reflection. When we do that, we discover how central religious beliefs and motivations are once again to an accurate so-cial analysis of the situation.

First, the writers see speaking out on the US economy as one of their responsibilities as lay Catholics taught by the Second Vatican Council:

> The apostolate of the social milieu, that is, the effort to infuse a Chris-tian spirit into the mentality, customs, laws, and structures of the com-munity in which a person lives, is so much the duty and responsibility of the laity that it can never be properly performed by others (*Apostolicam Actuositatem [The Document on the Laity]*, no. 13). (Lay Commission 1984, 1)

Pope John Paul II and all previous authors of Catholic social thought are criticized for failing to develop their understanding of two important issues: the institutional causes of economic creativity and the production of wealth. In a passage on the role of sin in society's life and institutional structures, the failure to develop Catholic economic thought is identified as one of the faults of the Catholic church (Lay Commission 1984, 2, 26–27).

This faith-based activity of producing *Toward the Future* also played sociological and political roles that solid social analysis needs to explicate. It claimed religious authority from the highest governing structure of the Catholic community, an ecumenical council. It set out to stir the patriotism and pride of US Catholics in their national systems. And it relativized and sought to "delegitimate" the teaching of US bishops on these matters that are "so much the duty and responsibility of the laity."

Finally, *Toward the Future* attempts to discredit the bishops' prophetic criticisms of the US political-economic system by suggesting that the American system's great success is in part the result of the separation of church and state. "The institutions established by the Founding Fathers, 'building wiser than they knew, the Almighty's hand guiding them'" give religion no direct role in governing society. The role of religion is to encourage the formation of the habits of association, cooperation, self-interest rightly understood, and all the virtues that make democracy and capitalism flourish. It is simply to be a teacher of the virtues needed for the society's success and progress:

> Not by accident has the American political economy been fertile in promoting the practice of association, the habits of cooperation, and the habits of the heart guided by self-interest rightly understood—that self-interest which reaches out to embrace the interests of others, near and far. Religion takes no direct part in the government of society, but in encouraging such habits, as Tocqueville recognized, it is the foremost of the political institutions of the land. (Lay Commission 1984, 24)

Theological Reflection: Evaluation and Action in Faith

The third moment of the pastoral spiral becomes a confrontation or a dialogue of theologies: the theology underlying the status quo and the theology of those engaged in the pastoral spiral process. It is the most authentic expression of our faith that we can identify that should guide the planning and action of the fourth moment.

Other chapters in this volume offer various ways to determine the greater authenticity. I personally draw upon two basic questions: Is the theology put forward *adequate* to the full gospel experienc; that is, does it accord with my personal experience and knowledge of God? Is it *appropriate* to this historical context?

I cannot elaborate here a full theological critique of the neo-liberalism we have been discussing, although I have given clear indications of how I would develop it. The presentation of God as creator, lawgiver, and judge does not do justice to the fullness of the Christian experience. Attention to God's redeeming work and the signs of the establishment of God's reign in history help to open our eyes to other elements in our context and sharpen our analyses. The theology of *Economic Justice for All: Pastoral Letter on Catholic Social Teaching and the US Economy* does an excellent job of providing a more sound and authentic theological foundation for a more just global economy.

In the fourth moment of the pastoral spiral, the planning and action, it will most often be necessary to include corrective theological and pastoral activities designed to expand religious awareness, responding to the specific religious focusing of experience and limiting of analysis brought about by the inadequate and inappropriate theologies supporting the unjust status quo.

Conclusion

This is not the place to take up the challenge offered by this theology, to evaluate it, and to propose a more adequate and appropriate religious vision. I have presented the neo-liberal theology briefly in order to make clear how faith, values, and religious institutions continue to play significant roles in shaping our experiences as well as justifying and maintaining the current injustices in today's globalizing society.

Our topic is how we see social analysis and the pastoral spiral after twenty-five years of experience with them. My principal points, therefore, are methodological. To use the pastoral spiral methodology fruitfully to uncover the unjust structural dynamics at play and sketch plans to make another, more just world possible, our "experience" or "insertion" observations should include the relevant religious elements confronting us. Any social analysis must include analysis of those theological factors shaping, legitimating, and sustaining the status quo. Our theological reflection must show that we have a more authentic faith vision to offer than the one currently operative. And our planning must include elements of religious motivation and guidance as well as religious structures of legitimation to support the work for social change.

These modifications of the pastoral spiral will help us to surface the profound importance of religious beliefs and values that often lie hidden at the base of our social-policy debates. Only by addressing those differences adequately can we hope to shape more just forms of globalization that will serve the authentic human social development of each and every one of God's people.

References

Gustafson, James M. 1975. *Can ethics be Christian?* Chicago: University of Chicago Press.

Holland, Joe, and Peter Henriot, SJ. 1983. *Social analysis: Linking faith and justice.* Maryknoll, NY: Orbis Books.

Hug, James E. 1983. *Tracing the Spirit: Communities, social action, and theological reflection.* New York: Paulist Press.

Lay Commission. 1984. *Toward the future: Catholic social thought and the US economy: A lay letter.* New York: Lay Commission on Catholic Social Teaching and the US Economy.

NCCB (National Conference of Catholic Bishops). 1986. *Economic justice for all: Pastoral letter on Catholic social teaching and the US economy.* Washington, DC: United States Catholic Conference.

The National Security Strategy of the United States. 2002. This document and the covering memo are available online at the US Department of State website.

Searching for Truth
and the Right Thing to Do

DEAN BRACKLEY

The Holland and Henriot pastoral circle lays out a path for understanding the world and responding to it better. This is no small achievement! Now, after twenty-five years of change, what can this method still teach us? How can it help new generations respond to these challenging times?

In 1980 Henriot and Holland foresaw a difficult road ahead: "In every area of life—economic, political, and cultural—we are moving into a grimmer future" (Holland and Henriot 1983, 77). They were right.[1] Today the world is a meaner and scarier place. The gap between rich and poor has widened, both within and among nations. Entire regions like sub-Saharan Africa, majorities in the poor countries, and Northern urban ghettos, especially in the United States, are cut off from a decent livelihood, mired in debt, and unable to climb out of poverty. As social spending contracts everywhere, a stigmatized underclass expands. Life-sustaining ecosystems groan under strain. As it becomes harder to conceal all this, cynicism and public lying are on the rise. So is reliance on force, with state violence, crime, and barbarism spreading on a world scale (see Castells 2000, chaps. 2–3). It is getting harder to tell the cops from the robbers. During the 1980s I watched neighborhoods, families, and egos crumble in the Bronx. Now the threefold crumbling seems to be globalizing—to San Salvador, Cairo, and Moscow.

In Latin America the social transformations that many were expecting in the 1960s and 1970s failed to materialize. In those heady days, pastoral agents and activists often misunderstood the aspirations of the poor (Comblin 1998, chap. 4), and repression far exceeded what people anticipated. Over the years bishops like those who committed the church to the poor at Medellín in 1968 have been replaced by more conservative church leaders, many of whom view with suspicion, or hostility, the theology and ministry that inspired the pastoral circle. Over the past three decades Christian base communities have declined in number and social relevance. More conservative "apostolic movements" now prosper in the Catholic church, and pentecostal Protestant congregations continue to grow (although some have matured over the years in their approach to social problems).

None of this means that radical transformation is less urgent today—in Latin America or elsewhere. However, people now look with more hope to groups in civil society than to traditional political actors (governments, parties, liberation movements). Some theologians, like Franz Hinkelammert in Costa Rica and Jung Mo Sung in Brazil, continue to develop a rich critique of the prevailing capitalist economy. Others, activists and theologians, focus on resistance to neo-liberal policies and nurturing the seeds of hope in local initiatives. They reflect on the wealth of indigenous and African American cultures and stress the need for equitable social relations, including gender relations, and defending the environment (see Fornet-Betancourt 2003).

Cultural Crisis and Pluralism

Changes in church and society have produced, and also reflect, worldwide cultural upheaval—part of what Joe Holland calls a "crisis of civilization" (Holland and Henriot 1983, xii). In this essay I respond to two challenges presented by this global cultural turmoil. In the first place, as several contributors to this volume point out, we are exposed today as never before to a wide range of world views and versions of "the good life." This pluralism touches every part of the globe and supercharges the most vital questions people face: How are we to understand our world? How should we respond to it? How can we stay human, and Christian, today? Second, the intellectual climate, including partisan polemics, challenges us to place the pastoral circle on a solid intellectual foundation. Frans Wijsen provides a vital contribution to that effort in this book. Here I complement his arguments from a different angle and, in so doing, specify the conditions for authentic searching for truth and right practice in our pluralistic world. In this way I hope to kill two birds with one stone: to show that the pastoral circle is strictly necessary for good discernment, and at the same time, to help postmodern searchers find their way and respond more generously to our broken world. In the end, these reflections outline a spirituality for searchers and especially for people within and beyond the church who are working for social change.

Pluralism is here to stay, and it can enrich us in many ways. We can learn from the great religions and the wealth of diverse cultures. At the same time, pluralism undermines the authorities, traditions, and institutions that help people make sense of life. And, unless we are careful, it can produce a paralyzing relativism.

Besides the gospel of Matthew, we are confronted with the gospels of Wall Street, MTV, and many others. Small wonder we feel less certain than our forebears about what is true and morally right. This uncertainty spreads today in poor countries as well as rich ones, in affluent and depressed neighborhoods alike, and especially among young people. In El Salvador it affects almost everyone. My students—from working-class, middle-class, and peasant households—are all exposed to multiple versions of what is going on in the world and what life is about. So are the youth of my urban parish, as well as all church professionals and the poor migrants who make their way north to the United States. Sooner or later the world views they all have inherited enter into crisis. In affluent societies the crisis is more acute. There, few seem to escape the painful collapse of their world and the difficult process of rebuilding. For some, this process becomes a recurrent, chronic drama. This is a major sign of our times.

In this situation, traditional communities "circle their wagons" to defend their identities and their traditions. Religions slide into fundamentalism. Some people despair of finding *the* truth about life's meaning and about morality, including intellectuals who cling to a narrow positivism. A climate of relativism grows: "You have your truth—and your morality—and I have mine." This is a sure-fire formula for sabotaging a social agenda and leaving society in the hands of its most powerful and least scrupulous members. Meanwhile, elites everywhere lay hold of the means of communication and broadcast a virulent political conservativism that discredits any serious critique of the status quo. Their aggressive discourse ridicules proposals for fighting poverty and demonizes movements for social change.

In this climate we need the pastoral circle more than ever. It provides a direct challenge to pseudo-scientific neo-conservatism. We must therefore demonstrate its validity and necessity. It is also an antidote to relativism. We must therefore show how it can guide people into greater light and help them discern what to do. Paraguayan theologian Juan Luis Segundo anticipated this challenge years ago. When Holland and Henriot first presented the pastoral circle, they referred to Segundo's "hermeneutic circle" (cf. Holland and Henriot 1983, 8; Segundo 1976, 7–9). Segundo points out how engaging social reality challenges the way we put our world together. The unsettling impact of injustice should provoke us to serious reflection with the help of basic sources, especially the Bible. That should, in turn, lead to a more adequate understanding of life and faith, and to more effective action. While Segundo is primarily concerned with theology, he locates theological reflection within the broader personal search for truth and right action. In other words, broadly understood, the pastoral circle is more than a tool for pastoral planning. It can also help individuals and groups make sense out of their lives and respond to the world better. This point of personal transformation is well exemplified in Singgih's contribution to this volume.

It is people who are searching like this that we will have to count on from now on to help make our world more livable. Will they rise to the challenge? Everything depends on how they (that is, we) conduct the search, as individuals and as groups, in a climate of ephemeral commitments, or commitment "lite," when pontificating and moralizing are automatic turnoffs. That is where the pastoral circle comes in. It is neither a set of doctrines nor a collection of moral norms; it is, rather, a discipline, a path. It specifies criteria for authentic searching. This is important, because authenticity remains one of the few values that can claim universal allegiance today. However, for the pastoral circle to make good on its potential, we must spell out in greater detail what its different elements entail. To do so, it will help to set the stage by pointing out what is at stake in people's searching today and the obstacles they face.

Cognitive Liberation: Bias versus Enriched Reason

Today people are not only searching for what is true and right but also for who they are and what to do with their lives. As they confront contradictory role models—a Mother Teresa on the one hand, the latest rock star on the other—identity crises multiply and postpone the consolidation of a solid (or is it rigid?) adult personality. In searching and in helping others search, we need to take this into account, and also the obstacles and pitfalls that lie in our path. Besides ignorance and diverse world views, these include the less obvious blind spots and biases that we all bring to the task.

Our cultural formation—by family, school, church, and the media—and our location, experience, and past choices circumscribe our imagination and intelligence. Besides the conscious concepts and customs we have inherited, unconscious assumptions underlie our thinking and acting. I mean the anthropological, cosmological, and moral myths and presuppositions that make up the horizon of each person's world, the "grid" through which we interpret and evaluate data. Thinkers like Marx, Freud, Nietzsche, sociologists of knowledge, and feminists have all labored to map this substratum of our conscious and rational life. Today some of their postmodern successors believe that our most basic assumptions rest ultimately on value commitments, including religious commitments, that are in the final analysis irrational. From this they conclude that our world views are mutually incommensurable, in the sense that we have no rational way to arbitrate among them. Pluralism slides into lazy relativism.

While pluralism is both insurmountable and beneficial, pessimism about getting closer to objective truth lets us off the hook too easily, insofar as our assumptions are unexamined and based on limited experience and unfounded prejudice. For, along with the benefits, we also inherit the biases and blind spots of our social class, race, age group, sex, religion, and nation. As a result, important problems escape our notice, and some questions fail to arise. To that extent, discovering truth and discerning action depend on unmasking the unconscious ignorance, falsehoods, and half-truths that stand between us and reality. If we ignore that challenge, our search remains unauthentic. We need the kind of cognitive liberation that reconfigures our world view, drawing what is really important from the margins toward the center of the canvass and displacing what is unimportant from the center and moving it toward the edges.

While we can't be blamed for distortions that we have simply inherited, we all seem to cling to them, at least to some extent. Why? We have a stake in our basic assumptions. They are rooted in our desires, which were first shaped by early interaction with our family and social environment. Our deep desires and inclinations are embedded, in the end, in our identity, so that to question them is to question who we are and to shake the foundations of our world. While basic assumptions are not to be blamed in the same way that deliberate actions are, our distorting prejudices have something in common with what Christians call original sin. Or rather, original sin has a cognitive dimension, what we might call original distortion. We are always already biased! In addition, personal, habitual, and structural sin also have cognitive consequences that we massively overlook in our "rational" debates: personal distortion, habitual distortion and systemic distortion. Whether it is culpable or not, we need to take bias seriously. Small wonder we find this a challenge!

Most moderns, and academics, prescribe more pure reason and awareness as the solution. As important as these are, they don't seem to be enough to dissolve the obstacles to understanding reality. Cognitive hygiene requires "conscientization," surely. But it also requires untangling the habits of our heart and ordering our commitments. Since these are rooted in our identity, it requires nothing less than personal transformation (conversion).

In other words, although reality may be reasonable, we need more than pure reason to understand it. We need *reason integrally considered*. I mean reason rooted in experience and practice and nourished by wisdom traditions, including revelation. We need reason liberated in personal transformation and enriched by imagination, affectivity, dialogue, and contemplation.

Authentic Searching

With its four moments—insertion, social analysis, theological reflection, and practical planning—the pastoral circle takes the obstacles to knowledge seriously. In what follows I propose three general criteria to guide our use of the pastoral circle in searching for understanding and for what to do. These criteria further specify what is involved in that search and what the pastoral circle's four "mediations of experience" (Holland and Henriot 1983, x) entail.

In general, searching for the truth and the right thing to do requires (1) *facing up to reality*, especially that of the victims of injustice (see Sobrino 1988, chap. 1); (2) *personal transformation* (conversion)—first, in order to free us from prejudice, and second, to enable us to follow the internal movement of the Spirit; and (3) a wisdom-bearing *community* to support and challenge us, since we cannot sustain a counter-cultural vision and commitment alone.

Observing these criteria is a matter of taking seriously the three poles of our experience—the world around us, our inner life, and the cultural word about the world. By drawing out the implications of these criteria, we can further identify the kind of reflection and the resources that authentic searching requires and in so doing demonstrate the validity and necessity of the pastoral circle method. Together, these criteria make up a discipline or way of proceeding. Although we could argue for most of them on strictly rational grounds—a great advantage in a time of pluralism—Christian faith helps us see their unity and coherence more clearly.

The Reality Principle

What we see depends on where we stand. That is the point of the first moment of the pastoral circle—insertion or contact—which Holland and Henriot drew from liberation theology. According to Gustavo Gutiérrez, theology is a second step, a reflection not only on praxis but *from* praxis. It presupposes commitment and assumes the perspective of the oppressed (Gutiérrez 1988, chap. 1; 1983, 200–1). Brazilians Leonardo and Clodovis Boff later provided a concise synthesis of the method of liberation theology (1987, chap. 3). For them, too, practical theology presupposes commitment (a kind of step zero). This is the context of the other three moments, which correspond to the "see, judge, and act" schema of Catholic Action. Each moment requires a "mediation" or tool: social analysis (the better to "see" reality), theological reflection proper ("judge"), and criteria for action ("act").[2]

The first step is vital. Entering new worlds and engaging people who are different from us broadens our horizon. Meeting people of different faiths and cultures can do this. However, suffering people, especially victims of injustice, do this in a unique and critical way. I frequently witness this in El Salvador. The foreign visitors who engage with poor communities provide an especially revealing example. Visitors from the North are both shaken by the hardship and injustice they witness and amazed by the hope and generosity of their hosts. This can be a life-changing experience for the pilgrims.

The humanity of the poor crashes through the pilgrims' defenses. As they see their reflection in the eyes of the poor ("They're just like us!"), they begin to feel disoriented. Their world—half-consciously divided into important people and unimportant people—begins to shake. The experience is a little like falling in love; in fact, something like that is happening. Their horizon broadens. They are entering a richer world.

The impoverished show us that the world is more cruel than we had thought, but more wonderful as well. When they accept us as we are, when they insist on celebrating life and sharing their few tortillas, they communicate hope. Sin abounds, but grace abounds even more (Rom 5:20).

"Insertion" opens our horizons. My middle-class tribe may be no worse than any other. The problem is that we are a minority laboring under the illusion—common to many minorities—that we are the norm. Technology and the media fortify that illusion. In reality, since we are removed from the daily struggle to survive, we easily fall into a chronic, low-grade confusion about what is most important in life, namely, life itself and love. The victims of injustice stop us short. Engaging them, we discover that they, not we, are at the center of the life-and-death drama. And that center is the best place for putting things in proper perspective.

The "insertion" moment normally involves *action*, which can itself sharpen understanding. People in Twelve-Step programs like Alcoholics Anonymous say that we need to act ourselves into a new way of thinking more than the other way around. We need to do the truth in order to know the truth (Jn 3:21; 7:17; 1 Jn 1:6). It is the person who practices compassion who sees straight. *Ama ut intellegas*: Love that you may understand. When linked to compassion, *religious practice* and *contemplation* also sharpen perception, including moral sensibility (Holland and Henriot 1983, x).[3]

The case of the visitors to Central America and similar experiences illustrate how understanding reality requires *conscientization*. The pastoral circle is all about that. Conscientization is an awakening to social reality—especially its cruelty, but also its promise. Discovering truth is more than a simple matter of pushing back the frontiers of ignorance. It requires unmasking the distortions that suffuse everyday discourse, including our inner discourse. Conscientization discloses the coverup of injustice and the "original prejudice" that some people are important and others (most) don't count. The key questions for conscientization are: Who suffers? Why? Who profits? Who has control? To whom are they accountable? How do these policies and institutions affect the weak? (Holland and Henriot 1983, 28).

Wherever we are located socially, we all resist having our world dismantled. Therefore, conscientization, like psychotherapy and conversion, requires time, effort, and mediators. It also requires social science.

Conscientization uncovers signs of hope. Few things paralyze like the pseudo-realism that is so clear-sighted about human selfishness and so blind to goodness and grace and the surprises they produce in history. This *realpolitik* cannot move us beyond the war on terrorism, nuclear deterrents, razor wire, and free-market anarchy. Since reality is pregnant with new possibilities, *utopian imagination* is essential to orient action (see Mannheim 1929; Gutiérrez 1988, 135–40; Bloch 1995). We not only have a right to dream, but we have a duty to dream. Utopian imagination is set in motion by questions like these: What kind of people do we want to be? What kind of society can we be? What kind of church? What kind of economy do we want? What kind of government? Like Martin Luther King's dream, utopian imagining awakens hope and inspires action. Unlike wishful fantasy, it springs from the kind of consolation that is rooted in faith and commitment.[4]

To sum up: Experience and action (especially engaging the victims), conscientization, utopian imagination, religious practice, and contemplation are all part of reason integrally considered. They are necessary for authentic searching according to the method of the pastoral circle.

Personal Transformation

In his "Afterword" to the second edition of *Social Analysis*, Peter Henriot stresses the importance of conversion for understanding (Holland and Henriot 1983, 96). Why? Since life is a moral drama, understanding it requires moral empathy. "Be transformed by the renewing of your minds," writes Paul, "so that you may discern what is the will of God—what is good and acceptable and perfect" (Rom 12:2). In the full sense, conversion is more than a change of values or even of behavior. It is a transformation of the person. Our ability to grasp what is at stake, morally, depends in the end on that. "Perception is a function of character," writes William Spohn. "Transformation of the person down to her most important values, therefore, is necessary to correct the vision of the heart" (1999, 86).

In this process we grow into our true self and our *vocation*. The idea of a vocation, so central to human dignity, is off the radar screen of today's dominant cultures. While postmodern capitalism might offer us a job or even a profession, it knows little of vocations, except for getting and spending. That cheapens us. Commercials telegraph the insult.

When we discover our vocation—as a painter, an athlete, or a chemist—something clicks inside us. Our life takes on a deeper meaning and purpose—something everyone is hungry for these days. Still, as much as we might identify with painting or chemistry, we do not identify completely. Our lives will still have meaning and purpose if, for some reason, we can no longer paint or do chemistry. Is there a deeper vocation that integrates our other callings? What gives our lives their ultimate meaning? What fulfills us as human beings? Along with others, Christians answer that we are created to love and serve. Only in giving ourselves do we find ourselves.

This is a calling that people "hear" in real life. Former UN Secretary General Dag Hammarskjöld wrote, "At some point I did answer 'Yes' to Someone—or Something—and from that hour I was certain that existence is meaningful and that, therefore, my life, in self-surrender, had a goal" (1964, 205). Hammarskjöld's vocation led him to work for peace, and he died in a plane crash pursuing peace in central Africa. Maryknoll sister Ita Ford, killed by Salvadoran guardsmen along with three companions in 1980, had written shortly before her death to her young niece, Jennifer, in the United States: "I hope you come to find that which gives life a deep meaning for you. Something worth living for—maybe even worth dying for—something that energizes you, enthuses you, enables you to keep moving ahead. I can't tell you what it might be. That's for you to find, to choose, to love."[5]

Ita invited Jennifer to discover her deepest calling. Life is short, and we only get to do it once. We want it to count. Our need for something worth living for, even dying for, converges with what the world needs from us. Yet, we can sleep through life, especially in consumer societies. The pastoral circle is designed to wake us up and keep us awake.

As the word suggests, vocations are called forth from within us. Spouses and children draw forth from some of us our vocation as wife, husband, parent. Martin Luther King Jr. discovered his vocation as leader and prophet in response to the challenges of the Montgomery bus boycott. Down-and-out working people drew forth from Dorothy Day her vocation as writer and revolutionary apostle of mercy. A lot depends on where we are. If King or Day had spent most of their time at poolside, few would remember them today. Suffering people are a privileged place for hearing our calling to serve. By penetrating our defenses and posing the crucial questions, the victims evoke our deepest calling. When that happens, something clicks deep within us. We feel drawn to serve, drawn with a sense of fullness and satisfaction that Ignatius of Loyola calls consolation. And consolation leads into the light.

While there is some truth to the common belief that feelings can cloud our thinking, that is only part of the truth. Just as affectivity is central to the problem of bias, it is also crucial to overcoming bias. That is in part a matter of *discerning interior movements,* as Ignatius shows.

Spiritual consolation and its opposite, desolation, are feelings that arise from our center and affect our interior state as a whole. Consolation is peace and joy, a sense of fullness that is disproportionate to its apparent causes. It directs us beyond ourselves in hope and generosity. Desolation is the opposite: sadness, inner turmoil, leaden discouragement (Ignatius Loyola 1992, nos. 316–17). These too-brief descriptions will have to do for now. The important thing is that, provided we are decidedly committed to seeking and doing what is right (rather than to mere self-satisfaction), consolation moves us toward greater self-transcendence. Desolation, on the other hand, indicates resistance to self-transcendence. The converted heart (not just any heart and not just any feeling) tends toward what is true and good.

In preparing this volume several contributors pointed out the importance of evaluation in the use of the pastoral circle, especially the importance of taking note of the good things that happen, however mundane. (Latin Americans stress the need to celebrate as well.) It is a vital point. In dark and discouraging times we dare not overlook the tiny and unexpected consolations that come our way and by which God nourishes our hope. They may well signal new beginnings—like the mustard seed, the leaven, and the small stone that can smash an empire.

Of special interest to the search for truth and practical discernment is the way consolation gives rise to images and concepts that expand our horizon and dissolve bias, while desolation narrows and distorts our vision. For just as the Father of Lies is behind desolation, the Spirit of truth is behind consolation (Jn 8:44; 14:17).

For example, consolation can erase the desolate feelings of guilt, loneliness, and impotence that lead us to misinterpret reality. It gives rise to a sense of pardon and acceptance, or of comfort, healing, or power—and corresponding images—that expand our horizon.

Engaging homeless people, people in jail, poor people, or other suffering people frequently provokes both consolation and desolation in well-disposed people. When visitors from the North encounter the poor in Central America, the experience stirs fear and discouragement on the one hand, and joy and enthusiasm, on the other, along with corresponding thoughts and images. Subversive thoughts and images (like a circle of equals) spontaneously arise out of consolation occasioned in this way. They clash with the original prejudice that some people are important and others are not. It might be our surroundings—a eucharist or other shared meal—that provide the new symbols that undermine the standard images of the social ladder and the political pyramid. By enabling us to see the world with new eyes, this kind of experience primes us to decode the lies behind official policy and common-sense discourse.

In short, consolation gives rise to thoughts, words, and symbols that unmask the distortions that discourage, sadden, and discriminate. It liberates from bias. Paul Ricoeur says that the symbol gives rise to thought (Ricoeur 1967, 347–57), to which we can add: Consolation gives rise to liberating symbols.

Community

Contemporary individualism generates a naive sense of self-sufficiency. In reality, the personal autonomy that is essential to maturity has nothing to do with self-sufficiency. We all need help in searching for truth and the right thing to do. We need a community that will support and challenge us. Not any community will do for this, but only one that draws on a deep tradition of practical wisdom. Of course, in the real world all such communities are imperfect, and all traditions accumulate negative elements over time. David Tracy explains how the biblical traditions stand out in the way they demand prophetic self-critique and purification (Tracy 1981, 236–37, 324–27, 420).

Contemporary pluralism offers communities the chance to benefit from dialogue with other traditions. What needs stressing today is that, unless we identify critically and creatively with such a community, we flounder about, shaped as much by markets and mass media as anything else. As Daniel Berrigan says, we can't go anywhere unless we're coming from somewhere.

As a wisdom-bearing community, the church nourishes an experience of transcendence and an alternative vision and praxis (Holland and Henriot 1983, xix–xxi). This is where theological reflection fits in our lives and in the pastoral circle.

In the Christian tradition Jesus of Nazareth with his commandment of love of neighbor is the humanizing norm of norms, the fundamental criterion that guides Christians in their search for truth and right action.

What does it take to search honestly and authentically? To sum up, according to *Social Analysis*, it takes insertion, social analysis, theological reflection, and practical orientation. I have argued that putting these moments of the pastoral circle into practice is a matter of (1) coming to terms with reality, especially the reality of the victims of injustice; (2) undergoing personal transformation and attending to the interior movements of the Spirit; and (3) identifying critically with a wisdom-bearing community. These three criteria require that we take seriously the three dimensions of experience: the world outside us, the world inside us, and the cultural word about the world. On a Christian reading, we must be open to the truth that comes from the Creator of all reality, from the Spirit who transforms and enlightens us from within, and from the word of God, the source of all true words.[6] A realistic appreciation of human limitations and biases obliges us to use reason integrally considered; that is, reason enriched by experience, practice, imagination, affectivity, and contemplation; reason liberated in personal transformation; reason that undergoes conscientization, that dialogues and that draws on traditions of wisdom.

Social Analysis presents the pastoral circle in explicitly Christian terms. While the discipline that I have proposed is also best understood in those terms, I have presented it in a way that should appeal to non-Christians as well. My argument is that all these touchstones mentioned are necessary in searching for truth and the right thing to do. To omit them would be unreasonable.

Conclusion

On a Christian reading, the three general criteria converge on the practical norm of love. This love, like that of the Good Samaritan, responds to suffering outside our family, tribal, and religious circles. This is solidarity. It is what the world needs most.

We have no clear road map to a more humane society and no precise blueprint for it. There are no more Winter Palaces for the Left to take; if there were, they would be quickly retaken through covert and overt operations. While politics remains important, today few expect traditional political actors to pull the world out of its crises. At most we hope they will support rather than block positive change.

Meanwhile, around the world, we are witnessing the burgeoning of citizens groups that are pushing for change from the bottom up and across the base of societies. Struggling neighbors, indigenous people, women, consumers, immigrants, ethnic minorities, environmental groups, human rights organizations, unions, small-size and medium-size businesses, cooperatives, and communal banks are sowing the seeds of a new social order. Many stress democratic participation and accountability, which is especially promising in what have been traditional authoritarian societies.

This effervescence of civil society reflects "the social and spiritual creativity of rooted communities networked in solidarity" (Holland and Henriot 1983, xvii). However, whether in Chicago or Kerala, local micro-initiatives are up against macro-obstacles. In Central America those who today openly challenge companies that are polluting the river may be found floating in the river tomorrow. The same goes for fighting official crime and corruption. Therefore, local activists and communities make friends with allies abroad: with Human Rights Watch, Greenpeace, sister parishes, and unions. Without such alliances the local groups have little chance against those who control the market and the means of violence.

Even with international allies, they are like small fish in a pond of sharks. Titanic competitors dominate the international arena: transnational capital, the G7 governments, international finance and trade institutions (the IMF, the WTO) with their political and economic power, and the ultimate backup of military force. And yet, powerful signs of hope brighten the international scene. Protests in Seattle, Bangkok, Prague, Quebec, and Geneva in recent years symbolize the growing challenge to global elitist hegemony. So do the 1996 global Land Mine Treaty, which more than thirteen hundred NGOs pushed through in record time, and the Jubilee 2000 coalition, which pressured the G7 countries to concede debt relief to some of the poorest countries. The World Social Forum has convened thousands of people these last few years in Porto Alegre, Brazil, and Mumbai, India, to explore creative strategies for positive change.

As legions of nongovernmental actors grow and network among themselves, they stir hope that another world is possible. But, again, populist micro-initiatives need allies to survive and thrive in an inhospitable environment. That is why we have to make this century a century of solidarity, especially international solidarity. As elites extend their power, globalizing markets, finance, and communications, the response can only be to globalize the practice of love. While that involves practical and technical challenges, the biggest challenge of all is to find committed people who are ready to hang in there over the long haul. These "new human beings" are indispensable. I mean people with hearts that respond to the suffering and heads prepared to address the complex causes of misery, including people in rich countries who know about trade, finance, and human rights law. Fortunately, many good people are stepping forward from professional life, unions, NGOs, colleges and universities, and the churches, with their unique potential to connect people across borders and their wealth of experience in service to the poor. However, we are still far from the critical mass of new human beings that is needed.

That is one reason why we need the pastoral circle. So many decent people, including church people, are unaware of the scope of structural poverty, the dimension of the environmental crisis, the scale of violence against women, child abuse and abortion in our societies, inhumane work conditions at home and abroad, and the pervasiveness of racism and patriarchy. If we take people's dignity seriously, and if we take the needs of the world seriously, we will question the hyper-tolerant individualism that undermines action. We will challenge people to search more authentically for the truth and help them respond better to our broken world.

Notes

[1] They were less prescient about the scope of conservative clerical restorationism that would take place in the Catholic church (Holland and Henriot 1983, 55, 84–85).

[2] The mediations of the pastoral circle must feed and complement each other. Neither social science nor practical reflection is completely autonomous (Holland and Henriot 1983, 13, 23, 92–101). In recent years many have stressed the importance of explaining the proper relationship between theology and social science (Milbank 1990; Mo Sung 1994). As Josef Elsner points out in this volume, the "see, judge, and act" methodology, which was used at Medellín in 1968 and Puebla in 1979, was discarded when the Catholic bishops convened in Santo Domingo in 1992.

[3] In the 1980s Gustavo Gutiérrez himself began to characterize theology as reflection on experience—not just practice—including in experience both action and contemplation. First silence (both action and contemplation), he said, then speech (1991, xiv).

[4] On consolation, see below. For a good example of prophetic-utopian thinking, see Ellacuría 1993, 299–300.

[5] I am grateful to Ita's brother, Bill, for providing me with this text.

[6] The first three (basic) agenda items that Johannes Banawiratma in this volume specifies for developing contextual communities and theologies seem to me akin to these three criteria: (1) being open church (the subject, which is in this case collective), (2) the poor, cultures, religions (the world), and (3) the gospel of Jesus Christ (the word, the ultimate criterion).

References

Boff, Leonardo, and Clodovis Boff. 1987. *Introducing liberation theology.* Maryknoll, NY: Orbis Books.

Bloch, E. 1995. *The principle of hope.* Cambridge, MA.: MIT Press.

Castells, M. 2000. *The information age,* vol. 3, *The end of millenium.* 2nd ed. Oxford: Blackwell Publishers.

Comblin, Jose. 1998. *Called for freedom: The changing context of liberation theology.* Translated by Phillip Berryman. Maryknoll, NY: Orbis Books.

Ellacuría, Ignacio. 1993. Utopia and prophecy in Latin America. In *Mysterium liberationis: Fundamental concepts of liberation theology,* edited by Ignacio Ellacuría and Jon Sobrino, 299–300. Maryknoll, NY: Orbis Books.

Fornet-Betancourt, R., ed. 2003. *Resistencia y solidaridad: Globalización capitalista y liberación.* Madrid: Trotta.

Freire, Paulo. 1970. *Pedagogy of the oppressed.* New York: Herder and Herder.

Gutiérrez, Gustavo. 1983. *The power of the poor in history.* Maryknoll, NY: Orbis Books.

———. 1988. *A theology of liberation: History, politics, and salvation.* Rev. ed. Maryknoll, NY: Orbis Books.

———. 1991. *The God of life.* Maryknoll, NY: Orbis Books, 1991.

Hammarskjöld, Dag. 1964. *Markings.* New York: Alfred A. Knopf.

Holland, Joe, and Peter Henriot. 1983. *Social analysis: Linking faith and justice.* Rev. ed. Maryknoll, NY: Orbis Books; Washington, DC: Center of Concern.

Ignatius Loyola. 1992. *Spiritual exercises.* Translated by George Ganss. Chicago: Loyola Univ. Press.

Mannheim, K. 1929. The utopian mentality. In K. Mannheim, *Ideology and utopia: An introduction to the sociology of knowledge.* New York: Harcourt, Brace, and World/Harvest.

Milbank, J. 1990. *Theology and social theory: Beyond secular reason.* Cambridge, MA: Oxford Univ. Press.

Mo Sung, Jung. 1994. *Economía: Tema ausente en la teología de la liberación.* San José, Costa Rica.: DEI.

Ricoeur, Paul. 1967. *The symbolism of evil.* Boston: Beacon Press.

Segundo, Juan Luis. 1976. *The liberation of theology.* Maryknoll, NY: Orbis Books.

Sobrino, Jon. 1988. *Spirituality of liberation: Toward political holiness.* Maryknoll, NY: Orbis Books.

Spohn, William C. 1999. *Go and do likewise: Jesus and ethics.* New York: Continuum.

Tracy, David. 1981. *The analogical imagination: Christian theology and the culture of pluralism.* New York: Crossroad.

Epilogue

As we indicated in the preface of this volume, the process of pulling together this collection of essays has had a long and winding journey. Looking back over the journey—marked as it was by an exchange of several hundred emails; meetings in Delhi, Aachen, Nairobi, Nijmegen, and Debre Zeit; and the sifting of dozens of drafts of articles—we three editors clearly learned much more than the mere mechanics of "going around the pastoral circle."

The first lesson came out of the struggle to choose an appropriate title for the book—one that would aptly sum up what the essays aimed to present, but one that would also attract attention (and sell copies!). From early on, it was clear that this was a book to commemorate the twenty-fifth anniversary of another book, the Holland and Henriot classic. So we first chose the title *Social Analysis Revisited*. But it soon became clear to us that it was the pastoral circle—of which social analysis was but one moment—that would make a much more interesting topic. How has the pastoral circle been used? In what areas of social and academic pursuits? With what effects on the situations and on the practitioners?

It quickly became clear that the original design of the pastoral circle—whose four "moments of mediation" are described in more detail in Appendix 1—had been adopted, adapted, modified, expanded, customized, and personalized in an extremely wide variety of ways. Teachers and researchers, social activists and organizational planners, persons "in the West and the Rest" (the phrase Frans Wijsen employs in describing the so-called developed world and the developing world) found ways of richly relating to individual and community experiences through the moments of contact, analysis, reflection, and response.

Central to what was occurring in the use of the pastoral circle was the experience of *transformation*. Since the original Holland and Henriot book had employed the subtitle *Linking Faith and Justice*, distinct *theological* and *social* emphases were emerging in the essays submitted for the new volume. We chose as an initial subtitle *Theology and Transformation*. But discussions among the authors and the contributors revealed that while the pastoral circle was being used for the transformation of theology, it was also facilitating a theology that was transforming: transforming societies, transforming churches, transforming academia, transforming people. Hence, the subtitle evolved into *A Critical Quest for Truth and Transformation*.

As we reviewed the essays we also noticed the frequent use of several words besides *transformation*. These were words such as *open, dialogue, critical, search, truth, pluralism, spirituality*. For us, this signaled that the pastoral circle was not simply a research tool for scholars or a planning tool for activists. In the diverse ways in which this pastoral circle has been used in the past twenty-five years (only some of which ways are exemplified in the essays in this volume), something more profound occurred.

Take, for example, the word *open*. Several of our colleagues noted that engaging in the pastoral circle process opened up situations to new perspectives, both analytical (based on contact with people involved in the dynamics of social change) and theological (based on faith dimensions made explicit through reflection on the analyzed situations). Brackley spoke of the helpfulness of the pastoral circle in the search for a truth beyond restrictive rationality. And Riley noted that engendering the pastoral circle opened up insights that the more traditional social teaching of the church overlooked in dealing with gender issues.

But there was also a clear need for a predisposition of openness in entering into the pastoral circle process. Without such openness, as challenging as it might be, nothing very helpful would emerge from the process. This need for openness is why Banawiratma could speak of the pastoral circle as a spirituality, and why de Mesa could challenge himself and others to search honestly for the truth of constants in theological reflection. Both Karecki and Singgih noted an initial reluctance on the part of more fundamentalist Christian students in diverse places such as South Africa and Indonesia to open themselves to what they might find following the steps of the pastoral circle.

But the pastoral circle seems to be difficult for some to follow not simply because of what is opening up before them in new social situations and new theological insights but also because of what is being demanded of them in terms of a commitment to a planned response. That, at least, is a lesson that can be drawn from the essays of Elsener, Luna, and Henriot when they speak of the reluctance of IMBISA bishops to follow through good analysis and theology with clear strategies for pastoral actions. It is noteworthy that Bodewes emphasizes that plans were integral to the use of the pastoral circle in the urban slums of Nairobi.

Pluralism and dialogue are experienced in different settings. From an Asian perspective, Amaladoss notes how cultural pluralism and religious pluralism give rise to theological pluralism, where unity can be found in the lived experience that the pastoral circle explores. In a European university setting, Wijsen argues for a grounded theology that bridges the gap sometimes highlighted between "scientific" and "committed" approaches to theology. This is also emphasized by Mejía, who is critical of teaching theology without addressing the questions raised in the real-life experiences of the students.

Our volume hopefully raises as many questions for the reader as it answers. For example, what are the dispositions that we bring as we enter into the pastoral circle process? Hug argues that we need to recognize the oftentimes implicit theology that informs our analysis. Holland acknowledges the strong influence of his own social background on his shaping of the pastoral circle process, but he questions the need to call for a first moment of "contact" with reality because we are always "inserted." This point, as well as other points raised by other essayists, can raise many an interesting conversation among our readers.

One final observation that we editors noted about the contributions to this volume is that they are heavily Third World in location. Is this because of the background of the authors—making them more knowledgeable about potential contributors who would come from this experience and location? Or is it because the pastoral circle is not so widely used in theological and social programs in the West?

Certainly one of the major lessons of this book, demonstrated repeatedly in the essays, is that the pastoral circle should never be a closed circle. (Hence the varieties of emphases upon *cycle* and *spiral*.) Therefore, as we come to the end of this book, we in no way intend to close our pastoral circle reflections! Rather, we are interested in being open to much wider sharing. As editors of this book, we would be very glad to receive comments and suggestions from readers and accounts of experiences with the pastoral circle. This will certainly enrich us all and possibly lead to yet another "revisiting" at some time in the future. Accordingly, we provide here our contact addresses.

Frans Wijsen
Institute for Missiology
P.O. Box 9103
6500 HD Nijmegen
The Netherlands
f.wijsen@theo.ru.nl

Peter Henriot
Jesuit Centre for
   Theological Reflection
P.O. Box 37774
10101 Lusaka
Zambia
phenriot@zamnet.zm

Rodrigo Mejía
Galilee Centre
P.O. Box 1399
Debre Zeit
Ethiopia
galilee@ethionet.et

Appendix 1

Steps in the Pastoral Circle

The pastoral circle is a process of answering four very basic questions about some experience that we have, either as individuals or in a community setting. These questions help us to respond more effectively to the experience through deeper understanding and wider evaluation.

In facing the experience, we ask these questions and pursue these approaches in a quest for answers.

1. *What is happening here?* Gather the data, stories, descriptions of what is going on in this situation. What are people undergoing, what are they feeling, what stories are they telling, how are they responding?
2. *Why is it happening?* Probe the causes, connections, and consequences of what is taking place. Who are the key actors and what roles do they play, what has been the history of this experience, what are influences both obvious and hidden?
3. *How do we evaluate it?* Understand the meaning of the situation in the light of our values, our belief systems, our community norms, and so on. What does a faith perspective bring to bear on the experience, what new questions and insights are suggested in the light of traditional resources of scripture or teachings?
4. *How do we respond?* Move through steps of planning, acting, and evaluating in order to effect the desired change in the situation. What strategies are called for, what short-term steps and what long-term steps are needed to bring change?

These four questions occur during four "moments" of what we call the pastoral circle. These moments mediate, or relate us to, the *experience* of the situation.

1. *Contact*: The moment of insertion, of touching the reality through objective observations and subjective feelings.
2. *Analysis*: The moment of asking questions of time, structures, and values, and their interconnections, in order to understand the deeper reality of the situation.
3. *Reflection*: The moment of discerning the meaning of the situation in view of our shared values, our faith commitments, the teaching of our scriptures, the norms of our communities, the wisdom of our ancestors (such as that found in proverbs).

4. *Response*: The moment of planning concrete actions, taking the necessary steps, and evaluating the results in order to plan anew.

These four moments are described as a circle because the experience that is *contacted*, *analyzed*, and *reflected upon* undergoes changes in the *response* taken, and therefore we must go around the circle yet again—and again.

But it is important to note that each of the moments in the pastoral circle must itself be subjected to critical examination. For example:

1. *Contact*: Where and with whom are we locating ourselves as we begin this process? Whose experience is being considered? Are there groups that are "left out" or whose experiences are less valued when experience is discussed? Does the experience of the poor and oppressed have a privileged role to play in the process? How much do gender concerns enter into our openness to contact with reality?
2. *Analysis*: What analytical tradition is being followed in this process and why? Are there presuppositions in these analyses that need to be tested? Is it possible to use a particular analysis without agreeing with its accompanying ideology (such as Marxism or neo-liberalism)? Do we enter into analysis with the presupposition that it is objective and value free or can we make explicit any biases that we bring?
3. *Reflection*: Are there methodological assumptions that underlie the reflection framework that we use? In what relationship does the analysis stand to the reflection? Is it complementary, subordinate, central, peripheral? How closely linked is the reflection to the actual existing social situation? Is the reflection "religious" or "theological"?
4. *Response*: What participates in the planning? What are the implications of the process used to determine appropriate responses? In the response, what is the relationship between the groups that serve and those that are served? Are we serious about the monitoring and evaluation that should accompany the implementation?

Appendix 2

Societal Structures

All social situations are affected by the organization, operation, and orientation of structures (institutions, organizations, policies, patterns, and so on) that determine the direction of events. For descriptive and analytical purposes, we can list the following seven societal structures:

1. *Economic* structures that determine the organization of *resources* (e.g., corporations, banks, tax measures, trade patterns, unions);
2. *Political* structures that determine the organization of *power* (e.g., parliaments, police, parties, local councils, constitutional guarantees of human rights);
3. *Social* structures that determine the organization of *relationships* (e.g., families, racial patterns, tribes, villages, recreation clubs, schools);
4. *Gender* structures that determine the organization of *male-female patterns* (e.g., work status and division of labor, decision-making participation, sexual expectations and limitations);
5. *Ecological* structures that determine the organization of *natural environments* (e.g., sustainable agriculture, weather patterns, population distributions, demographic patterns)
6. *Cultural* structures that determine the organization of *meaning* (e.g., traditions, language, art, drama, song, initiation rites, communications media); and
7. *Religious* structures that determine the organization of *transcendence* (e.g., churches, books of revelation, sacraments and rituals, moral commandments).

Obviously, these structures are not sharply discrete or isolated. In any given situation the structures are interrelated and connected. It is one of the tasks of social analysis to identify which structures are the most influential.

Appendix 3 _____

Selected Bibliography

Broderick, R., and C. Richardson. 1989. *Love your neighbour: Christian social analysis.* No. 27 of the Lumko Series. Delmenville: Lumko Institute.

Buthelezi, M. 1973. African theology and black theology: A search for a theological method. In *Relevant theology for Africa*, edited by H. J. Becken, 18–24. Durban.

Clarke, Th. 1983. A new way: Reflecting on experiences. In *Tracing the Spirit: Communities, social action, and theological reflection*, edited by James Hug. Woodstock Studies. Ramsey, NJ: Paulist Press.

———. 1986. *Playing in the Gospel: Spiritual and pastoral models.* Kansas City, MO: Sheed and Ward.

Cochrane, J., J. de Gruchy, and R. Petersen. 1991. *In word and deed: Towards a practical theology for social transformation.* Hilton, South Africa: Cluster Publications.

Elsener, Josef. 1998. *Action programme for the church in Africa proposed by "Ecclesia in Africa."* IMBISA Occasional Papers no. 2. Harare: IMBISA.

Freire, Paulo. 1990. *Education for critical consciousness.* London: Sheed and Ward.

Green, L. 1990. *Let's do theology: A pastoral cycle resource book.* London: Mowbray.

Healy, S., and B. Reynolds. 1983. *Social analysis in the light of the Gospel.* Dublin: Conference of Major Religious Superiors.

Henriot, Peter. 1998. Grassroots analysis: The emphasis on culture. In *Liberation theologies on shifting grounds*, edited by G. De Schrijver, 333–50. Leuven: Peeters Press.

Henriot, Peter, and Rodrigo Mejía. 2000. *Pastoral circle: A strategy for promoting justice and peace.* IMBISA Occasional Papers no. 5. Harare: IMBISA.

Henriot, P., et al. 2003. *Catholic social teaching: Our best kept secret.* Maryknoll, NY: Orbis Books; Washington, DC: Center of Concern.

Holland, Joe, and Peter Henriot. 1983. *Social analysis: Linking faith and justice.* Maryknoll, NY: Orbis Books.

Hope, A., and S. Timmel. 1984. *Training for transformation.* Handbooks 1, 2, 3. Gweru: Mambo Press.

Janssen, H. 1994. Der pastorale zirkel—eine Einführung. In *Inkulturation und kontextualität*, edited by M. Pankoke-Schenk and G. Evers, 221–30. Frankfurt am Main: Verlag Jozef Knecht.

Janssen, H. Hrsg. 1996. *Zeichen der zeit: Pastoraler zirkel, gesellschaftsanalyse, Bibel-teilen.* Aachen: Missio. Internationales Katholisches Missionswerk.

Kammer, F. 1995. *Salted with fire: Spirituality for the faithjustice journey*. New York: Paulist Press.

Karecki, Madge. 2002. Teaching to change the world: Missiology at the University of South Africa. *Missionalia* 30, no. 1: 132–43.

Killen, Patricia O'Connell, and John De Beer. 1994. *The art of theological reflection*. New York: Crossroad.

Mejía, Rodrigo. 1993. The new understanding of pastoral theology. In *A light on our path*, edited by C. McGarry, R. Mejía, and V. Shirima. Nairobi: Paulines Publications.

———. 2002. From life to practical theology: The pastoral cycle, and pastoral theology and the pastoral circle: The methodology and dynamics of the pastoral circle. In *New strategies for a new evangelization in Africa*, edited by P. Ryan, 111–20 and 111–28. Nairobi: Paulines Publications.

Singgih, E. G. 1981. *Dari Israel ke Asia: Masalah hubungan di antara kontekstualisasi teologia dengan interpretasi Alkitabiah*. Jakarta: BPK Gunung Mulia.

Wijsen, Frans. 1997. The pastoral circle in the training of church ministers. *African Ecclesial Review* 39, no. 4: 238–50.

About the Authors

Michael Amaladoss (India), a Jesuit, is director of the Institute of Dialogue with Cultures and Religions, Chennai, India. He was assistant to the superior general of the Society of Jesus, with special concern for evangelization, dialogue, inculturation, and ecumenism. He taught at Vidyajyoti Faculty of Theology and was editor of *Vidyajyoti Journal of Theological Reflection.*

Johannes Banawiratma (Indonesia) is professor of systematic theology at Duta Wacana Christian University, Yogyakarta, Indonesia. He taught Christology and social theology at Sanata Dharma University, Yogyakarta, and was director of the Center for Research and Training of Contextual Theology of this university.

Christine Bodewes (United States), a lawyer by profession, works as a Maryknoll lay missioner in Christ the King Parish in Nairobi, where she started a human rights office that provides legal advice, civic education, and advocacy on land and housing issues.

Dean Brackley (United States), a Jesuit, is professor of theology and theological ethics at the Central American University (UCA), San Salvador. Before joining the staff of UCA, Brackley worked in social ministry and popular education on Manhattan's Lower East Side and in the South Bronx, and taught at Fordham University.

José de Mesa (Philippines), a married lay theologian, is a professor of systematic theology at De La Salle University–Manila in the Philippines and Visiting Luzbetak Professor of Theology and Culture at the Catholic Theological Union in Chicago. He is also a member of an interfaith, interdisciplinary initiative of Catholic communicators of Asia, the Asian Communication Network, based in Bangkok, Thailand.

Josef Elsener (Switzerland), a member of the Bethlehem Mission Society, is on the research and teaching staff of Romero Haus, a formation and conference center in Lucerne, Switzerland. He worked as a missionary in Zimbabwe (1964–81 and 1994–2001) and South Africa (1993–94) and was the superior general of his Society from 1981 to 1993.

Peter Henriot (United States) is director of the Jesuit Centre for Theological Reflection, Lusaka, Zambia. A Jesuit and political scientist, he focuses his work on international development issues and on the social justice response of the contemporary church. He was director of the Center of Concern in Washington, D.C. in the 1980s.

Joe Holland (United States) is a professor of philosophy and religion at Saint Thomas University, Miami, and president of Pax Romana in Washington, D.C. He worked in Chile and was on the staff of the Center of Concern in Washington, D.C.

James Hug (United States), a Jesuit, is president of the Center of Concern in Washington, D.C. Specialized in spirituality and Christian ethics, he previously taught at the Jesuit School of Theology in Chicago and was on the staff of the Woodstock Theological Center in Washington, D.C.

Madge Karecki (United States), a member of the Sisters of St. Joseph–Third Order of St. Francis, is associate professor in the Department of Christian Spirituality, Church History and Missiology at the University of South Africa (Unisa). She has been in South Africa for twenty-one years. Before coming to Unisa she taught for twelve years at St. John Vianney Seminary in Pretoria. She has a special interest in developing innovative ways of teaching theological subjects and in the relationship between spirituality and mission.

Juan José Luna (Mexico) is the superior general of the Missionaries of Guadalupe, Mexico City, Mexico. He worked for many years in Angola and Zimbabwe and was the first secretary of the justice and peace office of IMBISA in Harare.

Rodrigo Mejía (Colombia), a Jesuit, is director of the Galilee Centre, Debre Zeit, Ethiopia, a center for human and spiritual renewal. He has been working as a missionary in Africa since 1964, serving the church in the Democratic Republic of Congo (1964–84), Kenya (1984–95), and since 1995 in Ethiopia. He was a professor of pastoral theology at Hekima College and at the Catholic University of Eastern Africa, Nairobi.

Maria Riley (United States), an Adrian Dominican sister, is on the research staff and is coordinator of the Global Women's Project at the Center of Concern in Washington, D.C. She is the initiator of the International Gender and Trade Network. She also initiated and chairs the Interfaith Working Group on Trade and Investment.

Gerrit Singgih (Indonesia) is a professor of biblical studies at Duta Wacana Christian University, Yogyakarta, Indonesia, and dean of its Faculty of Theology. He also teaches at Sanata Dharma University and Gadjah Mada State University, both in Yogyakarta. He is an ordained minister in the Protestant Church of Indonesia.

Frans Wijsen (the Netherlands) is a professor of mission studies, director of the Graduate School of Theology, and director of the Institute for Missiology at Radboud University Nijmegen, the Netherlands. As a lay missioner associated with the Society of African Missions, he worked in Tanzania (1984–88). He is also a visiting professor at Tangaza College in Nairobi, Kenya, and at Duta Wacana Christian University, Yogyakarta, Indonesia.

Index

action research, 120–22

Africa: colonialism and, 6, 119; conflicts in, 49–50; HIV/AIDS in, 52, 62–63, 67–68; pluralism in, 170; poverty in, 31–32, 36, 45, 52, 56–57, 115–16, 211; self-reliance in, 19, 44–45; Synod of, 19, 30, 37, 43–44; traditional culture in, 59, 115–17, 120, 147–49. *See also* IMBISA

African Forum for Catholic Social Teachings (AFCAST), 22

Amaladoss, Michael, 167, 169–82, 226

American Journey, The (Holland), 4

analysis: Bible and, 152–53; in Christ the King Church, Nairobi, 58–61; contextual, 80–81, 141; cultural, 25, 117–18, 144; education and, 138, 141–42, 144, 147; gender, 184–95; in Indonesia, 151–52, 156–57; interdisciplinary, 118–19, 132; interreligious dialogue and, 147; liberation theology and, 6–7, 42–43; Marxist, 4, 6–7, 118; pastoral theology and, 131–32; personal, 151–52; pluralism and, 170, 173–74, 214–18; Puebla and, 43; in South Africa, 141–42, 144, 147; symbolism and, 116–18; theological reflection and, 47–50, 167–68, 201, 203–9, 227; used by IMBISA, 20, 23, 25, 32–33, 36–37; used by SECAM, 48–50; in Zambia, 17, 18

Aquinas, Thomas, 99

Aristotle, 10–12

Asia: colonialism and, 6; pluralism in, 159–61, 170, 226; poverty in, 78–79, 154–56, 159–61, 211

Association of Member Episcopal Conferences in Eastern Africa (AMECEA), 19, 21

Augustine, 98

Ayoub, Mahmoud Mustafa, 80–81

bakas, sacrament and, 100–104

Banawiratma, Johannes, 13, 73–85, 151, 157, 226

basic Christian communities, 8–9, 17, 73–75, 178, 211–12. *See also* basic human communities; small Christian communities

basic human communities, 74, 84, 178–79. *See also* basic Christian communities; small Christian communities

Bible: analysis and, 152–53; religious pluralism and, 160–61; study groups, 46; theological reflection and, 7–8, 18, 67, 70–71, 153, 160–62

bishops: pastoral circle and, 19–21, 24, 30–38; synods of, 43–44

Bodewes, Christine, 13, 56–72, 226

Botswana, 121

Bourdieu, Pierre, 109, 116, 118

Brackley, Dean, 168, 211–24, 226

Cameroon, 119

Cardijn, Cardinal Joseph, 9–10

Catholic Action, 5, 6, 9–10

Catholic social teaching, 10, 18, 44, 199; gender analysis and, 193; pastoral circle and, 21–24; theological reflection and, 48, 133–34

Center of Concern, xix, 4–5

Centesimus annus (John Paul II), 78

Christ the King Church, Nairobi, Kenya, 56–72, 226; evaluation in, 68–69; insertion in, 58; *jumuiyas* (SCCs) in, 57, 58–64, 66–67, 69–72; pastoral circle and, 58–72; pastoral planning in, 62–64, 70; social/cultural analysis in, 58–61; theological reflection in, 61–62, 70–71

Church in Africa (John Paul II), 30, 44

conscientization, insertion and, 217–18

constants: theological reflection and, 93–97, 226; sacrament and, 97–104

237